THE PROSPECT OF DEEP FREE TRADE

BETWEEN THE

EUROPEAN UNION AND UKRAINE

THE PROSPECT OF DEEP FREE TRADE
BETWEEN THE
EUROPEAN UNION AND UKRAINE

Centre for European Policy Studies (CEPS), Brussels
Institut für Weltwirtschaft (IFW), Kiel
International Centre for Policy Studies (ICPS), Kyiv

Michael Emerson (Project Director)
T. Huw Edwards
Ildar Gazizullin
Matthias Lücke
Daniel Müller-Jentsch
Vira Nanivska
Valeriy Pyatnytskiy
Andreas Schneider
Rainer Schweickert
Olexandr Shevtsov
Olga Shumylo

Report prepared in fulfilment of contract 2005/S 89-085795 of the European Commission's
Directorate-General for Trade on the economic feasibility, general economic impact and
implications of a free trade agreement between the European Union and Ukraine.

The views expressed in this report are attributable only to the authors,
and not to the European Commission nor the Government of Ukraine.

CENTRE FOR EUROPEAN POLICY STUDIES
BRUSSELS

ISBN 92-9079-623-5

Centre for European Policy Studies
Place du Congrès 1, B-1000 Brussels
Tel: 32 (0) 2 229.39.11 Fax: 32 (0) 2 219.41.51
e-mail: info@ceps.be
internet: http://www.ceps.be

CONTENTS

PREFACE

This study of the feasibility of free trade between the EU and Ukraine was undertaken from September 2004 to January 2005, under contract from the European Commission. Extensive consultations were held in Brussels with the European Commission, first with the Directorates-General for Trade and External Relations, and subsequently with the several other directorates-general concerned with sectoral policy aspects of EU–Ukraine relations (transport, energy, enterprise, agriculture, information technology, heath and safety, economics and finance, competition). Consultations were also held in Brussels with UNICE, the European Round Table, COPA and steel industry interests. In Kyiv consultations were held with Ukraine's presidential staff, the Ministry of Economy, Ministry of Foreign Affairs and the Ministry of Justice (with special thanks to Olena Zerkal), the National Bank of Ukraine, the Ukrainian Agrarian Confederation, the European Business Association, steel industry interests, the Delegation of the European Commission, several embassies of EU member states, the offices of USAID, the World Bank, the IMF, the EBRD and the UNDP, along with several policy research centres.

All the authors worked in an independent capacity. Valeriy Pyatnytskiy was appointed Deputy Minister of Economy when the report was at an advanced stage of preparation.

This project is part of the broader work programme of CEPS on European Neighbourhood Policy, which is generously supported by the Compagnia di San Paolo and the Open Society Institute.

Michael Emerson
Project Director
March 2006

EXECUTIVE SUMMARY

1. Mandate

Our mandate has been to report on the possible content, feasibility and economic implications of Ukraine and the EU undertaking a free trade agreement (FTA) to follow on from Ukraine's accession to the World Trade Organisation (WTO).

The authors are a group of EU and Ukrainian economists, all of whom worked on the project in an independent capacity.[1]

The study was commissioned by the European Commission as a step in the EU–Ukraine Action Plan jointly agreed with the government of Ukraine in December 2004, in the framework of the European Neighbourhood Policy (ENP).

2. Context

The present study is intended to update an earlier study on this subject undertaken in 1999. There are indeed major new developments that warrant a fresh look at the question:

- Ukraine's economic recovery from the deep recession of the 1990s, with fast economic growth over the last five years;
- Ukraine's forthcoming WTO accession;
- the EU's enlargement in 2004 up to Ukraine's borders;

---

[1] Valeriy Pyatnytskiy participated fully in the larger part of the work of the group in an academic capacity, before his appointment as Deputy Minister of Economy in November 2005.

- the EU's new European Neighbourhood Policy and Action Plan with Ukraine; and

- the Orange Revolution in 2004, which marked the will of Ukraine to make the break from a phoney to a real democracy.

At the EU–Ukraine summit of 1 December 2005, EU leaders "reconfirmed the goal of promoting deep economic integration between the EU and Ukraine and, in order to achieve this, look forward to an early start of negotiations of a Free Trade Area once Ukraine has joined the WTO".[2]

3.   Methodological approach

A starting point for our work was the request to update an earlier study undertaken for the Commission on a possible free trade agreement (Brenton, 1999). We have approached the task of 'updating' in a more substantial way than just re-running model calculations quantifying the expected impact of free trade with more recent economic data. We took this decision because there have been important developments in the analytical methods of economists in recent years, reflecting better understanding of the processes of both the post-communist transition and contemporary European integration. We confirm the earlier conclusions that the simplest free trade agreement, merely removing customs tariffs, would have only a minor impact on Ukraine's macroeconomic performance, and even less on the EU's economy. On the other hand, deeper forms of market integration can have substantial impact, especially when they link to reforms of domestic economic governance in countries (such as Ukraine) where it is badly needed. We have thus drawn up two main scenarios for simple and deep free trade, and made quantified estimates for both. Whereas simple free trade is relatively straightforward to describe, a deep free trade agreement (FTA+) requires much more detailed specification of its possible contents, to which we therefore devote substantial attention.

4.   Current economic situation in Ukraine

Ukraine has succeeded in the last five years to climb out of the deep recession of the early years of post-communist transition. But this burst of fast growth owed much to a cyclical boom for metallurgical products in

---

[2] See the European Commission, Joint Statement, EU–Ukraine Summit held in Kyiv on 1 December 2005, 15222/05 (Presse 337), Brussels, 1.12.2005.

world markets, which has now come to an end, and to which is now added the rise in imported energy prices. Since Ukraine has only a moderate natural resource endowment, it has no option other than to become a highly open and internationally competitive economy in a diversified range of industrial and service sectors (the agricultural sector has a rich endowment of land, but will nonetheless be of declining importance in a growing economy).

To this end, Ukraine must establish a favourable business climate without delay, cutting out or streamlining a host of complicated, unpredictable and often corruptly administered business regulations, and so favour both domestic and foreign investment. Also, in the near future the government has to unwind the unsustainably populist fiscal policies of 2004. Yet Ukraine's capacity to attract strategically important foreign direct investments has recently been exemplified in the re-privatisation of its largest steel producer (Kryvorizhstal) and investment by an EU bank in one of its largest banks (Aval). Integration into European and international markets and supply chains, coupled with decisive measures to improve domestic economic governance and curb corruption, will have to be at the heart of an economic strategy to restore Ukraine to a fast-growth path.

5. From WTO accession to an FTA+: A continuum of possibilities

WTO accession primarily means:

- abiding by the principles of non-discrimination and transparency among WTO partners;
- fixing tariffs, mostly at low levels, with the most-favoured nation clause;
- excluding quota restrictions;
- opening many service sectors to free trade;
- adopting rules for customs procedures; and
- observing rules for non-tariff barriers, with the principle of non-discriminatory 'national treatment'.

The simplest or minimalist FTA would add to these WTO conditions the move to zero tariffs for trade in goods, further liberalisation of services, but perhaps with only limited liberalisation in some sectors.

Deepening the free trade package could mean drawing on the following:

- extending the zero tariff principle to embrace the free movement of all goods, services, capital and (doubtless with longer transition periods) labour as well;

- for trade in goods, substantial elimination of non-tariff barriers through harmonisation or mutual recognition of technical standards with those of the EU (or both);

- for trade in services, complete sectoral coverage and convergence on internal market regulatory rules of the EU or best international standards;

- stronger commitments in competition policy, corporate governance and internal market regulation that are anchored to EU practices, and for selective elements of environmental standards; and

- adoption of accompanying policies, including technical assistance, infrastructure investment, education and training.

6. Actual examples from the EU

The continuum of theoretical possibilities is illustrated by the variety of the EU's existing free trade and association agreements:

- The EU's first free trade agreements were with the European Free Trade Area (EFTA), and initially only covered free trade in goods.

- The Euro-Mediterranean agreements initially only provided for shallow free trade in goods, but extension to free trade in services is now being discussed.

- The EU-Chile agreement is already more extensive in the coverage of service sectors and other provisions.

- The EU and Turkey share a customs union for industrial products.

- The European Economic Area (EEA), bringing the EU together with Norway, Iceland and Liechtenstein, covers all 'four freedoms' and entails complete compliance with EU internal market laws and standards, and full mutual recognition. This is the extreme model of complete inclusion in the EU's internal market, yet without political membership of the EU.

- The current EU-Swiss model comprises a large selection of sectoral agreements linked to EU internal market norms, but this model is less complete than the EEA.

7.   Economic impacts of simple or deep free trade scenarios

For making quantitative estimates of the likely impact of free trade, the standard modelling (computable general equilibrium) technique is useful, but not fully adequate. This is because such models theoretically assume that trade barriers are separating otherwise competitive economies, which may be not too far from reality for the EU and US as trade partners, but is certainly not valid for Ukraine. In addition, the standard models generally fail to investigate the dynamic effects of improved institutional performance and economic governance or the curbing of corruption, which is now the most important deterrent to trade and investment for Ukraine.

In recent years, however, economists have progressed in analysing the impact of removing wider categories of trade barriers, such as incompatible technical standards, as well as the dynamics of deeper integration, especially between close neighbours where gravitational effects through proximity to large markets come into play. The recent experience of the enlargement of the EU into Central Europe, coinciding with the post-communist transition, has spurred research in these fields. There are now indications that deep free trade, of the kind discussed here for the EU and Ukraine, could have beneficial effects much greater than earlier estimates have suggested, including important benefits from both external liberalisation and domestic regulatory reforms in the main service sectors. Cuts in import tariffs on their own, such as in a simple FTA, will not lead to substantial income growth and welfare gains, although there would be significant changes in trade structure (which are detailed in chapter 4). Yet deeper free trade could deliver welfare gains of the order of 4-7% according to comparative static simulations; taking into account dynamic effects, welfare gains over time could be twice or three times as large. In addition, reductions in the cost of capital could lead to a further 4-5% welfare gain. Ukrainian exports to the EU could double, and EU exports to Ukraine could also grow very substantially.

Estimates of the impact of improved institutional quality for countries such as Ukraine are very large, with conceivable increases in GDP in the range of 20 to 30%. Fully opening the financial and other key service sectors such as telecommunications to foreign investment and best international practice would constitute a key element of such reforms, and could according to some new estimates alone raise the annual growth rate by 1.5%, compared with economies that have closed and unreformed markets. In interpreting these quantitative results it should be noted that they reflect different modelling approaches and are therefore not strictly comparable;

also, the reforms analysed are to some degree overlapping rather than strictly additional (the same is true for the estimated welfare effects).

Overall, a combination of opening the economy and transforming the quality of domestic economic governance could substantially raise the sustainable growth rate of the Ukrainian economy, possibly even approaching double digits for some time. This would mean a substantial catch up towards the GDP per capita levels of the new Central European member states of the EU. Ukraine has two key assets that could help to make this feasible, namely a well-educated human capital base and geographical proximity to the EU market – provided that the policy and institutional prerequisites are also satisfied. Furthermore, deep free trade may also lead to a more equal distribution of population income because enhanced competition will cut down monopoly profits.

The effects on the EU economy will be very minor at the macroeconomic level, even insignificant according to standard model calculations. But these simulations cannot take into account certain dynamic effects that could be of some importance to the EU economy. Notably there is the possibility that Ukraine's inclusion in the European supply chain could offer some EU industries, ranging from high-tech electronics to low-tech textiles, an opportunity to improve their competitiveness *vis-à-vis* the fast-growing Asian competitors by outsourcing labour- or resource-intensive parts of their production process. The example of the huge growth of US-Mexican trade and investment under the NAFTA agreement is suggestive here.

8. Concepts of feasibility

Feasibility, a key word in our terms of reference, is a complex concept. It is certainly not a static or purely technical matter, and it might be defined as having the following aspects in the present context:

- administrative capacity to legislate, implement and enforce requisite policy steps;
- political economy feasibility to undertake the requisite reform strategy;
- competitive capability of the economy to prosper under open market conditions; and
- educational capacity of the labour force for an advanced market economy.

In general terms, Ukraine's educational capacity is strong, its administrative capacity weak and its competitive capacity, with the exception of a few sectors, remains to be created. Political economy feasibility is surely a fluid and elastic matter, depending on the broad factor of political will, which is the product of political leadership, public understanding of the issues and perceptions of sectoral and national priorities on the part of different business and civil society interest groups. In this area, it is vital that the Ukrainian authorities invest more heavily in the normal processes of stakeholder consultation, for example for passing WTO-compliant legislation now, followed by that for an FTA. Given political will, administrative capacities can be strengthened, reform strategies implemented, and new competitive capacities created.

The broad picture is one of a trade-off, especially for Ukraine, between the ease of feasibility versus the scale of the benefits. Simple free trade is the most easily feasible, but its impact will be weak. Deep free trade is much more demanding in terms of feasibility, but offers the prospect of much larger economic advantages of strategic value.

9. How far to go in convergence on EU regulatory rules and standards?

How far or how fast the country should go in the direction of deep policy convergence on EU regulatory rules and technical standards requires detailed attention, i.e. to define the optimal package and time-path specifically for the case of Ukraine on the basis of cost-benefit analysis.

The recent experience of the new member states has underlined the heavy costs in the short run, for both public administrations and the private sector, of achieving full compliance with EU economic rules and standards. This was in fact achieved only with very substantial financial and technical assistance, along with the political incentive of full membership. Ukraine, however, is under no pressure to define a deep FTA in terms of complete compliance with EU market laws and standards, and so selective prioritisation is both possible and desirable. The parties can focus on defining the content of an FTA in accordance with objective cost and benefit criteria for the two parties.

10. A scenario for simple free trade (FTA)

Free trade in goods. Various precedents would suggest the elimination of tariffs asymmetrically over five to ten years. The EU might front-load its tariff cuts, possibly eliminating them all on the day of entry into force of the agreement, given its much greater competitive strengths. Ukraine would at the same time begin to reduce its tariffs. A long transition period, up to 10 years, has precedents in EU free trade agreements with Mediterranean countries. But the disadvantage of a long transition period is that the process may lose credibility and fail to energise the private sector, so we would suggest about five years.

WTO rules allow bilateral free trade agreements only on condition that substantially all products are included. Agriculture has been the main exception in many of the EU's free trade agreements. Particularly sensitive sectors could be handled with extended transition periods and limited partial exclusions.

Free trade in services. Ukraine's WTO offer already covers almost all service sectors, and will be one of the most liberal regimes of all WTO members. A few exclusions from the WTO offer, such as for road transport and civil aviation (see below), should be brought into the FTA.

Freedom of capital movements. Some restrictions remain at present for short-term capital movements, and these are understandable for a transitional period while the Ukrainian financial market is poorly developed, and while monetary policy is moving towards a floating exchange rate and inflation-targeting regime. Complete freedom for capital movements might be achieved by 2008.

11. A scenario for deep free trade and the reform of economic governance (FTA+)

Under the current Partnership and Cooperative Agreement with the EU, Ukraine has already been progressively approximating many of its external trade and internal regulatory policies to EU standards. Although important as preliminary investments in legal infrastructure, Ukraine's performance in implementation and enforcement has been lagging far behind. Our summary of the priorities for Ukraine would see a scenario with the following points, along with those outlined in the simple free trade scenario, and are illustrative rather than exhaustive:

i)   *Customs services* have to make a double quantum leap, first to eliminate corruption, and then to introduce technically advanced procedures that would logistically support Ukraine's entry into the European supply chain.

ii)   For *industrial product standards*, compliance with EU standards is of primary importance, and the EU Commission has proposed an ambitious plan to Ukraine for achieving a high level of harmonisation and mutual recognition by 2011.

iii) For *agricultural and food products* major investment is needed to enable compliance with EU sanitary and phytosanitary standards so that Ukraine might be able to export a diversified range of products to the EU.

iv) Ukrainian *competition policy* is being comprehensively aligned at the legislative level on EU practice, but major reinforcement of the political independence of the executive authority for controlling monopolies and state aid is needed, possibly with some external anchorage.

v) A *government procurement agreement* could be negotiated with the EU, taking into account whether Ukraine would first negotiate an agreement in this domain in the WTO.

vi) The *financial sector* is now being opened for foreign investment, and this is the crucial step at this stage towards improved resource allocation – by disconnecting the financial system from both government and domestic monopolistic power. Nevertheless, there should not be a premature attempt at total compliance with EU regulatory norms, which would be too costly.

vii) The *transport sector*, especially air and road transport, needs multiple initiatives beyond free trade in services, with convergence on EU standards and investments in infrastructures. Since the civil aviation sector is excluded from the WTO, bilateral negotiations between the EU and Ukraine are already beginning in this sector, and should aim at full inclusion of Ukraine in the 'Single European Sky'.

viii) The *telecommunications sector* has also recently been opened for foreign investment and competition, and here it is appropriate to converge on the EU's first generation of regulations of 1998 (rather than the more recent version, which relies on very advanced national regulatory authorities).

ix) In the *energy sector* there are already limited possibilities for connections with the EU electricity grid in the south-west region. But the bigger question of linkage of the entire Ukraine grid with the EU and south-east European grid now becomes conceivable, which would require strict compliance with EU standards. The gas crisis of January 2006 highlights the inevitable convergence of Ukraine's energy prices on world market levels, and the resulting burden of adjustment for its energy-intensive industries.

x)   In general, an essential requirement for the service sectors is for the *regulatory authorities* to have independence from both political and commercial interests, and to acquire state-of-the-art competence, for which twinning arrangements with European counterparts would be valuable.

xi) Ukraine's *corporate governance* standards are extremely weak and basic laws for joint stock companies, the protection of minority rights and for mandatory accounting and audit standards in line with European/international standards are still lacking.

xii) Regarding *environmental standards*, full compliance with EU standards would be extremely costly if implemented rapidly, although there are also the costs of non-action to consider, notably in the area of public health. The European Neighbourhood Policy (ENP) Action Plan therefore foresees step-by-step alignment with the environmental *acquis*, with EU financial support. Ukraine's accession to the Kyoto Protocol opens opportunities for accelerating the process in cooperation with the EU.

xiii) Concerning *labour regulations* there are urgent needs in Ukraine to improve safety standards, but this requires above all modern re-equipment in industries such as coal mining. The introduction of liability insurance systems would also be helpful. In this area there is no need to harmonise with the EU's often very burdensome regulations, such as those for part-time work. Mutual recognition of professional qualifications and coordination of social security would be natural complements to the other three freedoms.

xiv) With regard to the *movement of persons*, it is already highly positive for both parties that Ukraine has scrapped visa restrictions for EU citizens. Asymmetry is appropriate here in the interests of both parties for the next several years. Visa-free travel would be appropriate when Ukraine has achieved a higher level of prosperity and border control. Visa facilitation negotiations have now begun for Ukrainians travelling to the EU.

xv) Ukraine's *human capital* is high, especially in the natural sciences, but has a huge need for modernisation in the social sciences and management studies. With the projected doubling of the EU's grant assistance from €50 to €100 million in the near future, we advocate scholarships in higher education as a major priority, with a rapid build up from the few dozens per year of Ukrainian students in the EU as at present, to a thousand by 2008.

12. Benchmarks and checkpoints

The negotiation and implementation of an FTA+ could be subject to a number of major benchmarks or checkpoints, for example from the entry into force and review after a number of years to moving towards an even more advanced relationship. The main strategic requirement, for an FTA+ to become strongly beneficial, is for Ukraine to switch to a transparent, consistent and largely de-corrupted regime of economic governance, and therefore to acquire a reputation for these qualities in the eyes of the international business community. Examples of conditional checkpoints could include some vital laws for creating conditions for sound economic governance that need to be passed, notably the current draft laws for joint stock companies, minority shareholder rights and competition policy for state aid, which have been rejected by the parliament during the last year, but have not been pre-conditions for WTO accession.

In any event, enforcement of EU-compliant legislation will be monitored under the ENP Action Plans, and this could link to the intention to make aid under the new European Neighbourhood Policy Instrument (ENPI) dependent on performance according to governance criteria. This could further link with and reinforce conditionalities set by the international financial institutions (IFIs). Indeed, classic trade policies are in general not suitable instruments for fine-tuning in relation to wider economic policy conditions. On the other hand, where an FTA+ forms part of a wider transition strategy and European integration process, there will be opportunities for attaching EU and other IFI finance to policy reforms that would be crucial for the success of an FTA+.

13. From sensitive sectors to a rebranded Ukrainian economy

We have had a close look at certain sectors that are currently the most heavily protected in either or both the EU and Ukraine, and where the most lively opposition to free trade might be expected.

For both parties agriculture is a heavily protected and politically sensitive sector. In Ukraine this is because the modernisation of the agricultural sector has only recently begun, beyond the essential first step of privatisation. For the EU there are already major political difficulties in agreeing conditions for opening the WTO's Doha Round agenda, especially for liberalisation of agricultural trade.

For the EU, steel and textiles have been sensitive industrial sectors for several years. In any case, the EU's quota for steel imports from Ukraine will have to be scrapped with Ukraine's accession to WTO, and an FTA will not add to this sector's challenges. It is already apparent that EU and Ukrainian steel producers are beginning to see opportunities for complementarity and mutual integration through investments. For textiles Ukraine is not at present a major player, but with an FTA+ there would be useful opportunities for intra-industry trade in textiles and clothing, with the proximity of low labour costs in Ukraine next to the high value-added parts of the supply chain in the EU.

The challenges are more heavily weighted on the Ukrainian side, where virtually every sector of the economy, including for example a poorly competitive automobile industry, still faces the prospect of deep restructuring and renewal. The extent of the poor international competitiveness of Ukrainian industry and service sectors makes it pointless to try and identify individual branches that might justify special protection. This is why a strategy of total commitment to openness and steady improvement of the business environment is indispensable. Once Ukraine achieves a reputation for such a strategy, which means a 're-branding' of the Ukrainian economy, there is every reason to expect a strong flow of domestic and foreign investment. Already there are signs that major industrial sectors, for example electronics manufacturers, are seriously considering the option of locating an important part of the European supply chain in Ukraine, which could also become a plus for the EU's global competitiveness, in light of the Asian challenge it faces.

14. Implications for Ukrainian-Russian trade relations

There will be many aspects of an EU FTA+ affecting relations between both parties and Russia. Both the EU and Ukraine would want an FTA+ to be compatible with positive and constructive relations with Russia, as illustrated in the following two examples:

- There could in principle be possibilities for free trade between all three parties. For Ukraine the main objective should be to have free trade with both the EU and Russia. Russia also advocates a customs union with Ukraine (and Belarus and Kazakhstan); however, this idea is being rejected by Ukraine since it would indeed be incompatible with free trade between Ukraine and the EU.

- For the highly complex domain of technical standards for industrial and agricultural goods, convergence on a single set of standards is desirable. Ukraine is converging on European standards. Here it would be helpful if Russia more clearly agreed to also converge on European standards in the framework of the (EU–Russia) Common European Economic Space.

15. What is feasible? What is necessary?

Unfortunately, as noted earlier, the main policy options come in the form of a trade-off between the ease of feasibility and the scale of likely benefits.

The least ambitious and simplest free trade area, merely eliminating tariffs with the exception of agriculture, would be rather easily feasible, but of little benefit since the most important barriers to trade and investment in Ukraine remaining after WTO accession will be the well-known problems of economic governance (lack of transparency in business relations, lack of predictability in government policies and pervasive corruption).

It would clearly not be feasible, on the other hand, to seek within a five-year time horizon, full inclusion into the EU's internal market in the manner of Norway in the European Economic Area. The burden of full compliance with EU law for the legislature, government agencies and the private sector would certainly be excessive for Ukraine over such a short period.

An FTA+ along the lines set out above would fit with the needed reform agenda of Ukraine. Its feasibility would certainly be more difficult than for simple free trade, and would depend on the capacity of the Ukrainian government, parliament, business interests and civil society to find together the political will to work towards this end. This condition cannot be taken for granted at present, since the current parliament has refused to pass a number of laws required even for WTO accession, and which would be essential parts of a comprehensive strategy to improve economic governance. It remains to be seen therefore what will prove feasible with the next parliament following the elections of March 2006.

The ongoing experiences of the post-communist transition in wider Europe point to a model that is not as simple as the idea of a naturally continuous process. The picture seems rather to be one of two models emerging: the model of countries converging fast on advanced European standards of economic governance and democracy with law-abiding societies, versus a model of corrupt oligarchic governance, pseudo-democracy and poor living standards. Regrettably, it seems that the second as well as the first of these models is self-sustaining. The Ukraine of the Orange Revolution was seen to be trying to break out of one to join the other. But the economic forces that sustain the vicious circle of corruption and poor living standards are formidable, which is why a strong and deep free trade formula, rather than a shallow one, is advisable.

At this stage the future of the Orange Revolution and Ukraine's European choice hang in the balance, and cannot be considered irreversible. A credible reform strategy needs to be anchored in the short run to a progression, beginning with the conditions for WTO accession and leading on to those for deep free trade, or an FTA+, with the EU. In the long run, Ukraine can only become a prosperous and stable democratic society with a diversified economy if as a general rule it converges on international standards of economic governance and competitiveness. Convergence on European standards fits as a strategic anchor both as a matter of the political 'European choice' and as proxy for general international standards.

1. Introduction
Some Principles and Paradigms

This study concerns the possible content, implications and feasibility of a free trade agreement (FTA) between the European Union and Ukraine. The EU–Ukraine Partnership and Cooperation Agreement (PCA), which entered into force on 1 March 1998, foresaw the possible establishment of an FTA between the two partners. A study of the Tacis programme in 1999 (referred to below as the '1999 study') examined the issues in depth. The present study is intended to update that work[3]

The new political context

Since the 1999 study, there have been no less than five substantial changes in the context for the relationship between the EU and Ukraine:

- The EU has enlarged to 25 member states, with Poland, Slovakia and Hungary all directly bordering Ukraine, and Romania due to follow soon.

- The EU has developed a new European Neighbourhood Policy (ENP), which embraces Ukraine and greatly extends the agenda of EU–Ukrainian integration measures, including a stake in the internal market. Thus the idea of free trade is already overlapping with that of deeper integration.

---

[3] See P. Brenton, *Study on Evaluating the Economic Feasibility, General Impact and Implications of a Free Trade Agreement between the European Union and Ukraine according to the Partnership and Cooperation Agreement*, Executive Summary, CEPS, Brussels, 1999.

- Over the past five years, Ukraine's economy has impressively resumed economic growth, compensating for the heavy losses of the early period of independence. These gains relied heavily on an exceptional boom in world metallurgical demand, however, which is now over. Therefore new and sustainable sources of economic growth are urgently required.

- Meanwhile, Ukraine's negotiations for accession to the WTO have been gradually advancing, and the government is attaching the highest priority to now bringing them to a rapid conclusion, which would satisfy a major prerequisite for opening negotiations for free trade with the EU. Yet continuing parliamentary opposition to some necessary WTO-enabling laws means that there remains some uncertainty over the timing of the country's accession to the WTO.

- In the last year, Ukraine has seen its dramatic Orange Revolution, which aimed at making a decisive break in favour of sound democratic governance, followed by the announcement of ambitious objectives for European integration. Nevertheless subsequent developments are a reminder that the objective of democratic stability is not achieved overnight.

At the EU-Ukraine summit of 1 December 2005, EU leaders, "reconfirmed the goal of promoting deep economic integration between the EU and Ukraine and, in order to achieve this, look forward to an early start of negotiations of a Free Trade Area once Ukraine has joined the WTO".[4]

All these developments make the elaboration of a strategy for trade liberalisation and economic integration between the EU and Ukraine a much more relevant and pressing concern for policy-makers.

Forms of free trade

Free trade has traditionally been defined in a simple way, namely the removal of tariffs and quotas for trade in goods. For free trade to exist between the EU and Ukraine, it is understood by both parties that Ukraine's accession to the WTO is in any case a prior step. Once this is achieved, the further move to the simplest form of free trade with the EU would be a rather modest step, since the tariffs bound with WTO accession

---

[4] See the European Commission, Joint Statement, EU–Ukraine Summit held in Kyiv on 1 December 2005, 15222/05 (Presse 337), Brussels, 1.12.2005.

will be relatively low on average, and the rules of the WTO exclude quota restrictions as a general rule. More precisely, WTO accession means:

- fixing tariffs, mostly at low levels;
- excluding quota restrictions;
- opening many service sectors for free trade;
- conforming with rules for customs procedures; and
- conforming to rules for non-tariff barriers, with the principle of non-discriminatory 'national treatment'.

The simplest and shallowest FTA would therefore add to these WTO conditions only the move to zero tariffs for trade in goods, but perhaps with some limited exclusions such as those applying to agriculture. This simplest form of free trade would surely be feasible as it adds rather little to the conditions for WTO membership, which is expected in the near future in any case.

Deeper forms of economic integration, which we call 'deep free trade', or 'FTA+', could in principle include the following further elements:

- for trade in goods, substantial elimination of non-tariff barriers through harmonisation or mutual recognition of regulatory rules and technical standards (or both);
- for service sectors, complete coverage of and convergence on internal market regulatory rules, leading to harmonisation or mutual recognition of regulatory standards (or both);
- extension to capital and labour, no doubt with various conditions and transition periods, for goods and services;
- commitments to European models and methods of competition policy, corporate governance and internal market regulation;
- alignment with European environmental standards in the long run, but starting now; and
- accompanying policies, including technical assistance, infrastructure investment and programmes for education and training.

How far or how fast the country should go in these directions requires detailed attention in order to define the most advisable package and time-path, and we advocate careful cost-benefit analysis of the options. The deep free trade concept covers a continuum of conceivable packages or of sequencing of different components, and our report assembles (in chapter 6) one view of a plausible package of priorities. While many alternative packages are conceivable, we do not encourage 'shopping' to simply to pick out the easiest elements. As pointed out below, there are important synergies to be achieved between the different sectoral items, such that a holistic approach is in our judgement advisable. The main variable in fine-tuning the package should be in sequencing and lengths of transition periods for various reforms.

Concepts of feasibility

With a view to free trade between Ukraine and the EU, there are several concepts of feasibility or capacity to be considered.

Administrative capacity to legislate and implement the requisite policy steps. Ukrainian administrative capacities in the public sector are undoubtedly still weak, but in the context of free trade the important distinction is between those measures that are pure acts of liberalisation, versus those that involve sophisticated regulatory capabilities. The agenda for simple free trade will actually reduce burdens on the public administration through removing the task of collecting customs duties (although not eliminating the need for proper customs controls), reducing or eliminating licensing requirements for entry into service sectors and capital movements, and – as was done by Ukraine in 2005 – by simply scrapping visa requirements for visitors from the EU. On the other hand, the deep free trade agenda, with convergence on the EU *acquis* or best international regulatory practice, would require serious institutional reform and capacity-building. This first concerns the technical functions of regulatory authorities in the executive branch of government, which require a high degree of professional knowledge. Second, it concerns the functioning of law enforcement and judicial authorities. Third, it requires a correct separation of powers between the executive, legislature and judiciary. On all these accounts, Ukraine's ratings, according to international surveys undertaken by the International Bank for Reconstruction and Development (IBRD) and the European Bank for Reconstruction and Development (EBRD), are still weak.

Political economy feasibility to undertake a reform strategy. So far it has not proved politically feasible to obtain parliament's agreement to significant parts of the economic reform agenda needed to create a newly diversified and internationally competitive economy. In particular, oligarchic interest groups in the parliament, with strong links to the executive, have hampered attempts to introduce some basic legislation for accession to the WTO and to establish sound ground rules for corporate governance. Oligarchic business interests have both bought influence in the parliament and secured a very high level of direct representation within it. That being said, civil society has become forceful in protesting against corrupt governance – such was the essence of the Orange Revolution. Whether the next political period can produce a power structure that will be willing and able to undertake a deep reform agenda is unknown at the time of writing.

Competitive capability of the economy to prosper under open market conditions. Ukraine has delayed the structural adjustment of its economy to competitive, world market conditions. Ukraine has, however, built up very large trade surpluses since 2000, which provide a favourable basis for trade liberalisation. These surpluses will now be reduced as a result of weakening demand for metallurgical exports and rising prices for energy imports. The rise in energy prices towards world market levels, long delayed, is now being imposed on Ukraine, which therefore has no option but to develop a more energy-efficient and internationally competitive economy. This step will require new and rapid growth in many branches of the industrial and service sector economy. That in turn requires a favourable business climate by international standards, which leads back to the case for the deep free trade agenda.

Educational capacity of the labour force for an advanced market economy. All the former communist states of Europe achieved high educational standards. International surveys show that for the more easily comparable mathematical and scientific disciplines the levels of educational achievement in both the EU's new member states and Ukraine, Russia and Belarus actually exceed those of Western European countries. Aptitudes to adapt to new technologies are good, as for example in the rapid development of a service sector in information technology software. This primary prerequisite for deep integration with the EU is therefore satisfied.

The feasible and the necessary. What is feasible depends in the short run on the level of ambition of the project. Over a medium-term time horizon, however, the political-will factor is key to making more ambitious projects feasible, and notably so for Ukraine since the general educational level satisfies a key prerequisite for deep integration with Europe. The simplest free trade proposition is clearly the most feasible in the short run, since it eases problems of weak administrative capacity and the economy starts with a healthy trade surplus. But it is unlikely to produce important benefits. By contrast, the political and administrative demands made by a deep free trade and reform agenda are much more onerous. Whether this heavier political agenda is going to prove feasible in the period ahead is uncertain at this stage. The political-will factor is certainly not a static matter, resulting as it does from the constant interaction between political leaders, the perceptions of public opinion and the influence of business and civil society. At this time the need for profound economic reform should become all the more obvious by the end of cheap imported energy supplies. Moreover when the political situation is manifestly unsettled and unstable, as is understandable for a country mid-way through the post-communist transition, the need for external anchorage of the reform process is all the greater.

Cost-benefit analysis for the optimal FTA+ package

The precise choice of the optimal extent and speed of Ukraine's approximation of EU internal market law and practice is a highly complex matter. There is a need for operational criteria to define the best way forward for the foreseeable future. The criteria should in principle be based on analysis of the costs and benefits for Ukraine to converge, to fuller or lesser degrees, on the regulations and standards of each chapter of the EU's external and internal market policies (known as the EU *acquis communautaire*).[5]

The cost and benefits of adopting given market laws and policies may be identified as follows:

- Costs
  - *for the public sector* in recruiting/retaining skilled personnel in government departments and in allocating material resources for technical agencies;
  - *for the private sector* in changing the technical specifications of products to satisfy reach EU standards or to enable service sectors to respect regulatory norms; and
  - *for accelerated economic restructuring* with the scrapping of investment in the previous system and transitional unemployment.

---

[5] The term *'acquis'* is the French expression used very commonly in EU circles as shorthand for the 'acquired' stock of EU laws, regulations and standards. New member states are required to become completely *'acquis* compliant', and EEA members have to become completely compliant with the internal market *acquis.*

- Benefits
  - through obtaining improved EU market access;
  - through accessing conditional financial incentives offered by the EU and IFIs; and
  - through embedding improved domestic economic governance, leading to better economic performance.

While the main issue on the cost side is the burden of implementing regulatory rules and standards, a distinction needs to be made in the cost-benefit analysis between:

- mandatory *standards*, which must be adopted by the entire sector, as is typical for the financial sector; and
- voluntary *standards*, which may be applied by the individual enterprise if it so wishes, as is typical for industrial products (Box 1).

The voluntary standards system is an important part of the market economy paradigm, whereas the generalisation of mandatory standards (rather than their selective choice in accordance with externalities) is part of the centrally-planned economy paradigm, of which the *Gosstandards* system is a relic.

Box 1. Examples of costs and benefits in some cases of possible EU compliance

A Ukrainian manufacturer can choose voluntarily to adopt the EU product standard and gains access to the EU market. The costs should not be too onerous, since companies have the option not to comply. The EU and IFIs may grant technical assistance to help set up the testing and conformity assessment agencies. The benefits in terms of economic governance are, however, small.

The prudential regulations for financial services are mandatory for all banks, in line with basic EU and international standards. The costs of compliance may initially be heavy, but the benefits in terms of domestic economic governance are very important, and investment aid from the IFIs could be significant. Yet for Ukrainian banks to have full access to the EU market, obtaining the 'European passport', the regulatory system would have to be exactly compliant with all EU directives, which would be a great additional burden for little benefit at this stage.

Accounting and auditing standards, in line with EU and international practices, are currently voluntary in Ukraine, but could be made mandatory for all large companies. The costs of compliance are initially quite high for the private sector and there are no direct benefits in terms of market access for trade. But the benefits in terms of access to international capital markets, in improved domestic governance and in creating a favourable business environment for foreign investment are very important.

More generally, the criteria for judging the desirable degree of EU compliance include: i) whether it facilitates deeper market integration; ii) whether the EU law or standard is in line with best international practice; iii) whether it helps the transition of the reform process; and iv) whether it can help overcome obstacles to reform from domestic interest groups. These are the criteria that are taken into account later in this report, especially when looking in some detail at the market-opening and reform agendas for the service sectors.

Synergies from a holistic approach

While each individual act of adopting EU norms and standards can be assessed as single items, this may only be a first step in the assessment, since there will often be synergy between multiple actions in a given sector (see Box 2).

Box 2. An example of possible synergies between multiple elements of EU compliance

The prospects for the civil aviation sector in Ukraine might be dramatically improved with a 'freedom of the skies' agreement with the EU concerning market access, but only on the condition that Ukrainian airlines can buy new aircraft competitively without import duties (*thus free trade in goods and services together*). In addition, the main airports would need to be upgraded to meet European safety standards along with major infrastructural investment following privatisation, which could also attract foreign investment (*thus further adding regulatory compliance and infrastructural investment*). The potential synergies culminating from these multiple actions would be decisive, while isolated actions would not yield a favourable cost-benefit result.

This point links to an even broader argument concerning the construction of a nation's reputation, image and identity. International investors wish to synthesise masses of detailed information in making their investment strategies. For this purpose credible anchorage on a robust set of rules, with further qualities of predictability for future policy-making are vital for the building of a reputation for a favourable business climate. The new member states of the EU have evidently been through an extremely demanding process of becoming comprehensively compliant with EU rules and standards, backed up legal enforcement mechanisms. For Ukraine, 'European choice' is the chosen label, but to give credibility to this image there has to be a very substantial commitment to EU standards. This stance does not have to represent a total commitment as for accession candidate states, but there has to be a critical mass. Otherwise, there will be no reputational benefit, as was indeed the case during the Kuchma regime. The Orange Revolution created the opportunity to construct a new reputation, and deep free trade with the EU could be a strategic mechanism for achieving it.

2. MACROECONOMIC AND STRUCTURAL DEVELOPMENTS IN UKRAINE

Ukraine has arrived at a crossroads on its way from a Soviet past to a European future. While the external environment is becoming less favourable, a big leap forward is necessary for creating a market-based economy, namely one that would allow for structural change by the entry of new enterprises offering new products or more efficient lines of production. This advance means using the momentum created by the Orange Revolution and combining negotiations about better access to external markets with sweeping reforms at home, so as to signal to domestic and foreign investors that Ukraine is going to exploit its comparative advantage as a low-cost producer bridging European and Asian areas.

2.1 Macroeconomic performance

It is excellent that the Ukrainian economy has been able to grow rapidly in the last few years, recovering from the deep recession of the early years of the post-communist transition. The macroeconomic situation is now becoming more difficult, but assuming that monetary stability is assured, the starting condition for the years ahead looks broadly favourable.

Ukraine experienced a strong recovery in the six years after the 1998 crisis (IMF, 2005 and World Bank, 2005a). GDP growth totalled 50% for the period 1999–2004. At 12.1% in 2004, Ukraine's growth rate was the highest in Europe, but this recovery came from a low starting base. Ukraine's output contraction in the 1990s was more pronounced than in most other transition countries and the country's GDP has not yet reached the level it recorded in 1990. Ukraine's per capita GDP of €1,200 at market prices is less than half that of Russia or Romania and not even 10% of that in the EU-15 (although at purchasing power parity, this disparity is considerably less).

The acceleration in economic growth has initially been driven by exports. Rapid growth in China has boosted Ukraine's steel exports, while continued growth in Russia has benefited Ukraine's machinery exports. Additionally, the cheap exchange-rate policy since the 1998 crisis has improved competitiveness considerably. Consequently, annual export growth has averaged 25% since the end of 2002, yielding a sizable current account surplus (10.5% of GDP in 2004) and foreign reserve accumulation. These favourable external conditions have helped to fuel an investment and construction boom, with domestic demand playing an increasingly important role. The trend was also supported by the surge in credit to the private sector and rising disposable incomes. Until 2004, economic growth allowed for a significant improvement in the fiscal position, which led to a greatly reduced debt-to-GDP ratio (from 61% of GDP in 1999 to less than 27% of GDP in 2004). The economy has also experienced significant growth in the real demand for money owing to increased confidence and rising incomes. The macroeconomic stability achieved by Ukraine in 2004 was remarkable in absolute but also in relative terms, when comparing Ukraine's inflation rates, budget balance and public debt with EU-accession candidate states (see further below) and the standards set by the euro area (Vinhas de Souza et al., 2005).

Now, however, Ukraine's macroeconomic environment is deteriorating fast, with much slower growth, and rising inflation and budget deficits (World Bank, 2005a and ICPS, 2005a). Since the elections of late 2004, real growth has slowed while inflation pressures have mounted. In the period January-August 2005, GDP growth decelerated to 2.8% compared with a year earlier. Cutbacks in public investment together with continuing uncertainty about policy interventions caused a substantial fall in investment demand. The contribution of net exports also declined, partly because of the appreciation of the Ukrainian *hryvnya* in April. Meanwhile, consumption growth, fuelled by fiscal stimulus, has remained strong. Industrial production decelerated to 3.5% in January-August 2005. A considerable part of the slowdown can be attributed to the metals (–3.2% in January-July) and oil refining (–8.6%) sectors. Metal production declined as a result of the reversal of the growth of world metal prices, reduced import demand in China and tensions associated with the re-privatisation. The oil refinery sector suffered from the demand decline associated with the surging prices and the earlier government's attempts to control prices and limit exports (abandoned in May). Agricultural output grew by only 2.5%

in 2005, as compared with 20% in 2004. Investment uncertainty resulted in a 7.7% decline in construction during January-August 2005. By contrast, the food industry grew at 14% in 2005, reflecting households' real income growth.

Rising inflationary pressures reflect increasingly tight capacity constraints, large terms-of-trade gains, massive hikes in public wages and pensions and rigidity in the supply response to higher demand in some food markets (e.g. meat). At the same time, the impact and persistence of these shocks on inflation has been enhanced by a monetary policy framework that tends to transmit exchange-rate market pressures directly into changes in monetary conditions. As a result, annual CPI inflation has been on an upward trend since early 2003 and reached 14.9% in the period between August 2004 and 2005.

In the macroeconomic framework, the most pressing issue is the exchange rate targeting policy.[6] In an environment of strong external surpluses and a virtually stable exchange rate there are increasing inflationary pressures, albeit after a period of rather limited inflationary effects stemming from a re-monetisation and reduction of 'barter' payments (Vinhas de Souza et al., 2005). The appreciation of the *hryvnya* in early 2005 may be interpreted as a step towards a more flexible exchange-rate system, a step supported by the international financial institutions, and the authorities have announced their intention to move to an inflation-targeting system. Indeed, an over-long continuation of the current exchange-rate peg may become unsustainable and feed speculative pressures (van Aarle et al., 2004). It is therefore advisable that Ukraine gradually moves towards more exchange rate flexibility in order to gain greater control over monetary aggregates and so avoid the build up of financial vulnerabilities. Unfortunately, whereas there is broad agreement

---

[6] In 2000, a free-floating exchange-rate regime was introduced, but de facto the *hryvnya* has been kept at an almost constant rate with respect to the US dollar by means of foreign-exchange market interventions. Since 2000, the trade and current accounts have shown surpluses, leading to an increase in the money supply, as often the monetary authorities refrained from sterilising these inflows. The main reason behind the lack of effective sterilisation was the lack of sterilisation instruments and the ineffectiveness of the National Bank of Ukraine rates as a monetary policy tool (Bilan, 2004). Also, owing to the success of the stabilisation policy, the demand for financial assets increased. This led to high growth rates of money supply and a credit boom (IMF, 2005).

on the need for such a change, there is much less agreement on the best alternatives (see Yushchenko, 2000) given the practical difficulties that remain in implementing monetary policy in Ukraine (as in other CIS countries – see Esanov et al., 2004). To mention two of the difficulties, the monetary transmission mechanism is still unstable (see Bilan, 2004, Golodniuk, 2004 and Leheyda, 2004) and there is a potential –and growing – 'fear of floating' problem, when one looks at the level of the dollarisation of liabilities in the financial system (IMF, 2005). Money supply or interest rate rules coupled with a floating exchange rate are difficult to implement in Ukraine, because there are neither the stable structural relationships nor the deep financial markets needed to support such monetary rules. The problem also applies to other transition countries such as China (Diehl & Schweickert, 2005),

Assuming that macroeconomic stability remains a high priority, and driven by the early Yushchenko reforms and favourable external conditions, the starting point for the years ahead is still broadly favourable. The National Bank of Ukraine (NBU) developed a solid reputation through its smooth introduction of a new currency in the mid-1990s and remains one of the country's more respected and better-led institutions (EIU, 2005). Good starting conditions together with the reputation of the central bank should allow Ukraine's politicians to concentrate on badly needed institutional reforms.

2.2 Institutional reforms for structural change

While the metallurgical boom has driven the recent rapid economic growth, the necessary diversification away from traditional sectors has been delayed by vested interests and inadequate modernisation of the legal, regulatory and institutional framework. Institutional reform now has to be the first priority for structural change.

The year 2000, when Viktor Yushchenko was Prime Minister, represented a milestone from an historical perspective since it marked the start of Ukraine's economic recovery (World Bank, 2004a). Yet the strong growth since 2000 has reflected low marginal costs for expanding production in many areas owing to excess capacity after the free fall in output in the 1990s. Under these conditions, growth in domestic demand impacted more on output than prices. Yet marginal costs are now increasing as capacity constraints become more binding, which makes fixed capital investment, along with a more efficient allocation of existing resources, increasingly important as a determinant of future growth potential.[7] Although investment levels in Ukraine appear adequate to support economic growth in general, it is not clear if they will be sufficient to support a sustained period of rapid growth over the medium term.

Restructuring in Ukraine has been delayed by vested bureaucratic and economic interests eager to preserve elements of the centrally planned system and by the lack of consensus among political and business leaders over the desirability of market reforms (EIU, 2005). The recent very rapid recovery in growth relied heavily on low value-added (or even value-subtracting) manufacturing sectors, particularly metallurgy (see Tables 2.1 and 2.2). This led to concerns about the longer-term sustainability of the recovery, which was not the result of far-reaching reforms or large-scale investment of the sort needed to reorient the manufacturing sector towards higher value-added output and developed markets. These concerns eased somewhat when in the last few years the ongoing recovery in manufacturing became less driven by traditional industries, and suggested a somewhat broader and more sustainable basis for growth. During this period, higher value-added sectors (including the engineering sector, food and light industries) became increasingly important contributors to growth. Since 2003, machine-building, a relatively high value-added sub-sector, has emerged as the fastest-growing component of the manufacturing sector. The rapid expansion in machine-building is the result of strong Russian demand for railway carriages and locomotives, and a surge in demand among Ukrainian consumers for low-budget, domestically assembled automobiles.

Nonetheless, the metal sector still plays a crucial role. In 2003-04, it returned to strong double-digit growth, having recovered from a sharp production slump in the first months of 2002 (because of weak world prices and proliferating trade restrictions). The sector's recovery reflected improved prices and the successful re-orientation of exports to newer

---

[7] The energy and utility sectors deserve special attention as energy demand continues to increase while the infrastructure deteriorates. In addition to robbing the energy sector of needed investment resources, low energy prices and continuing problems in payment discipline encourage wastefulness and distort the production input mix towards energy-intensive technologies.

markets in the Middle East and Asia. But with about 75-80% of Ukraine's metal production still oriented towards foreign rather than domestic consumers, the sector's vulnerability remains an issue. So too does the growing domestic shortage of scrap metals and coke, two key inputs in steel production. Controversial government measures – including a duty on scrap exports – have failed to dissuade Ukrainian scrap exporters from taking advantage of the higher prices available elsewhere. As a result, Ukraine's success in diversifying away from traditional sectors has been gradual at best. Privatisation and foreign investment have proceeded more slowly in Ukraine than in former communist countries in Central Europe, such as Poland and Hungary.

Table 2.1 Gross value-added by sector, 2002-07 (% of real change)

	2002	2003	2004	2005	2006	2007	% of GDP in 2003
			Est.	Forecast	Forecast	Forecast	
Agriculture, hunting and forestry	2.0	–11.0	19.5	3.0	1.0	3.0	12.7
Extraction	2.4	5.4	4.2	5.0	3.0	3.0	4.0
Processing	9.5	17.4	14.7	3.0	7.0	7.0	23.4
Utilities (power, gas and water)	1.7	4.5	–1.0	3.0	3.0	1.0	3.6
Construction	–2.6	28.2	18.4	–3.0	8.0	10.0	5.0
Wholesale/retail trade	7.8	21.5	17.8	–1.0	5.0	6.0	14.6
Transport	7.4	11.1	10.3	7.0	7.5	8.0	13.2
Education	–0.5	10.4	6.7	5.0	6.0	7.0	4.7
Healthcare and social security	4.6	9.0	5.5	5.0	6.0	6.0	3.2
Other types of economic activity	–	8.3	8.1	8.0	7.0	6.4	15.9
Net tax on products	0.5	2.9	12.6	6.0	5.0	5.0	–
GDP	5.2	9.6	12.1	4.0	5.5	6.0	–

Source: ICPS (2005a).

Table 2.2 Industrial output (2002-07)

	2002 (UAH millions)	Arc (%)	2003 (UAH millions)	Arc (%)	2004 (UAH millions)	Arc (%)	2005 Arc (%)	2006 Forecast Arc (%)	2007 Arc (%)
Total industrial output	171,206.7	7.0	220,605.1	15.8	326,543.9	12.5	5.0	6.5	6.0
Extraction	19,822.0	2.3	21,900.4	5.5	26,881.6	4.1	3.0	3.0	3.0
Fuel extraction	13,026.5	-0.8	13,778.7	3.6	15,014.3	1.9	1.0	1.0	1.0
Non-fuel extraction	6,795.5	7.7	8,121.7	9.1	11,106.3	7.6	6.0	6.0	6.0
Processing industry	126,186.0	8.9	171,592.6	18.2	253,706.3	14.6	6.0	7.0	7.0
Food industry and processing of farm output	30,883.6	8.4	38,409.0	20.0	49,150.7	12.4	10.0	8.0	8.0
Textiles/apparel	2,216.9	0.4	2,498.1	4.0	3,434.0	13.6	4.0	7.0	7.0
Timber production and wood products	1,002.4	23.4	1,499.4	23.6	1,931.8	25.5	20.0	10.0	10.0
Pulp & paper, printing and publishing	3,327.6	8.4	4,294.7	25.7	6,261.5	25.9	10.0	15.0	10.0
Coke production and petroleum refining	9,837.3	25.5	16,896.9	8.7	27,831.4	3.4	-8.0	4.0	2.0
Chemicals and petrochemicals	10,789.4	6.5	14,523.1	16.8	21,204.9	14.4	10.0	6.0	5.0
Other non-metal mineral products	5,378.7	5.3	6,797.3	17.9	9,149.1	19.3	12.0	15.0	25.0
Metallurgy and metal processing	39,031.0	3.9	53,650.9	14.3	86,674.2	12.0	2.0	0.0	-2.0
Machine building	21,309.4	11.3	30,091.4	35.8	43,782.0	28.0	9.0	14.0	15.0
Utilities (electricity, gas and water)	25,198.7	1.1	27,112.1	4.7	45,955.9	-1.1	3.0	3.0	1.0

Note: Arc = annual real change.

Source: ICPS (2005a).

The fundamental challenge will be to modernise the legal, regulatory and institutional framework required for a functioning market economy. Sustained progress in building market-based institutions is a *sine qua non* condition for EU enlargement and neighbourhood policies. Ukraine is characterised by widespread state ownership, an oligarchic business structure (a big part of the economy is controlled by a few industrial clans), inefficient bureaucracy and endemic corruption. The importance of the private sector has risen (to 65% of GDP and 45% of fixed assets), but the composition of the private sector is strongly skewed towards heavy industry, while the service sectors and SMEs remain underdeveloped (ICPS, 2004b). Hence, a strong move towards the implementation of market–based institutional reforms should have been a natural first priority for the new government when it came to power in January 2005. Yet the political arena became fully occupied by counterproductive discussions, which led to a standstill in the essential reform process (Åslund, 2005). The government's interventions in the energy and food sectors, the surge in government expenditures and the re-privatisation drive brought investment and reconstruction to a painful halt. The exceedingly high tax burden harms business and investment, while rising costs neither stimulate enterprises nor calm the surging inflation.

The recent update of the Blue Ribbon report (BRC, 2005) for Ukraine points exactly at the institutional deficits as a bottleneck for structural changes.[8] The report foresees that years will pass before the full positive impact of these changes could be felt, and the steps needed to achieve them will arouse fierce conflicts of interests. But credible signals that the government has adopted a reform course can be expected to improve public confidence. With trade negotiations already on the agenda, tax policy, privatisation, competition policy and better financial intermediation

---

[8] The report proposes five priorities for reform. The first area of priority includes political reform, administrative reform, reform of relations between the central state and local governments and judicial reform. Social reforms are a second priority area. A third priority area consists of further tax reform and the development of the financial sector. The fourth priority targets respect for private property — something that has been discredited by the current relations between the state and private business in post-Soviet Ukraine. The fifth priority area is Ukraine's international integration, which is vital for the country's economic development.

are the reform areas where the government could take immediate steps that help structural change.[9] In the absence of reforms in these areas, the country will have a low investment rating, which discourages foreign capital inflow, while domestic capital flees offshore.

Institutional reform should be the first priority for structural change. The main obstructions on the way from a Soviet past to a European future are domestic. Without a clear signal to the public and to the business sector of a big leap forward in building reliable, market–based institutions, which allow restructuring by the market entry of new enterprises with new products, there is clearly a risk that Ukraine may not use the momentum created by favourable macroeconomic conditions and the spirit of the Orange Revolution, and get stuck on its way to a modern market economy.

2.3 Patterns of trade and foreign investment

Ukraine's trade has roughly doubled over the last decade in US$ value terms, with a major diversification of exports away from the initially dominant Russian market. Exports to Asian markets have grown hugely, while the volume of exports going to the EU-25 plus south-east Europe is now double that for Russia. The new trade structure sees Ukraine having to export to the EU and Asia in order to pay for its oil and gas imports from Russia.

Largely as a result of booming metal exports, Ukraine's level of trade openness has increased considerably (imports and exports are equivalent to 90% of GDP), and is now comparable to other countries in the region. In the medium term, however, the sustainability of the export trend remains uncertain and the export sector faces severe shortcomings (World Bank, 2004a): Ukraine's export elasticity on foreign incomes has been low,

---

[9] An effort should be made to simplify and unify the code, while reducing overall taxation. Another task is to make sure that refunds of value-added tax (VAT) for exporters actually work, so that they are not being punished with an unlawful levy of no less than 20%. Also, the number of taxes as well as the tax burden should be reduced from the current high level of 39% of GDP to a more moderate rate of 25–30% of GDP. The state also continues to control the most capital-intensive enterprises: two-thirds of the capital assets of the real sector remain in state owner-ship, especially in the energy and transport industries, telecommunications, public utilities and military-industrial sectors. Coupled with a completion of privatisation, a more robust and consistent competition policy should be developed (Vinhas de Souza et al., 2005)

Ukrainian exports remain highly concentrated (as shown in slow changes in Ukraine's diversification indicators) and, finally, Ukrainian exporters face far more problems at home than abroad.

Nevertheless, the regional structure of trade is changing continuously. After the enlargement in May 2004, the EU became the largest trade partner of Ukraine. Trade with the EU-25 is estimated to account for approximately one-third of merchandise exports and imports in 2004, with total trade turnover at almost €15 billion. In spite of this fact, it is still substantially below the share from the eight new EU member states from Eastern Europe several years prior to their EU accession. For example, the share of Ukraine's exports to the EU-15 (20% in 2003) is three times lower than that of Poland. The role of Russia — although it is still the largest single-country trade partner for Ukraine — has been substantially declining. The most significant area of that decline is registered for Ukraine's exports to Russia, which dropped by more than half as a share in Ukraine's total exports, from 36% in 1996 to 16% in 2004 (see Tables 2.3 and 2.4). Export flows were redirected towards both the EU-25 and the rest of the world, in particular Asia. As for imports, the decrease in trade with Russia was far less significant, primarily because of its importance as a source of energy products for Ukraine. The structure of Ukraine's trade with the EU-25 and with Russia differs quite significantly (see Figures 2.1 and 2.2). In the most simplified terms, trade flows in Ukraine include westward movement of raw materials and semi–processed goods, and eastwards the opposite movement of final products, primarily investment goods. These features characterise both Ukrainian–EU and Ukrainian–Russian trade relations (Vinhas de Souza et al., 2005).[10]

---

[10] Ukraine's competitive position in world trade on the basis of revealed comparative advantage index shows that Ukraine has a comparative advantage in metals, agro–food products (including vegetable and animal oils and fats) and inedible crude materials. Also Ukraine had, but lost, comparative advantage in chemical products. Exports of these products face more trade restrictions in the case of the EU market (anti–dumping cases against metal and chemical products, limitations of the GSP scheme, etc.), than in the case of the Russian market. Free trade agreements and similar trade regulations inherited from the past and still partially functioning make the Russian market relatively more open than the EU market.

Table 2.3 Ukraine's changing trade structure for exports from 1996 to 2004

Exports to:	1996 ($ million)	2004 ($ million)	1996 (%)	2004 (%)
EU-15	3,196	6,432	22.2	19.7
CEECs-10*	1,123	3,349	7.8	10.2
SEECs**	849	1,820	5.9	5.6
EU + CEECs + SEECs	5,168	11,600	35.9	35.5
Russia	5,572	5,886	38.7	16.0
Rest of the World	3,626	15,177	25.2	46.5
Total	**14,400**	**32,666**	**100.0**	**100.0**

Source: International Monetary Fund, *Directions of Trade.*

Table 2.4 Ukraine's changing trade structure for imports (from 1996 to 2004)

Imports from:	1996 ($ million)	2004 ($ million)	1996 (%)	2004 (%)
EU-15	2,710	6,439	15.4	22.2
CEEC-10*	1,091	2,506	6.2	8.6
SEECs**	563	606	3.2	2.1
EU + CEECs +SEECs	4,364	9,551	24.8	32.9
Russia	8,819	12,127	50.1	41.8
Rest of the World	4,418	7,316	25.1	25.2
Total	**17,603**	**28,996**	**100.0**	**100.0**

* The 10 Central and Eastern European countries (CEEC-10) comprise the new EU member states of Estonia, Latvia, Lithuania, Malta, Poland, Slovak Republic, Slovenia, Hungary, Czech Republic and Cyprus.

** The south-eastern European countries (SEECs) comprise Bulgaria, Romania, Bosnia/Herzegovina, Macedonia, Albania, Croatia, Yugoslavia and Turkey.

Source: International Monetary Fund, *Directions of Trade.*

Figure 2.1 Structure of Ukrainian exports (2002)

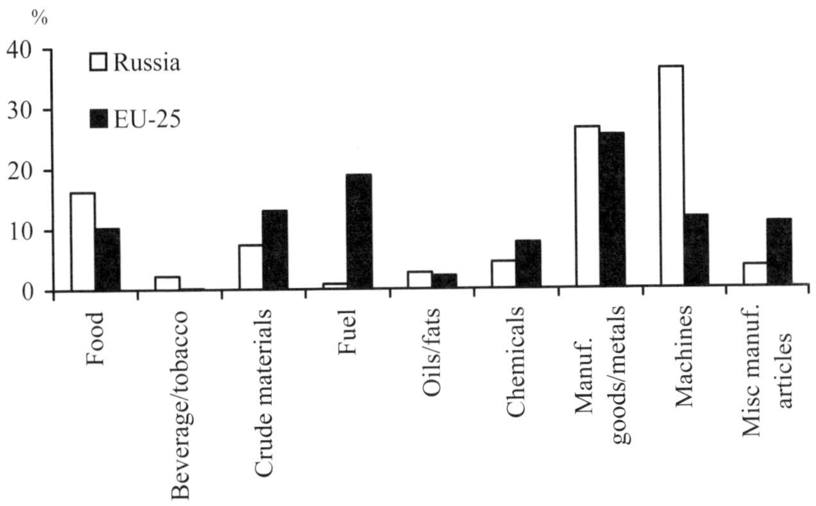

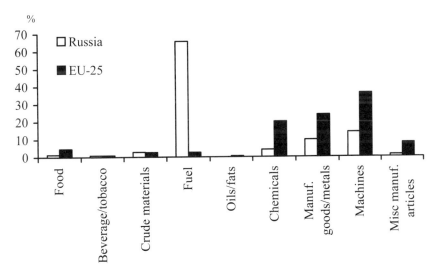

Source: Vinhas de Souza et al. (2005).

Figure 2.2 Structure of Ukrainian imports (2002)

Source: Vinhas de Souza et al. (2005).

Ukraine's dependence on Russia's fuels is partly a consequence of natural resource endowments, but partly also a heritage of the former Soviet Union, which meant an extremely inefficient structure of energy consumption. Ukraine is the most energy-consuming economy in the region. The introduction of energy-saving technologies, as well as the diversification of energy suppliers and types of energy used is expected to reduce Ukraine's dependence upon Russia. In terms of exports, the EU's market seems potentially much more attractive, being the largest neighbouring market both in terms of population and GDP. But it is also more demanding, and increasing export share in this market will mean meeting very high demand standards; however, it would also facilitate entering other world markets with quality products.

Another indicator of regional integration is capital movements between the regions concerned and, in particular, flows of foreign direct investment (FDI). Despite all the benefits FDI can bring to a transition economy, Ukraine has failed to attract a significant amount of capital from abroad. As for the origin of current foreign investors present in Ukraine, the EU is by far the largest, with more than one-third of total FDI inflow (for just the EU-15, so the figure for the EU-25 would be higher).[11] It is followed by the US, a set of so-called 'offshore zones' (Cyprus, an EU-25 member and the Virgin Islands, a British dependency) and CIS countries – mainly Russia (see Figure 2.3). All together, these four groups account for three-quarters of the total FDI stock.

FDI originating from different regions goes into different industries. As shown in Table 2.5, Russian capital is concentrated in the fuel and energy sector. Russian oil companies have acquired almost all Ukrainian oil refineries, which in the era of the former Soviet Union were constructed specifically for processing Russian oil. EU investors are mostly companies in the food, chemical and machine-building industries. The wholesale and retail trade sector has also received a significant portion of the funds coming from the EU. Hence, capital from the more advanced economies of the EU can bring benefits that are more relevant for the long-term growth

---

[11] The figure of FDI flow from the EU-25 is not reported, since the enlarged EU includes one very large off-shore zone, Cyprus, which accounts for a substantial portion of FDI into Ukraine. It is difficult to identify the true origin of capital coming from offshore zones. Potentially, investors of all countries (including Ukrainian) may use these regions for tax-optimisation schemes.

and development of the Ukrainian economy. But without a big leap forward in terms of the institutional reforms outlined above, Ukraine is likely to miss its chance to exploit a comparative advantage as a low-wage location with access to both the EU and the CIS markets. On its own, a simple free trade regime with either EU or CIS will not do the trick. The experience of the new EU member states showed that domestic reforms linked to European integration led to an increase in FDI inflows on a scale sufficient to boost economic growth. Trade policy, to be discussed below, has to be seen as a catalyst for internal reforms and an element in an aggressive strategy to increase domestic investment and FDI inflows.

Figure 2.3 Origins of FDI inflows to Ukraine (2003)

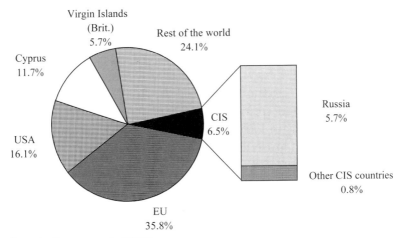

Source: Vinhas de Souza et al. (2005).

Table 2.5 Sectoral distribution of FDI from the EU-15 and Russia (2003)

	EU-15		Russia	
	($ million)	(%)	($ million)	(%)
All sectors	2,383.4	100	377.7	100
Agriculture	61.6	2.6	5.9	1.6
Industry	1,340.2	56.2	159.4	42.2
Mining	32.7	1.4	1.1	0.3
Manufacturing	1,297.0	54.4	158.3	41.9
Food industry	581.0	24.4	10.6	2.8
Light industry	55.0	2.3	0.1	0.0
Wood–processing	45.2	1.9	0.5	0.1
Publishing	73.0	3.1	0.8	0.2
Coke and refined oil products	10.2	0.4	103.7	27.5
Chemical industry	141.1	5.9	0.6	0.2
Other non-metallic mineral products	109.4	4.6	2.3	0.6
Metallurgy and metal processing	46.0	1.9	20.0	5.3
Machine-building	205.0	8.6	8.5	2.3
Other	29.5	1.2	11.1	2.9
Production and distribution of electricity, gas and water supply	10.1	0.4	0.0	0.0
Construction	50.3	2.1	14.7	3.9
Wholesale & retail trade	373.3	15.7	26.9	7.1
Hotels and restaurants	24.9	1.0	6.3	1.7
Transport and telecommunications	174.9	7.3	39.4	10.4
Finance	186.1	7.8	28.5	7.5
Real estate	108.1	4.5	17.3	4.6
Education	1.2	0.1	0.0	0.0
Healthcare	5.2	0.2	77.9	20.6
Other community, social and personal services	57.6	2.4	1.4	0.4

Source: Vinhas de Souza et al. (2005).

2.4 Ukraine and comparator countries

Relative to comparator countries, such as Turkey, Romania and some other EU candidate and new member states, Ukraine's fiscal and external balances and indebtedness situation is relatively favourable, and provides a sound basis for the reform of domestic economic governance and institutions.

When trying to gauge the effects of economic integration between Ukraine and the EU, it is important to appreciate the fact that Ukraine is different from other countries that are either part of the enlargement process or the European Neighbourhood Policy (ENP). With 600,000 km², the country is slightly bigger than France and its 48 million inhabitants are equivalent to two-thirds of the total population that entered the EU during the 2004 enlargement. Economically, the characteristics of Ukraine are somewhat of a mixture between Poland (the largest of the recent accession countries, with substantial heavy industry), Romania (a large and poor accession candidate with a significant agricultural sector) and Turkey (a large country of geo-strategic importance on the European fringe). Despite these similarities, Ukraine is unique in the combination of its features: its large size, its low income level, the depth of the structural adjustment challenges ahead, the size of its steel and heavy industry, as well as its huge and potentially highly competitive agricultural sector.

A precondition for Ukraine's progress is to secure the macroeconomic stability achieved so far. As regards inflation, Ukraine figures in the last position with Romania and Turkey (Vinhas de Souza et al., 2005). But Ukraine's performance with respect to fiscal data was much better. The fiscal deficit in 2004 was even lower than the EU's 3% (Maastricht) criterion. Together with the Baltic countries, Bulgaria, Romania and Slovenia, Ukraine outperforms the euro area in this regard. Turkey appears again at the end of the scale, with a fiscal deficit more than double that of Poland, the new member state with the highest fiscal deficit. A similar picture appears with respect to public debt, where Ukraine is again in the group with the best performance, whereas Turkey has the highest public debt. All in all, the macro picture on the basis of inflation and fiscal data reveals that Ukraine still needs to undergo some additional nominal convergence. This is only in absolute terms, however, as in relative terms Ukraine performs quite well when compared with the new member states. Turkey is the only country in the sample that fails to meet any of the three criteria discussed here. Hence, according to the Maastricht criteria, Ukraine is considerably closer to Brussels than Turkey.

A more critical matter of concern may be the external position. Table 2.6 shows some indicators on the external position comparing the five non–member countries with the new member states in this respect. Ukraine shows the lowest external debt and short-term debt ratios of all, whereas some new member states (such as Estonia and Latvia) and candidate countries (such as Bulgaria, Croatia and Turkey) have heavily exposed external debt burdens. A similarly favourable position for Ukraine is seen with respect to the current account deficits adjusted for FDI inflows.

Table 2.6 The changing structure of Ukraine's trade (1996-2002)

	EU-25				Russia			
	1996		2002		1996		2002	
	$ million	(%)*	$ million	(%)*	$ million	(%)*	$ million	(%)*
Exports								
Regional exports	2,793.8	19.4	4,449.9	30.9	5,170.0	35.9	2,462.6	17.1
Exports by the Level of Procession								
Raw materials	810.2	29.0	890.0	20.0	206.8	4.0	73.9	3.0
Semi-processed products	894.0	32.0	1,379.5	31.0	2,326.5	45.0	763.4	31.0
Final goods	922.0	33.0	2,002.5	45.0	2,688.4	52.0	1,625.3	66.0
Exports by the factor intensity								
Capital intensive goods	1,005.8	36.0	1,513.0	34.0	2,843.5	55.0	1,354.4	55.0
Labour intensive goods	335.3	12.0	801.0	18.0	361.9	7.0	295.5	12.0
Raw material intensive goods	1,201.3	43.0	1,780.0	40.0	1,499.3	29.0	615.6	25.0
Imports								
Regional imports	3,802.2	21.6	5,316.1	30.2	7,815.7	44.4	6196.3	35.2
Imports by the level of procession								
Raw materials	418.2	11.0	152.1	4.0	2,509.5	66.0	2,509.5	66.0
Semi-processed products	646.4	17.0	874.5	23.0	380.2	10.0	418.2	11.0
Final goods	2,623.6	69.0	2,623.6	69.0	950.6	25.0	874.5	23.0
Imports by the factor intensity								
Capital intensive goods	1,749.0	46.0	2,205.3	58.0	836.5	22.0	912.5	24.0
Labour intensive goods	798.5	21.0	950.6	25.0	152.1	4.0	190.1	5.0
Raw material intensive goods	836.5	22.0	342.2	9.0	2,737.6	72.0	2,623.6	69.0

* In percent of total exports/imports in the case of regional exports/imports; in percent of regional exports/imports otherwise.

Sources: Vinhas de Souza et al. (2005), World Bank (2005a) and authors' calculations.

Hence, the still favourable macroeconomic setting could provide the basis for a big advance in terms of institutional reforms. The fact that this is so badly needed is seen in the World Bank Governance Indicators (WBGI), which demonstrate the challenges (see Figure 2.4). In a sample of European countries, Ukraine together with Moldova, perform worst. In contrast to naïve expectations about the transition process, not all countries' institutions have improved over the years. By far the largest progress has been made by Bulgaria and Croatia. In fact, Croatia shows positive developments in all indicators. In the case of Turkey, there is a strong deterioration in the indicators for regulatory quality and control of corruption and no progress with respect to government effectiveness or the rule of law. In Ukraine the poor quality of almost all institutions had even been deteriorating further before the Orange Revolution. The Kuchma heritage was clearly disastrous. Up to that point, the transition process had not translated into better institutions, whereas the case of the Baltic states and now that of Croatia, illustrates how EU integration may help to focus the reform process of accession countries (Schweickert, 2004 and Hammermann & Schweickert, 2005).

Figure 2.4 Institutional quality in the EU and non–EU Europe (2004)

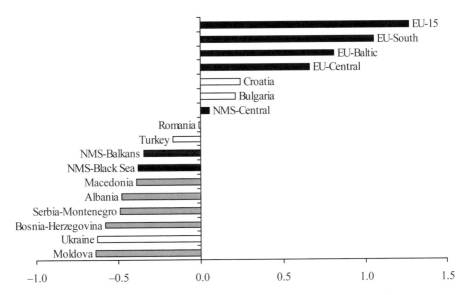

Notes: EU-15 comprises the EU member states before 2004; EU–South refers to Portugal, Spain, Greece; EU–Baltic refers to Estonia, Latvia, Lithuania; EU–Central refers to Poland, Czech Republic, Slovak Republic, Hungary, Slovenia; NMS–Central refers to the non-EU member states Bulgaria, Romania; NMS–Balkans comprises the non-EU member states of former Yugoslavia; NMS–Black Sea refers to Ukraine, Moldova and Turkey.

Sources: Kaufmann et al. (2005) and authors' calculations.

Based on the indicators analysed in this chapter, the macroeconomic situation is still favourable. The fiscal and external debt figures in particular are better than in comparator countries. On the negative side, there is a considerable backlog with respect to the development of institutional capacities and a potential for macroeconomic instability owing to monetary expansion, rising inflation rates and real exchange-rate instability. As a consequence, the process of structural adjustment in Ukraine remains at an early stage. Like much of the former Soviet bloc, independent Ukraine inherited an economy based on heavy industry and reliant on technology that had largely been superseded in the West. Ukraine's main challenge is to diversify away from many of the industries that depended heavily on government subsidies and to develop a viable production and export structure on the basis of a comparative advantage as a low-wage producer located between European and CIS markets. This leads to the conclusions that Ukraine urgently needs to develop market-based institutions that foster structural change. Together with sustained macroeconomic stability, this is a precondition for establishing stable trade relations with its neighbours and for exploiting potential benefits from an FTA with the EU.

Table 2.7. Major macroeconomic indicators for Ukraine by indicator and year (1998-2007)

	1998	1999	2000	2001	2002	2003	2004 est.	2005 forecast	2006 forecast	2007 forecast
Economic activity										
GDP, UAH billions	102.6	130.4	170.1	204.2	225.8	267.3	344.8	412.1	486.5	542.6
Real GDP, apc*	–1.9	–0.2	5.9	9.2	5.2	9.6	12.1	4.0	5.5	6.0
Real industrial output, apc	–1.0	4.0	13.2	14.2	7.0	15.8	12.5	5.0	6.5	6.0
Real agricultural output, apc	–9.8	–5.7	7.6	10.2	1.2	–11.0	19.9	3.0	1.0	3.0
Gross investment, % GDP	20.8	17.5	19.8	21.8	20.2	22.0	19.1	19.4	18.9	19.6
Real gross fixed investment, apc	2.6	0.1	12.4	6.2	3.4	15.8	10.2	–2.0	7.0	9.0
Real total consumption, apc	–0.1	–3.7	2.0	9.3	5.0	12.8	12.1	13.1	7.6	7.8
Net FDI, $ millions[a]	747	489	594	769	688	1,411	1,711	1,700	2,000	2,500
Real disposable household income, apc[b]	–5.8	1.2	11.1	10.0	18.0	9.1	16.5	19.5	6.0	6.5
Real retail trade, apc	–6.6	–7.1	8.1	13.7	15.0	20.5	20.0	17.0	13.0	10.0
Prices										
Consumer price index, apc	20.0	19.2	25.8	6.1	–0.6	8.2	12.3	13.5	11.5	7.0
Producer price index, apc	35.3	15.7	20.8	0.9	5.7	11.1	24.1	11.0	6.0	6.0
Labour market										
Population, millions	50.1	49.7	49.3	48.4	48.0	47.6	47.3	47.1	46.9	46.7
Average monthly real wages, apc*	–3.9	–8.9	–0.9	19.3	18.2	15.2	23.8	15.0	8.0	7.0
Unemployment rate, % (ILO methodology)	–	11.9	11.7	11.1	10.1	9.1	8.6	8.2	8.0	7.8

Table 2.7, continued

Foreign economic activity										
Exports of goods & services, apc	−13.4	−7.3	18.0	8.0	10.7	24.0	37.2	13.0	7.0	8.0
Imports of goods & services, apc	−14.0	−19.1	17.8	14.1	5.0	28.7	26.0	20.0	13.0	15.0
Current account balance, % GDP	−3.1	3.0	4.0	3.7	7.7	5.8	10.5	6.0	2.8	−0.3
Budget										
Revenues, % GDP (consolidated) [c]	27.3	24.7	26.2	26.9	27.4	28.5	26.5	30.0	29.0	29.0
Balance, % GDP [c]	−2.7	−2.4	−0.8	−0.3	0.7	−0.2	−3.2	−3.0	−2.0	−1.0
Financial indicators										
Monetary base, apc	22	39	39	37	34	30	34	39	23	15
M3, apc	25	41	45	42	42	47	32	38	30	22
NBU gold/forex reserves, $ millions	793	1,094	1,475	3,089	4,417	6,937	9,252	14,475	16,176	17,146
Official exchange rate, UAH/$ (average annual)	2.45	4.13	5.44	5.37	5.33	5.33	5.32	5.11	5.04	5.09
Loan interest, % pa (average annual) [d]	55	53	40	32	25	18	17.5	15.9	13.3	9.0

* Apc = annual percentage change.

(a) according to the NBU.

(b) starting in 2002, indicator of aggregate disposable household income.

(c) calculation using IMF methodology.

(d) commercial bank loans, UAH.

Source: ICPS (2005a).

Table 2.8. External balances in the new member states, accession countries and Ukraine in 2004 (%)

	External debt/ GDP	Short-term debt/ exports	Debt service/ exports	Current account/ GDP	FDI/ GDP	Current account + FDI	Reserves/ M2	Real effective exch. rates (change)
Czech Republic	35.5	21.8	6.2	−4.6	4.6	−0.0	36.8	−0.2
Estonia	80.3	36.6	13.5	−14.5	5.5	−9.0	34.8	0.9
Hungary	57.2	14.2	24.5	−9.1	2.3	−6.8	27.6	3.8
Lithuania	46.0	29.9	14.4	−8.5	3.0	−5.5	53.3	−0.9
Latria	74.4	112.5	14.8	−10.9	3.8	−7.1	34.4	−0.4
Poland	41.7	20.0	16.0	−1.4	1.7	0.2	36.8	−2.1
Slovenia	45.5	0.8	14.7	−0.3	−0.5	−0.8	44.6	0.0
Slovakia	46.1	20.5	8.0	−3.6	3.9	0.3	52.4	9.0
NMS-8	**53.3**	**32.0**	**14.0**	**−6.6**	**3.0**	**−3.6**	**40.1**	**1.3**
Bulgaria	61.9	23.1	12.4	−7.0	9.7	2.7	60.0	3.0
Romania	35.5	6.0	14.4	−6.0	5.5	−0.4	71.5	2.2
Turkey	51.1	32.0	36.9	−3.6	0.7	−3.0	24.7	−0.1
AC-3	**32.5**	**9.7**	**8.9**	**−4.3**	**5.1**	**0.8**	**43.8**	**1.7**
Croatia	78.9	3.3	20.4	−5.3	2.4	−2.9	37.5	−0.4
Ukraine	27.3	1.2	12.9	10.2	2.3	12.5	38.7	−7.5
NAC-2	**53.1**	**2.3**	**16.7**	**2.4**	**2.3**	**4.8**	**38.1**	**−4.0**

3. UKRAINE'S TRADE POLICIES

This chapter reviews recent developments in Ukraine's trade-related policies and outlines the government's options. Ukraine's negotiations on WTO accession are currently the focal point of reforms in trade-related policies. Although important in its own right, WTO accession will also help to resolve some current bilateral trade-policy issues, such as by ending EU quotas on steel imports from Ukraine. Also reviewed is progress to date in Ukraine's institutional approximation to EU law (*acquis communautaire*) in key areas as defined by the EU–Ukraine Partnership and Cooperation Agreement (PCA). Finally we discuss how far Ukraine's integration with the Commonwealth of Independent States (CIS) can go without prejudicing an EU–Ukraine FTA.

3.1 WTO accession process

Ukraine's average tariff rate for WTO accession is likely to be a little under 5% for industrial goods and about 11% for agricultural produce. Ukraine's offer for service sector liberalisation is very bold and goes beyond what many existing WTO members have done. Yet there are still problems in getting some WTO-compliant legislation adopted by the parliament.

WTO accession is a precondition for free trade between the EU and Ukraine. But even by the standards of WTO accession negotiations, Ukraine's accession process has been protracted since it first applied for membership in 1993. At least one meeting has been held by Ukraine's accession working party each year since 1995. An offer on market access for imports of services was first submitted in 1997 and an offer on goods in 1999. A first draft of the working party's report (which normally signals that all substantial disagreements have been essentially resolved) is dated 16 March 2004; the newest draft is dated 24 August 2005. A working party meeting planned for 29 September 2005 was postponed. Still, if parliamentary support can be ensured for the required legislative changes, it is entirely possible for Ukraine to accede to the WTO in 2006.

Ukraine's negotiations on market access for goods and services are almost complete, following extensive bilateral and multilateral talks. But substantial issues remain to be resolved, mostly with Australia and the US. On the Australian side, concerns include agricultural subsidies to be retained by Ukraine as well as the proposed tariff rate quota for sugar (Australia wants Ukraine to double the tariff-free quota). American concerns focus on the implementation in national legislation and effective enforcement of WTO rules on the protection of intellectual property rights, as well as on market access in audio-visual services. On the US side, complex congressional procedures are currently being activated to permanently waive the application of the Jackson–Vanik amendment to Ukraine, which is a precondition for Ukraine to enjoy the full benefits of WTO membership in its trade relations with the US.

In bilateral and multilateral negotiations, practically all import tariff lines for goods have been agreed. Although detailed information about Ukraine's recent comprehensive tariff offer consolidating the results of these negotiations is formally restricted, its key features are widely known. Import tariffs (most-favoured nation or MFN rates) on agricultural products will decline from an average of 15% at present to about 11% at the end of the implementation period around 2010. The average MFN tariff on industrial goods will remain roughly constant at just below 5% as bound rates are reduced slightly during the implementation period but still remain marginally higher on average than the current applied rates. These conclusions apply broadly to both weighted and unweighted average tariffs. The view that no large cut in the average tariff is likely to be required reflects the fact that import tariffs in Ukraine have already been fairly modest in recent years.[12]

In 2004, Ukraine submitted a services offer that will bind fairly liberal rules for market access across a wide range of service sectors. There will be no limitations on i) cross-border supply, ii) consumption abroad, or iii) commercial presence for 139 out of 155 service (sub)sectors (see Box 3.1).

---

[12] See World Bank, *Ukraine Trade Policy Study*, Report No. 29684, Washington, D.C. (2004a) for a comprehensive review of the Ukrainian trade regime since the early 1990s.

Box 3.1. Ukrainian offer to the WTO in services

Sectors covered by the standard formula with no limitations on cross-border supply, consumption abroad or commercial presence:

- Professional services – legal, advisory, accounting, taxation, etc.
- Computer and related services – data processing, software and repair services
- Research and development services in natural and social sciences
- Real estate services
- Rental & leasing services
- Other business services – advertising, consulting, personnel, etc.
- Telecommunications services – telephone, mobile, e-mail, leased circuits, etc.
- Construction services for buildings & engineering works
- Distribution services – wholesale, retail, franchising, agencies
- Environmental services
- Banking & financial services
- Tourism and travel-related services
- Recreational, cultural & sporting services
- Transport services – maritime, inland waterway, railway & fuel pipelines

Sectors with limitations are:

- Health & related services
- Agricultural land – ownership only by Ukrainian citizens
- Notarial services – only performed by Ukrainian citizens
- Auditing services – a foreign auditor's conclusions must be confirmed by a Ukrainian auditor
- Medical & dental services – professional qualifications will be assessed according to Ukrainian law
- Postal services – the licensing system for mail & packages applies universally to service providers
- Education, schools & other academic institutions– only Ukrainian citizens can head educational institutions
- Insurance services – licensing required for branches (but not subsidiaries)
- Hospital services – professional qualifications are assessed according to Ukrainian law
- News agencies – foreign investment is limited to 30%
- Audio-visual sector
- Road transport

Source: Government of Ukraine.

Ukraine does not commit itself with respect to restrictions on the movement of natural persons except for senior employees (who may stay in Ukraine for up to five years) and a widely defined group of service providers who may stay in Ukraine for up to 180 days in any calendar year. This offer has been accepted by the members of Ukraine's accession working party, with only minor issues still to be settled, and is outstandingly liberal by the standards of many WTO member states; further many of the limitations (as in Box 3.1) concern regulatory issues that do not restrict market access.

Implementation in national legislation. Although negotiations with trading partners have almost been completed, there is a considerable amount of legislation that still needs to be passed by parliament for Ukraine to become WTO-compliant. The government has made repeated efforts since the summer of 2005 to push through large packages of the required measures. Parliamentary opposition has remained a problem, however, with alliances of various interest groups ranging from communists with ideological objections to oligarchs with specific business interests.

Changes in national legislation are needed not only to implement the results of market access negotiations for goods and services. In addition, Ukraine needs to implement the WTO Single Undertaking, i.e. all binding WTO rules that affect a wide range of trade-related policies. For example, with respect to trade in goods, these include the national treatment of imported goods in terms of domestic taxes or standards for customs valuation of imports. With respect to the protection of trade-related intellectual property rights, the WTO Single Undertaking includes minimum standards of protection for various categories of intellectual property rights as well as rules on effective enforcement.

The government has recently adopted a series of necessary but politically difficult changes in government regulations, including some related to investment incentives and the price regulations for alcoholic drinks. The parliament has implemented required changes in customs tariffs following Ukraine's recent tariff offer, removed restrictions on the imports of used cars, liberalised financial and audit services, and reduced export restrictions on ferrous metal scrap and some agricultural products. Apart from several outstanding legislative changes of a fairly technical nature (sanitary and phytosanitary standards, technical barriers to trade), delays in adopting the draft laws necessary for WTO accession persist in sensitive sectors such agriculture (export restrictions on hides and skins and the lowering of barriers to sugar imports) and metallurgy (reductions in – but no abolition of – export duties on metal scrap). With the March 2006 parliamentary elections looming as well as persistent pressure from the big metallurgical lobbies, it is unclear whether essential legislative changes can be made before the elections.

3.2 Trade relations with the EU

Under the existing trade policy regime the EU grants tariff preferences to Ukraine, as to many partner states under the Generalised System of Preferences (GSP), but also has made considerable use of the anti-dumping defensive instrument. The EU recognised Ukraine's market economy status in December 2005. WTO accession will make an important difference to EU–Ukrainian trade relations, since the EU's steel import quota will have to be scrapped and the scope for anti-dumping actions will be more strictly constrained.

Ukraine's bilateral relations with the EU are based mainly on the PCA, which was signed in 1994 and entered into force in 1998 for an initial 10-year period. A future EU–Ukraine FTA would presumably become part of a new agreement that might replace the PCA after 2008. Other significant bilateral agreements relate to trade in textiles and clothing (now fully liberalised), trade in steel products and cooperation in the field of controlled nuclear fusion.

EU imports from Ukraine have benefited from the Generalised System of Preferences (GSP) since 1993. Currently, imports can be divided into three categories, each accounting for approximately one-third of import value: goods imported tariff-free under the GSP (non-sensitive products), goods imported under GSP preferential tariff rates (sensitive products) and goods imported at MFN tariff levels. It has been estimated that GSP preferences reduce EU import tariffs on Ukraine's exports by up to 2 percentage points from a hypothetical average of about 4% under MFN rates. It is noteworthy that GSP treatment is not granted to many of Ukraine's most important export commodities, such as iron and steel, fertilisers, fishery products, grain, seeds, fruit or plants (for more details, see World Bank, 2004a, pp. 73-86). Overall, however, average tariffs on EU imports from Ukraine are already quite low; an EU–Ukraine FTA will lead to little additional market access for Ukraine through tariff reductions.

Many Ukrainian exports to the EU as well as to other countries have been subject to anti-dumping duties in recent years. According to the WTO, Ukraine ranked 13th in the world as a target of anti-dumping measures between January 1995 and June 2004, with 51 anti-dumping actions imposed by various trading partners (a share of anti-dumping measures about ten times greater than Ukraine's share of world trade). Of these, eight originated in the EU-25 (typically in the range of 25-50%) and affected a group of metallurgical and chemical products. As these product groups comprise roughly half of Ukraine's total exports (to all destinations), it is highly likely that anti-dumping duties had a major impact on Ukrainian exports to the EU.

The large number of successful anti-dumping procedures against Ukrainian exports is partly explained by the fact that during that period Ukraine had not yet been accorded market economy status by the EU. As a result, Ukrainian exporters found it more difficult to disprove allegations of dumping by EU special interest groups. Issues that prevented Ukraine's graduation to market economy status (MES) included deficiencies in bankruptcy legislation and state intervention in price-setting mechanisms. These concerns should diminish as Ukraine addresses the implementation of relevant WTO rules (such as Art. XVII of GATT 1994 on state trading enterprises) in its national legislation upon acceding to the WTO. While concerns about soft budget constraints in Ukraine should certainly not be minimised, it is noteworthy that Russia was granted MES by the EU as early as 2002. The state of the systemic transition is broadly similar in Russia and Ukraine. The EU finally granted Ukraine MES in December 2005.

Ukrainian (as well as Russian and Kazakh) exports of many steel products to the EU are still limited by a quota system that will expire automatically when Ukraine accedes to the WTO. Thus WTO accession will remove a market access barrier that would otherwise have to be dealt with by an EU–Ukraine FTA.

3.3 Approximation to EU law

Ukraine has been making considerable efforts to bring its market legislation in line with EU standards and laws in line with commitments made in the PCA, even during the politically inhospitable environment of the Kuchma administration. The results so far have only been partial.

Among many other provisions, the EU–Ukraine PCA sets out the objective of approximating Ukrainian economic laws to the EU's regulations and norms. Art. 51 states that:

> an important condition for strengthening the economic links between Ukraine and the Community is the approximation of Ukraine's existing and future legislation to that of the Community. Ukraine shall

endeavour to ensure that its legislation will be gradually made compatible with that of the Community.[13]

Art. 51 goes on to specify 16 domains for approximation. Since 1996, considerable legislative work has been done in these areas, coordinated by the Ministry of Justice and supported by EU technical assistance. In a recent stocktaking exercise for all 16 domains, the EU-financed Ukrainian-European Policy and Legal Advice Centre (UEPLAC) used the following definitions to broadly characterise the degree of approximation to EU norms of every key legal instrument in each of the 16 domains. The results of this stocktaking exercise are summarised in Table 3.1, although it must be stressed that it only gives an impression of a highly complex field. Out of a total of 234 legal instruments analysed, 26 are described as fully approximated; approximation is considered advanced in 62 instruments and underway in 113; 33 legal instruments are held not to be approximated. Among the 16 domains, approximation of legal instruments in the broad field of service sector regulation seems especially, while the least progress has been made in areas under the heading of economic governance. Nevertheless, significant legislative efforts have been made in all domains.

The Ministry of Justice is currently (mid-November 2005) completing its own review of legal approximation in the 16 domains; while their report is not yet available, we have received impressions of their views from interviews and a short paper prepared by the ministry (see Box 3.2). The overall picture is similar to that painted by the UEPLAC review, although again this can only be taken as a broad brush view. While identifying outstanding issues in each domain, the ministry notes that there has been a continuing harmonisation process that could be substantially completed by the time the PCA expires in 2008. The ministry rightly stresses that this scorecard relates to the legal texts and does not assess the effectiveness of enforcement. Still, it seems a significant achievement that these legal reforms were largely developed during the Kuchma administration in a less than favourable environment for EU–Ukrainian institutional integration.

---

[13] See Council and Commission Decisions No. 98/149/EC, ECSC, Euratom of 26 January 1998 on the conclusion of the Partnership and Cooperation Agreement between the European Communities and their Member States, of the one part, and Ukraine, of the other part OJ 049, 19.02.1998, pp. 0001-0002.

Table 3.1 Approximation levels of Ukrainian legislation in relation to the EU acquis in the 16 domains of Art. 51 of the PCA – Assessments as of 2004

Sector of policy	Number of Ukrainian laws			
	Approx-imated	Approx-imation advanced	Approx-imation under way	Not approx-imated
Trade and product regulation				
1. Customs	–	1	4	–
2. Technical standards	–	–	11	3
3. Food safety	8	3	24	2
4. Indirect taxation	–	4	4	–
Service sector regulation				
5. Banking	2	2	2	–
6. Financial markets, insurance	–	1	14	–
7. Transport	4	10	13	–
8. Nuclear energy sector	3	3	-	–
Economic governance				
9. Competition & bankruptcy	1	10	-	1
10. Public procurement	–	5	-	1
11. Intellectual property rights	5	9	-	6
12. Taxation	–	1	1	4
13. Civil code	–	–	6	–
14. Consumer protection	–	–	9	4
15. Labour protection	2	7	9	10
16. Environment	1	6	16	2
Totals	**26**	**62**	**113**	**33**

Notes: Approximated = the given legal instrument is very similar to the respective EU legislation.

Approximation advanced = the main elements of the examined legal instrument are present in the domestic legal system and it has been developed along a similar line to that of the EU.

Approximation underway = first steps towards implementing the given legal instrument have been taken, or there is a comprehensive legal draft in progress or in front of the government or parliament.

Not approximated = this area of law is at such an early stage of development that a particular legal instrument is missing from Ukraine's legal system.

Source: UEPLAC (2004).

Box 3.2. Evaluation of Ukraine's approximation to EU law

Trade and product issues

Customs: There is substantial compliance with the EU and the WTO, but implementation is still lagging for customs evaluation and rules of origin. Amendments to the customs code are still needed in 2006.

Product standards: So far, 16 technical regulations and 2000 out of 5000 specific standards have been adopted in compliance with EU and international standards.

Food standards: Current statutory acts are not totally compliant with the EU or the WTO. A draft law has been submitted, but implementation will be difficult.

Indirect taxation: VAT compensation (for exporters?) is still a flagrant issue of non-compliance.

Service sector regulation

Banking: This area is largely compliant with the EU; the area is open, but some procedures are unduly complex.

Financial services: Adaptation of laws is ongoing; it is anticipated that this area will become EU-compliant.

Insurance: This field is largely open and compliant.

Transport: This area still needs essential privatisation and reforms. There is a Ministry of Transport plan for 2005-07.

Energy: Ukraine has joined and ratified the European Energy Charter. Wholesale markets for electricity, oil and gas still need further liberalisation and reform.

Economic governance issues

Competition: Most competition law is compliant with the EU. Implementation and procedural issues remain, for which a new law in 2006 is planned.

Public procurement: This area is only partly compliant, with new a programme for 2005-10 aiming at EU compliance.

Bankruptcy law: Several problems remain, notably provisions concerning companies with state participations.

Intellectual property: Substantial work needs to be done towards EU compliance, but draft laws are still to be passed.

Company law: There is partial compliance with more draft laws planned for 2006.

Company law and accounting: Work towards EU compliance is ongoing, with revisions of laws planned for 2006.

Consumer protection: This area is only partly EU compliant; revisions of the related laws are ongoing.

Environment: Development of environmental law is ongoing but patchy.

Labour law: Current laws do not meet EU standards and new ones are needed.

Source: Ministry of Justice, Ukraine.

What seems appropriate is a *two-pronged strategy with an active and a passive component*: active *acquis* convergence would be pursued in priority areas, where the *acquis* either makes a significant contribution to domestic economic development or to deeper cross-border integration. Economic development will be promoted by those parts of the *acquis* that are in line with international best practices, are suited for Ukraine's state of development, are relatively easy to implement (cost-benefit analysis) and address pressing reform needs. This report argues that priority areas for *acquis* convergence include product standards, competition policy and the backbone areas of telecommunications, transport, energy and financial services. Passive *acquis* convergence would be pursued in all non-priority policy areas, by screening all new pieces of legislation on their *acquis* compatibility. In other words, new legislation would be modified but not initiated out of the desire to comply with the *acquis*. The Ministry of Justice has a department in charge of legal approximation to the EU and could fulfil that function.

Ukraine's key challenge regarding *acquis* compliance is *not the adoption of new legislation, but its effective enforcement*. In many policy areas, the country has relatively modern laws, but they are not sufficiently implemented or complied with. In the EU internal market, however, enforcement is the key. To make progress on this front, Ukraine will have to address a number of structural problems: its weak government institutions, a highly deficient judicial system, poorly developed regulatory authorities, pervasive corruption and the strong grip of the oligarchs with their shady business practices on large parts of the economy. Unless these problems are solved, Ukraine will not be able to make real progress on *acquis* compliance.

3.4 Ukraine–Russia/CIS/Common Economic Space

Ukraine's participation in the Single Economic Space (SES) with Russia, Belarus and Kazakhstan raises issues of compatibility with an FTA+ with the EU. Free trade with both the SES and EU are entirely possible, but customs union would not be.

Since trade among the former Soviet republics collapsed in the early 1990s, Ukraine has participated in various CIS-wide and bilateral agreements that have sought to revive the traditional trade linkages among them. Many of these agreements, especially multilateral ones such as the CIS Economic Union, the CIS free trade zone, the CIS Common Agricultural Market, etc., have suffered from very weak implementation and have remained virtually irrelevant. Nevertheless, working bilateral agreements are in place with key CIS trading partners that effectively establish bilateral free trade areas, albeit with some exemptions for sensitive products. For example, the 1993 free trade agreement with Russia covers all goods except sugar, tobacco goods, certain spirits, chocolate and candies, while the Ukrainian–Russian steel trade is regulated by special quotas on Ukraine's steel exports to Russia.

In 2003, Ukraine was invited to join an ambitious effort at deeper integration (the SES project) with Russia, Belarus and Kazakhstan. These three countries are already linked by a customs union; their systemic transformation has advanced to a broadly similar degree (at least as regards Russia and Kazakhstan); and many policy-makers probably share similar protectionist preferences with respect to the design of trade-related policies. With only four member countries (compared with the CIS's twelve) and with Russia clearly playing a leading role, this new effort at integration is potentially more promising than previous ones at the CIS level. The objectives stated by the SES are ambitious, with the creation of a customs union without exceptions or limitations, involving a unified policy on tariff and non-tariff regulations, unified rules for competition, the use of subsidies and other forms of state support and without contingent protection affecting intra-union trade. Further steps would involve the harmonisation of macroeconomic policies and network regulation.

Ukrainian participation in the SES project was rendered politically feasible by the explicit understanding that these ambitious objectives are to be implemented gradually, with each country independently determining the speed of its integration (the so-called 'multilevel' and 'multi-speed integration'). Eventually, however, a single commission in which each member state will have a voting weight proportional to its economic size would govern all policies; clearly, decisions by this commission would be dominated by Russia.

Ukraine's participation in an effective SES customs union along these lines would be incompatible with an EU–Ukrainian FTA because Ukraine would have to give up its sovereignty over certain trade-related policies to a supranational SES decision-making body. Technically, the EU could conclude an FTA with the SES customs union. But at best it will take a long time for this body to develop a sufficiently robust institutional structure to act as a counterpart in an agreement with the EU.

Therefore, Ukraine faces a crucial choice: either to integrate more closely with the EU through a deep FTA while seeking to maintain and extend the existing free trade agreements with CIS countries (for example, by reducing the list of goods exempted from free trade); or it could opt for deeper SES integration with its envisaged customs union and institutional provisions. In the latter case improvements in EU–Ukrainian trade relations might be limited to what would come with WTO accession, such as an end to the quota system for steel products and the granting of market-economy status, which would make it more difficult to impose anti-dumping tariffs on Ukrainian exports to the EU. It is notable, however, that Ukraine's political declarations since the Orange Revolution have excluded Ukraine's accession to the customs union of the SES.

Interestingly, Ukraine's bilateral free trade agreements with some CIS member countries contain provisions on the conduct of WTO accession negotiations. There was an early understanding among many CIS countries that they would closely coordinate their negotiating strategies and aim at joining the WTO at the same time. This coordinated approach made sense because many difficult issues – such as state trading enterprises, the legal implementation and enforcement of intellectual property rights, etc. – applied similarly to most CIS countries. In practice, this coordinated approach translated into Russia taking the lead in negotiations while governments that were so inclined (including Belarus, Kazakhstan and for some time Ukraine) would follow closely – on the understanding that, should Russia accede first, it would then use its newly gained influence to accelerate the other countries' accession process. If Ukraine makes integration with the EU the clear priority, these provisions would lose relevance.

There would still be many aspects of an FTA+ where the choices made will necessarily affect relations between both parties and Russia. It is entirely possible for there to be free trade between all three parties. Yet in the absence of this condition there should be no customs union between any of the parties.

For the highly complex domain of technical standards for industrial and agricultural goods it is desirable that there be convergence on a single set of standards. Ukraine is converging on EU standards. Here it would be helpful if Russia also converged on EU standards in the framework of the (EU-Russia) Common European Economic Space, and there are signs that Russian practice is tending to move in this direction. Nevertheless, Ukrainian enterprises could still seek to supply both EU and Russian markets in conformity with their respective standards where these are different, so there is no necessary conflict of norms.

In the electricity sector, grid connections require technical compatibility. Ukraine now has a small regional grid connection with its EU neighbours, known as the 'Burshtyn Island', while the rest of the Ukrainian grid is connected to the Russian grid. If Ukraine joined the south-east European grid, as has begun to be discussed, it would mean alignment with EU standards. That step would have implications for the present Ukrainian–Russian grid connection, unless there is also progress in EU–Russian electricity trade, which only seems to be a long-term prospect.

4. ECONOMIC EFFECTS OF SIMPLE OR DEEP FREE TRADE SCENARIOS[*]

This chapter reviews and updates the findings of the 1999 feasibility study on the likely economic effects of an EU–Ukraine FTA. Given the limited time available for preparing this report, it has not been possible to undertake a fresh, detailed empirical analysis of all possible effects on trade and production patterns, income growth and distribution, and social welfare. Yet by updating the earlier analyses as well as drawing on recent literature, it is possible to discuss rough orders of magnitude of the main effects.

The first section of this chapter (section 4.1) reviews the changing geographical and commodity composition of Ukraine's international trade since 1997.[14] Section 4.2 reports the simulation results from an updated and somewhat extended version of the computable general equilibrium (CGE) model that was employed in the earlier study. These findings provide insights into the direction and possible order of magnitude of trade and sectoral output effects of trade integration. But comparative-static CGE models cannot capture the medium- to long-term welfare gains and income growth that would result from an improving investment climate as a result of Ukraine approximating key economic institutions to the EU model in the

---

[*] The authors thank Alexander Freese, Alexandra Horst and Ece Turgay for their research assistance in this chapter.

[14] Annex 4, section 3 provides additional detail on recent trends in several indicators that were used in the 1999 study to gauge possible trade creation and diversion effects from an EU–Ukraine FTA.

context of a deep EU–Ukraine FTA. Section 4.3 draws on recent related literature to provide a sense of the orders of magnitude of such effects.

4.1 Gravity models and Ukrainian trade trends

The evolution of the geographical composition and sectoral pattern of Ukraine's international trade since 1997 confirms the conclusion of the earlier study (Brenton, 1999) that the EU and Ukraine are natural trading partners.

The lingering impact of Soviet-style central planning on the international trade patterns of Ukraine has diminished since 1997. The Soviet economy had been fairly insulated from the rest of the world – even from the member countries of the Council for Mutual Economic Assistance. As a result, during the first half of the 1990s, the share of Commonwealth of Independent State (CIS) countries in Ukraine's international trade was far larger than one would expect on the basis of their geographical location and economic size (GDP per head and population). Also, the commodity composition of exports differed from traditional (CIS) markets where final goods played a significant role in line with the structure of output in Ukraine, and the EU and other industrialised countries where exports consisted more of commodities and intermediate goods.

With respect to the geographical composition of trade, the 1999 study (Brenton, 1999, ch. 3) used a gravity model of bilateral trade flows to predict a substantial growth of the EU's share in Ukraine's exports. The gravity model describes bilateral flows as increasing in the economic weight of the two countries, measured by per capita income and total population, and decreasing in their distance, which may be reflected in geographical distance as well as other factors that either facilitate or impede transactions across the border (e.g. common language or currency, a free trade agreement and adjacency). While the EU-15 accounted for about one-third of Ukrainian non-fuel imports and less than one-fifth of exports, its potential share, based on a 'normal' trade pattern estimated with a gravity model, was thought to be closer to one-half of both non-fuel imports and exports (Brenton, 1999, ch. 3, Fig. 3).

Figure 4.1 demonstrates that Ukrainian exports have indeed evolved towards a more 'normal' geographical composition while growing rapidly since 1997. Whereas exports to Russia and other CIS countries almost doubled from $4.6 billion to $8.6 billion in 2004, exports to the EU-25 countries tripled to $9.8 billion. Exports to the rest of the world, chiefly to developing countries in Asia, the Middle East and the Western hemisphere, more than doubled from $6.5 billion to $14.3 billion. Preliminary data for

2005 suggest, however, that exports to Russia continued their strong growth from 2004, whereas exports to the EU were stagnant. If confirmed by annual data, this new trend would suggest that many Ukrainian firms are able to take advantage of strong demand growth in Russia, fuelled by high world market prices for energy. Clearly, many Ukrainian firms are still more familiar with the Russian market than with Western Europe; at the same time, a shared history and language may give them an edge over their competitors in the Russian market.

Figure 4.1. Ukraine: Exports by major destinations, 1997-2004
(US$ billion)

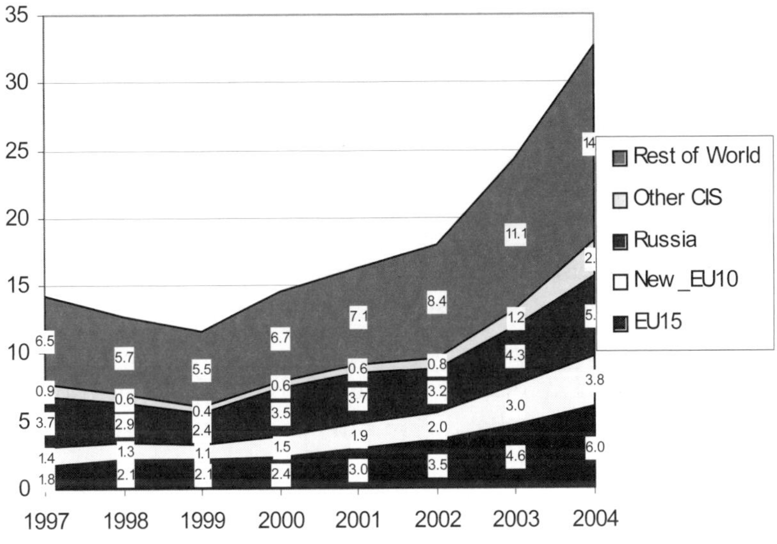

Source: IMF, Direction of Trade Statistics.

A less clear picture emerges for Ukraine's imports (Figure 4.2), possibly in part because the sharp energy price increases in recent years inflated the value of Ukrainian imports from Russia (predominantly energy) relative to imports from the EU. Total imports declined sharply between 1997 and 1999 owing to the regional economic crisis. From 1999 to 2003, import growth was particularly strong for the EU-25 ($7.7 billion in 2003 versus $5.0 billion in 1997) and the rest of the world ($6.9 billion versus $3.6 billion); imports from Russia and other CIS countries grew less rapidly. In 2004, however, imports from CIS countries jumped to $15.2 billion from $9.6 billion in 2003, probably in large part because of increases in energy prices.

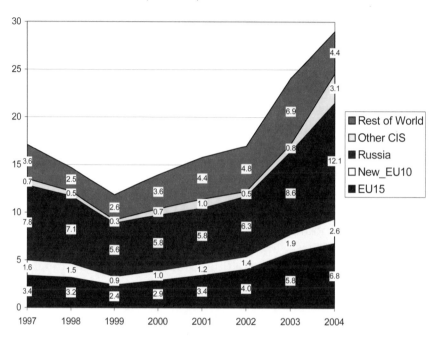

Figure 4.2. Ukraine: Imports by major countries of origin, 1997-2004
(US$ billion)

Source: IMF, Direction of Trade Statistics.

The gravity model does not permit us to predict how long the reorientation of Ukraine's trade patterns towards a more 'normal' pattern with a substantially larger share of the EU in Ukraine's exports and imports will take. In the short run, the relative weight of trading partners fluctuates along with exchange rates and world market prices for key commodities; trade patterns are partly driven by path dependencies (such as existing pipelines for natural gas transport); and in any case, coefficient estimates and hence the 'normal' trade pattern assumed for Ukraine obviously depend on the database that is used to estimate the gravity model. Nevertheless, the model as well as the strong growth of trade with the EU since 1997 suggests that the EU and Ukraine are natural trading partners, based on geographical proximity and the EU's large GDP. Therefore, any trade diversion that may be caused by an EU–Ukraine FTA is unlikely to be large and will probably be compensated for by efficiency gains from trade creation.

On the other hand, Russia and other CIS countries are currently as important to Ukraine as export markets as the EU – and even more important as sources of imports. Therefore, it would be desirable for Ukraine to maintain and further develop the free trade agreements that cover Ukraine's trade with the CIS countries. To the extent that deeper integration involves the harmonisation of institutions, such as in standardisation and certification, it would be desirable for Ukraine's CIS trading partners to also persuade their institutions to approximate to EU norms, rather than maintain idiosyncratic rules.

Neither the commodity composition of Ukraine's exports and imports, nor the EU-25 trade share in individual product categories, have changed much in the course of the rapid growth of international trade since 2001 (Tables 4.1 and 4.2).

On the export side, where the EU-25 accounted for 30% overall in 2001 as well as 2004, its shares are still relatively high for many raw and semi-processed commodities, such as mineral products (47% in 2004), hides and skins (61%), and wood and wood products (71%). By contrast, EU-25 shares for many processed commodities and final goods are much lower, with machinery at 31% and base metals and articles thereof at 21%. For the latter, exports to the EU are restricted by a quota regime that will automatically expire when Ukraine accedes to the WTO.

Since the remaining exports go mostly to Russia and other CIS countries, these figures document the difficulties that Ukrainian producers of final goods still face in meeting the demands of the relatively sophisticated EU markets for differentiated goods (see section 2.3 for a more detailed discussion). There are encouraging counter-examples, however. Textile and clothing exports are destined largely to the EU (76% in 2004), probably reflecting production networks with EU firms where Ukrainian firms perform labour-intensive operations outsourced from Western Europe (see section 4.3 for a more thorough discussion of the role of such networks). Similarly, exports of instruments (HS Section XVIII), another labour-intensive sector, have grown sharply, with 46% of all exports going to the EU. These examples suggest that Ukraine's international trade patterns are indeed becoming more 'normal' – not only with respect to the overall direction of trade, but also in the sense that Ukrainian exporters are overcoming the Soviet legacy of insulation from the world market and are learning to successfully serve relatively sophisticated markets such as the EU.

Table 4.1 Ukraine's exports to the EU vs. the rest of the world by commodity (2001 and 2004)

HS section Of which HS chapter		Total exports ($ million)		Of which exports to EU-25 (%)	
		2001	2004	2001	2004
I	Animals & animal products	454	648	16.5	3.9
II	Vegetable products	693	1,136	48.9	28.4
III	Animal or vegetable fats	225	546	19.8	38.1
IV	Prepared foodstuffs	451	1,141	13.1	13.9
V	Mineral products	1,750	4,324	57.4	51.8
27	Mineral fuels, oils, distillation products, etc	1,186	3,387	51.6	47.2
VI	Chemical products	1,478	2,782	30.1	29.7
28	Inorganic chemicals, precious metal compounds, etc.	550	786	19.5	20.4
29	Organic chemicals	203	500	58.0	47.3
VII	Plastics & rubber	256	439	18.1	30.3
VIII	Hides & skins	130	207	81.8	60.8
IX	Wood & wood products	230	516	81.7	70.8
X	Wood pulp products	287	393	17.4	10.2
XI	Textiles & textile articles	614	883	74.2	81.5
62	Articles of apparel, accessories, not knit or crocheted	420	554	80.6	75.7
XII	Footwear, headgear	85	122	69.5	58.3
XIII	Articles of stone, plaster, cement, asbestos	141	281	19.5	39.2
XV	Base metals & articles thereof	6,720	13,048	18.6	20.7
72	Iron and steel	4,977	10,766	13.8	17.7
73	Articles of iron or steel	649	1,448	13.6	32.2
XVI	Machinery & mechanical appliances	1,714	3,032	34.1	31.3
84	Nuclear reactors, boilers, machinery, etc	1,249	1,803	33.4	24.2
85	Electrical, electronic equipment	466	1,229	36.0	41.8
XVII	Transportation equipment	549	2,035	18.3	10.8
XVIII	Instruments - measuring, musical	77	592	25.4	60.9
XIX	Arms & ammunition	93	171	47.2	56.9
XX	Miscellaneous	11	0	99.2	66.9
XXI	Works of art	305	370	10.1	26.8
	Total	**16,265**	**32,666**	**30.4**	**29.9**

Source: Ukrainian national statistics.

Table 4.2 Ukraine's imports from the EU vs. the rest of the world, by commodity (2001 and 2004)

HS section		Total imports ($ million)		Of which imports to EU 25 (%)	
Of which HS chapter		2001	2004	2001	2004
I	Animals & animal products	183	315	26.5	35.3
II	Vegetable products	266	439	43.0	24.1
III	Animal or vegetable fats	86	149	50.4	44.3
IV	Prepared foodstuffs	590	1,005	28.9	35.2
V	Mineral products	6,725	10,845	3.1	4.2
VI	Chemical products	1,127	2,248	59.7	59.0
29	Organic chemicals	186	340	41.7	39.2
30	Pharmaceutical products	343	745	69.2	67.3
38	Miscellaneous chemical products	192	313	69.3	72.8
VII	Plastics & rubber	697	1,407	49.7	50.0
39	Plastics and articles thereof	463	1,071	61.9	57.3
VIII	Hides & skins	66	73	71.3	75.4
IX	Wood & wood products	73	156	73.7	75.8
X	Wood pulp products	538	785	54.0	60.3
XI	Textiles & textile articles	647	992	61.1	63.4
52	Cotton	96	171	47.5	52.4
54	Manmade filaments	105	115	58.6	69.7
55	Manmade staple fibres	129	175	63.3	62.7
XII	Footwear, headgear	44	43	30.3	42.2
XIII	Articles of stone, plaster, cement, asbestos	185	391	57.9	50.3
XV	Base metals & articles thereof	821	1,753	39.2	31.2
XVI	Machinery & mechanical appliances	2,378	4,741	50.6	56.5
84	Nuclear reactors, boilers, machinery, etc.	1,661	3,214	46.8	54.3
85	Electrical, electronic equipment	717	1,526	59.4	61.0
XVII	Transportation equipment	746	2,494	44.0	41.8
87	Vehicles other than railway, tramway	637	2,247	46.3	43.9
XVIII	Instruments – measuring, musical	260	560	46.0	45.7
XIX	Arms & ammunition	114	242	70.2	54.2
XX	Miscellaneous	1	1	20.4	16.6
XXI	Works of art	228	356	39.4	49.4
	Total	**15,775**	**28,997**	**29.5**	**32.6**

Source: Ukrainian national statistics.

4.2 CGE model simulations

Cuts in import tariffs on their own, such as in a simple FTA, will not lead to substantial income growth and welfare gains. But deeper free trade could deliver welfare gains of the order of 4-7% in comparative static simulations. If dynamic effects are also taken into account, the orders of magnitude could over time be twice or three times as large. Additional estimates on the effects of reductions in the cost of capital could amount to further welfare gains of 4-5%. If this deeper free trade were limited to Ukraine, there would be a potential for trade diversion from other CIS countries. Therefore, a comprehensive approach for trade liberalisation and institutional harmonisation covering the whole region would be desirable.

The 1999 feasibility study used a small comparative-static CGE model to estimate the production and trade effects of an EU–Ukraine FTA. We have reviewed and updated this model with more recent data, while leaving its basic structure unchanged owing to time constraints. Our model predicts trade flows and output changes for six regions: Ukraine, the EU-15, the 2004 Central and Eastern European accession countries (CEECs), south-eastern European countries including Turkey (SEECs), Russia and the rest of the world (ROW). Its sectoral focus is on trade in goods because available data for trade in services are at best fragmentary, especially in terms of disaggregation by trading partners. Thus we separately identify the following sectors: agriculture, minerals, food products, light manufacturing, heavy manufacturing, textiles, metals and services, and other activities. It would be desirable to distinguish between plant and animal products within agriculture, but this was precluded by lack of data.

The model is based on data drawn from the Global Trade Analysis Project (GTAP) database complemented by Ukrainian national sources. While the GTAP data are available only for 2001, information on Ukraine has been adjusted to reflect the rapid growth of Ukraine's GDP and international trade since then. We assess the sensitivity of our simulation results by employing two alternative sets of assumptions about elasticities of substitution between factors of production and elasticities of transformation across outputs; these 'low' and 'high' elasticity cases correspond approximately to 'short-term' and 'long-term' effects. In the low (high) elasticity case, the elasticity of substitution is 2 (4) between the same class of goods from different countries and 1.25 (1.25) between different classes of goods. The elasticity of transformation in production is 2 (4). A detailed description of the model and fuller discussion of the assumption is in annex 4.

Data on import tariffs are from the GTAP database for 2001, complemented with national data for Ukraine. In an extension of the 1999 model, we use a gravity model of bilateral trade flows to estimate the implicit non-tariff trade barriers among the regions of our model. Regression estimates are obtained for each sector from GTAP trade data for 2001. Technically, these estimates are based on the coefficients of dummy variables for relevant country groupings in the gravity regressions (for example, to indicate that a given bilateral trade relationship involves trade among EU-15 countries, or between an EU-15 country and an accession country, or between an EU-15 country and the rest of the world). The resulting estimates of the *ad valorem* equivalents of implied trade barriers are large, roughly ranging from 20% for textiles to 40% for food products, over and above the formal and informal barriers still encountered by trade flows between EU countries.

We develop three highly stylised scenarios involving progressive degrees of trade liberalisation and institutional approximation. Scenario (i) represents the eastern enlargement of the EU plus Malta and Cyprus as well as the future accession of south-eastern Europe (especially Romania and Bulgaria). This scenario involves eliminating the estimated non-tariff barriers between the EU-15, CEECs and SEECs. This scenario is included in part to assess the possible disruption to Ukraine's trade with the CEEC and SEEC regions because of their accession to the EU. Scenario (ii) adds a simple FTA with the EU-15, the CEECs, the SEECs and Ukraine, with import tariffs fully abolished, but EU versus non-EU non-tariff barriers still in place. Scenario (iii) represents the move from a simple to a deep FTA, eliminating non-tariff barriers between Ukraine and the extended EU-25 with the aid of considerable institutional and regulatory convergence.

In interpreting the simulation results from this small comparative-static model, it is important to be clear about its limitations. For this particular exercise, the stocks of all factors of production are assumed constant and fully employed. Reductions in trade barriers will lead to an elimination of waste (non-tariff barriers are represented by a cost per unit of output), as well as to a more efficient allocation of factors of production across sectors and additional trade; but increases in output for one sector inevitably involve decreases in output elsewhere in the economy. Thus the model does not account for the added investment and income growth that would result from the efficiency gains arising from trade liberalisation and institutional approximation. Still, some rough indications are given below of the possible size of the dynamic effects, which would be additional to the comparative-static effects generated by the model.

Table 4.3 summarises the changes in Ukraine's international trade and sectoral structure of output owing to progressive trade liberalisation in line with our scenarios. Considering trade flows by trading partner first, the eastern enlargement scenario (i) causes trade between the EU-15 and Ukraine to decline slightly.

Table 4.3 CGE simulation results - Trade by partner country and sector (percent change)

	Scenario (i) EU eastern enlargement (change)		Scenario (ii) EU-Ukraine simple FTA (change relative to eastern enlargement)		Scenario (iii) EU-Ukraine deep FTA (change relative to simple FTA)	
	Short term	Long term	Short term	Long term	Short term	Long term
Exports of Ukraine						
EU-15	0.0	-0.7	19.8	64.8	15.8	58.0
CEECs	2.4	27.3	23.8	94.1	11.8	37.2
SEECs	3.1	26.4	21.9	76.8	6.7	34.9
Russia	-4.4	-10.4	0.2	-0.2	-10.7	-15.5
Rest of world	0.4	-0.2	0.2	0.0	-8.0	-11.5
Imports of Ukraine						
EU-15	-4.8	-11.7	5.9	11.4	18.3	53.6
CEECs	22.2	86.3	8.4	15.9	15.3	32.9
SEECs	17.0	82.5	8.3	15.5	3.6	28.8
Russia	-5.2	-13.7	-4.8	-10.8	0.2	-7.0
Rest of world	-4.7	-12.5	-3.0	-6.7	-1.9	-13.6
Exports by sector						
Agriculture	2.0	4.8	5.2	11.7	5.1	31.2
Minerals	-3.1	-7.7	1.3	1.5	-24.8	-37.1
Food processing	1.2	3.5	14.0	35.2	7.5	15.2
Light manufacturing	-5.4	-10.4	14.4	34.6	6.2	21.9
Heavy manufacturing	-1.3	3.6	4.0	10.1	7.5	13.2
Textiles	4.5	8.5	5.6	13.8	9.0	8.8
Metals	-0.5	-1.3	79.4	495.5	10.6	63.5
Other activities	3.9	3.7	1.4	1.8	16.2	75.2
Imports by sector						
Agriculture	4.3	18.0	10.8	35.2	9.8	34.5
Minerals	-0.2	3.9	0.7	5.5	-12.7	-20.7
Food processing	0.8	1.7	-4.4	-15.2	7.4	12.7
Light manufacturing	-1.1	-1.7	-1.4	-5.4	2.7	6.4
Heavy manufacturing	-5.0	-4.8	-7.3	-8.3	9.1	15.2
Textiles	1.9	3.2	1.0	2.9	12.8	19.1
Metals	-1.2	0.8	4.9	7.8	0.9	2.3
Other activities	-1.1	-2.9	-2.9	-5.5	11.4	42.4

Source: Authors' simulations.

Table 4.4 CGE simulation results - Trade with the EU-15 and CEECs (percent change)

	Scenario (i) EU eastern enlargement (change)		Scenario (ii) EU-Ukraine simple FTA (change relative to eastern enlargement)		Scenario (iii) EU-Ukraine deep FTA (change relative to simple FTA)	
	Short term	Long term	Short term	Long term	Short term	Long term
Exports to EU-15						
Agriculture	0.7	-1.4	22.1	49.6	56.8	103.4
Minerals	0.0	-3.6	3.6	7.4	21.4	142.7
Food processing	1.3	0.8	40.8	98.5	54.2	18.1
Light manufacturing	0.7	-9.1	28.1	65.4	41.5	18.1
Heavy manufacturing	-4.1	-3.4	10.2	22.4	13.8	9.1
Textiles	1.4	0.0	11.0	25.1	20.2	3.0
Metals	-1.0	-4.1	314.4	1,714.9	402.0	76.1
Other activities	5.9	8.3	1.4	1.8	48.0	194.3
Imports from EU-15						
Agriculture	-3.9	-9.7	1.7	36.6	24.1	48.7
Minerals	-5.3	-13.9	30.8	2.9	9.0	-2.7
Food processing	-2.8	-7.5	16.2	64.7	8.8	6.7
Light manufacturing	-2.0	-18.8	4.0	25.6	7.8	-5.4
Heavy manufacturing	-10.0	-18.6	1.9	7.4	9.0	-6.9
Textiles	-0.6	-3.4	10.7	4.5	10.4	8.7
Metals	-4.6	-17.9	-0.2	20.8	18.7	18.5
Other activities	0.1	1.1	5.9	0.1	35.1	140.3
Exports to CEECs						
Agriculture	2.0	38.8	24.0	48.5	25.8	184.4
Minerals	6.7	40.0	6.3	7.1	17.7	242.2
Food processing	-7.0	9.5	40.1	97.1	8.3	27.8
Light manufacturing	-37.7	-31.8	27.7	65.3	9.1	-11.8
Heavy manufacturing	20.4	62.1	10.2	22.3	7.6	83.5
Textiles	14.2	40.3	11.1	25.0	6.5	45.1
Metals	22.9	111.4	307.0	1,460.8	21.1	238.3
Other activities	-21.2	-55.5	0.9	1.6	38.5	21.4
Imports from CEECs						
Agriculture	33.9	131.9	11.2	21.9	24.0	282.1
Minerals	23.8	86.0	0.0	-0.5	8.6	109.0
Food processing	24.4	83.3	32.0	68.5	8.6	112.2
Light manufacturing	-11.3	57.8	22.2	41.1	7.8	83.7
Heavy manufacturing	21.7	62.8	7.0	13.8	9.1	87.3
Textiles	16.7	53.7	11.1	24.1	11.4	74.6
Metals	44.7	198.1	8.6	12.4	18.3	307.4
Other activities	-16.3	-54.6	5.9	13.3	35.0	8.6

Source: Authors' simulations.

But this effect is compensated for by a substantial increase in trade between Ukraine and the new (recent and future) EU members, as they adopt the more liberal import regime of the EU. In scenario (ii), with import tariffs eliminated on trade with the enlarged EU, the earlier reductions in trade with the EU-15 are more than reversed while trade with the CEECs/SEECs continues to grow. In scenario (iii), putting trade between Ukraine and the enlarged EU on a more equal footing with intra-EU trade, Ukraine's trade with the EU-15/CEECs/SEECs grows very substantially. In all three scenarios, some trade is diverted away from Russia and the rest of the world as a result of lower trade barriers between Ukraine and Western Europe.

Because of the high level of sectoral aggregation and highly stylised representation of the production side in this small CGE model, it is especially important to view the sectoral change generated by the simulations as an indication of the mechanisms at work, rather than as a forecast. With this caveat, under both a simple and a deep FTA (scenarios (ii) and (iii)), Ukraine's total exports rise across nearly all sectors (except agriculture under a deep FTA). Metallurgical exports increase disproportionately, largely as a result of the elimination of the EU import quota, which is subsumed under the simple FTA scenario (although technically it will occur whenever Ukraine accedes to the WTO; see also annex 2).

For Ukraine's trade with the EU-15 and the CEECs the model predicts large increases in both Ukrainian exports and imports in agriculture and food processing (see Table 4.4 above). This result suggests that additional export opportunities for Western European producers will appear alongside higher competitive pressure from Ukrainian exports not only across, but also within broadly defined sectors. The impact of the lifting of the EU quota regime on Ukrainian metallurgical exports (subsumed under the simple FTA scenario) is also prominent. In reality, however, the surge in exports will probably be dampened by the ongoing price increases for imports of energy materials from Russia (e.g. the price increases decided early in January 2006). As a result the external competitiveness of the Ukrainian iron and steel industry will suffer. This sector is more energy-intensive than its worldwide competitors, with more than 40% of output still from open-hearth furnaces. On the other hand a wide range of sectors that are less energy-intensive stand to gain, especially if the energy price increases also result in some compensatory depreciation of the Ukrainian currency.

Our model also generates estimates of the comparative-static income and welfare effects for Ukraine from progressive trade liberalisation and institutional approximation. For the 'eastern enlargement' scenario (i), welfare gains are up to 3%, similar in size to the gains for the CEECs and SEECs themselves. For a simple FTA (scenario (ii)), the gains are negligible whereas for a deep FTA (scenario (iii)), they are 4-7% on top of the gains through eastern enlargement (see annex 4 for details).

Broadly, these estimates are in line with the findings of other recent papers on the impact of trade liberalisation in CIS countries. For example, using a single-country model to study the impact of Ukraine's WTO accession, Pavel et al. (2004) arrive at welfare gains of around 4%, largely through the elimination of subsidies rather than cuts in import tariffs. Recent studies of the CEEC accession states (Le Jour et al., 2001 and Edwards, 2005) show that the effects of harmonisation and mutual recognition agreements are potentially far more significant for trade and for economic welfare in particular than tariff and quota removal alone. From related literature it is also known that when additional investment resulting from higher efficiency is taken into account, such comparative-static effects translate into full dynamic effects that may be two to three times as large.[15]

The following calculation explores how a deep EU–Ukraine FTA would affect investment in Ukraine more specifically, namely by reducing the cost of capital in at least three ways. First, the cost of capital goods will be reduced by cheaper imports. As a rough guide, our simulations suggest that the price of capital goods (compared with average output prices for Ukrainian industry) could fall by up to 3%. Second, institutional approximation to the EU to rebrand Ukraine as a more reliable place in which to do business will reduce risk premia for investors. A conservative estimate puts the consequent reduction in the cost of capital (measured as the annual rental cost) at 10%. Further, increased competition in the

---

[15] Annex 4 also discusses several other welfare-improving effects of trade liberalisation and institutional integration that are difficult to estimate but are widely acknowledged by recent empirical research to be quantitatively important. These include: increased competition and lower monopolistic price mark-ups (which are important in Ukraine where many markets are highly monopolised); reduced corruption (though lower monopoly rents); and productivity gains through firm-selection effects because exporting firms would grow faster than other firms and exporters tend to be high-productivity producers.

banking sector could reduce the cost of capital by 5%. Altogether, the price of capital could fall by up to 17%.

Cheaper capital affects welfare via a complex route. First, the stock of capital employed will rise by between 15 and 30%, depending on elasticity assumptions (short-term versus long-term). GDP will rise by between 4% (short-term) and 9% (high elasticity), compared with our basic CGE simulations with fixed capital. This will increase wages in Ukraine by up to 10%. Still, it is plausible that most of the extra capital will be in the form of foreign direct investment (FDI); hence, there will be an offsetting outflow of interest, profits and dividends. Nevertheless, cheaper capital goods mean lower costs for existing Ukrainian firms, while a lower risk premium reduces welfare losses through uncertainty for all. Lower profit margins in financial intermediation, however, imply lower profits for Ukrainian banks. Taking all these effects into account, the lower cost of capital raises welfare in Ukraine by between 4 and 5%, in addition to the trade gains identified in our comparative static simulations. Thus the overall welfare gain from a deep EU–Ukraine FTA would be estimated as well above 10%.

4.3 Impact of institutional reforms and approximation

Estimates of the impact of improved institutional quality for countries such as Ukraine are very large, with conceivable increases in GDP in the range of 20 to 30%. Fully opening the financial and other important service sectors to foreign investment and best international practice would constitute a key element of such reforms.

While the comparative-static CGE model gives a useful indication of prospective structural change in international trade and production owing to an EU–Ukraine FTA, the model does not adequately account for how a lasting improvement in the quality of institutions in Ukraine through deep integration with the EU would lead to additional investment and GDP growth. This section reviews recent literature on medium- to long-term growth effects of regional integration schemes and institutional reforms and applies the findings to a deep EU–Ukraine FTA. Two strands of literature are considered: i) case studies based on the experiences of recent major regional integration projects, such as NAFTA and the EU's southern enlargement; and ii) econometric studies that relate improvements in the quality of institutions to GDP growth.

Piazolo (2001, ch. D) reviews case studies of the growth effects of regional integration between rich and poor countries. It is often argued that by 'anchoring' key institutional reforms on an international agreement, poor-country governments may enhance their credibility, improve the investment climate and accelerate GDP growth. Regional integration with institutional approximation to the rich partner is a strong signal of the commitment to reform, renders arbitrary policy changes more difficult and costly and thereby strengthens the incentives for the government to stay the course. The influence of different national interest groups is reduced, further enhancing the credibility of reforms.

The history of NAFTA shows these mechanisms at work. Fernandez-Arias & Spiegel (1998) argue that the primary impact of NAFTA does not lie in the further reduction of already low tariffs between the partners, but in a fundamental change in the attractiveness of Mexico as a location for investment. They extend the traditional analysis of customs unions to allow for international capital movements and show how a trade accord may improve the ability of the less developed partner to attract capital. Beyond this, it has been argued from a political economy perspective that the existence of NAFTA indirectly helped Mexico to overcome the peso crisis of December 2004 because, without NAFTA, the US government would not have mobilised the large financial resources needed by the Mexican government to avoid default. In this respect, regional integration provided 'insurance' cover to Mexico, reducing planning uncertainties for the economic agents. The NAFTA experience is particularly relevant to a deep EU–Ukraine FTA, which would fall short, in terms of the strength of commitments and extent of financial support, of full EU membership; nevertheless, it is notable that NAFTA has been an effective mechanism for enhancing economic reforms in Mexico.

The example of Mexico and NAFTA also showcases one key channel through which improvements in the investment climate lead to higher investment and income growth. A large proportion of output growth in Mexico comes from trade and production networks between US and Mexican plants. While the outsourcing of low-skilled, labour-intensive activities from the US was the primary driving force, more complex patterns of interaction are emerging. In this respect, Mexico's experience mirrors that of many other developing and transition economies where manufactured exports have expanded rapidly. Typically, a wide variety of trade and production networks involving local and importing-country firms have evolved (see for example Luecke & Szalavetz, 1999). In these networks, importers perform functions that are initially beyond the capacity of local firms, e.g. marketing in the export market, product design, quality control, finance or logistics. Local firms are free to focus on manufacturing operations where their comparative advantage presumably lies. Over time, learning by doing as well as by more formal transfers of technological and managerial know-how allow many local firms to move into higher value-added activities and become more independent of their importing-country partners.

Although such trade and production networks may involve different ownership patterns, including FDI, they do invariably require importing-country firms to make a substantial investment – in terms of effort, time and money – in the relationship with the local firm. Therefore, a good investment climate and business environment is a precondition for successful network formation (and by implication, expansion of manufactured exports) even when no FDI is involved. It is in this context that regional integration, such as through a deep EU–Ukraine FTA, has a crucial role to play.

This is especially true in Ukraine where trade and production networks are only beginning to evolve. Ukrainian clothing producers and similar low-skill, labour-intensive industries have benefited from some outsourcing by Western European firms. A problematic business environment makes it difficult, however, especially for small and medium-sized firms to attract the kind of involvement and support from foreign firms that would enable them to expand sophisticated manufactured exports. A recent case study on the potential for electronics manufacturing in Ukraine (ICPS, 2005b) finds that many fundamental conditions are good, especially regarding the availability and wage levels of skilled workers. But for Ukrainian firms to be able to integrate into international production networks, efficient customs procedures and high-quality producer services – especially in transport and logistics – would be required. A deep EU–Ukraine FTA, by improving the quality of market-enabling and market-supporting institutions in Ukraine, could significantly help to overcome the obstacles that are still holding back the participation of Ukrainian firms in trade and production networks.

While case studies on the effects of regional integration schemes such as NAFTA are instructive, they normally cannot quantitatively disentangle the 'net' effect of a regional integration agreement from other determinants of income growth such as domestic reforms. Econometric studies of the growth effects of institutional change seek to overcome this difficulty; they tend to be based on cross-section country data and follow one of two basic conceptual approaches: (i) they assume that the quality of institutions is a parameter in a macroeconomic production function and estimate the output elasticity of institutional quality; or (ii) they estimate Barro-type growth regressions that explain GDP growth over the period of observation as a function of initial per-capital income, investment ratios in human and physical capital, and various additional variables – including institutional quality – that may be viewed as influencing the efficiency parameter of the production function that underlies the growth model.

Of the studies that directly estimate the output elasticity of institutional quality, the estimates by Piazolo (2001, ch. D) may be the most directly applicable to EU–Ukrainian institutional approximation. Piazolo uses the transition indicators of the European Bank of Reconstruction and Development (EBRD) (published annually in the EBRD Transition Report) to measure the extent to which reforms in the EBRD sample of transition economies during the 1990s have created institutions of the same quality as the EU's. The EBRD transition indicators cover major areas of systemic reform (corporate governance, markets and international trade, the financial sector and legal infrastructure) and range from 1 (indicating little or no reform in the particular area) to 4+ (institutional quality equivalent to the *acquis communautaire*). The average score for Ukraine in 2005 was less than 3; it seems reasonable to assume that an ambitious, deep FTA with the EU could bring the average score to around 4 during a reasonable implementation period.

Piazolo's estimates suggest that an improvement in institutional quality by one-third, as measured by the EBRD index, would increase the level of GDP by at least one tenth purely through the greater efficiency of resource use (conceptually similar to the comparative-static effect that we estimate with our CGE model; see section 5.2). The total increase in GDP, allowing for additional investment over time, could be in the 20 to 30% range. Clearly, even though these numbers (and similar results in the literature) are based on solid econometric work, they are not 'exact' estimates but indications of the likely order of magnitude of possible income effects of effective institutional approximation between Ukraine and the EU. At the same time, these numbers do provide a more realistic sense of the potential benefits of a deep EU–Ukraine FTA than the small comparative static efficiency effects generated by our CGE model, notwithstanding other important insights that may be gained from the CGE model. (These estimates are similar in magnitude and partly overlap conceptually with the indication given in the preceding section that full dynamic effects may multiply comparative-static results by a factor of two to three).

Several econometric studies have recently been undertaken on the impact of services liberalisation on GDP growth (for a summary of the literature, see Lücke & Spinanger 2004). These are of particular relevance to a deep EU–Ukraine FTA as it would cover significant areas of service sector regulations. With respect to financial services, François & Schuknecht (2000) find that financial sector openness (i.e. the presence of foreign banks in the domestic market, not necessarily involving capital account liberalisation) is strongly and positively associated with competition in the sector; furthermore, competition is strongly associated with economic growth, on top of the separate effect of financial sector development on growth. In other words, a highly competitive and highly developed financial sector is associated with a higher GDP growth rate than a less competitive and similarly developed sector.

Overall, the *annual* GDP growth rates of countries that had fully opened their financial services industries were 1.3 to 1.6 percentage points higher than for countries with the 'most closed' type of financial services regime. Similarly, Mattoo, Rathindran & Subramanian (2001) find from cross-country growth regressions that countries with fully open telecommunications and financial services sectors *annually* grew up to 1.5 percentage points faster than other countries. These are huge growth effects from services liberalisation; for example, with a 1.5 percentage point difference in annual growth rates between two countries, after 20 years GDP is 35% higher in the richer country. As cross-country growth regressions may be interpreted as indicative of long-term growth effects allowing for higher investment, a 20-year time horizon would appear quite appropriate for a 'back-of-the-envelope' calculation along these lines. The regression results suggest that for Ukraine, comprehensive services liberalisation, institutional reform and approximation to the EU through a deep FTA with the EU have potentially large benefits.[16]

---

[16] This conclusion is further supported by recent research on southern Mediterranean neighbourhood partner states (Egypt and Tunisia) that suggests very substantial gains from service sector liberalisation (Müller-Jentsch, 2004). Similarly, a literature survey by the OECD concludes that the gains from future services liberalisation will be at least as large as that for goods, as service sectors remain considerably more protected in many developing and transition economies (OECD, 2001).

5. A SCENARIO FOR SIMPLE FREE TRADE

In this chapter we review the basic ingredients of a simple free trade scenario for goods, services and capital.

5.1 Free trade in goods

A plausible scenario would be for tariffs to be eliminated asymmetrically, to be front-loaded for the EU and for Ukraine over a period of years, probably close to five. A period of 10 years would be too long for the needs of Ukraine's reform agenda. Remaining export duties would be scrapped. Any exceptional treatment for agriculture should be simple, such as eliminating tariffs soon for some commodities, but with extended periods for others.

There are many precedents for free trade agreements made by the EU, with some recurrent patterns seen in the Europe Agreements and the Mediterranean Association Agreements.

Tariffs. Given that quantitative restrictions will have been eliminated with WTO accession, the main variable would be the elimination of tariffs, with a number of negotiation variables with respect to transition periods and possible exclusions.

For Poland, for example, tariff dismantling was asymmetric in its Europe Agreement, with the EU eliminating its tariffs over a period of up to five years after entry into force of the agreement, and with Poland doing so over up to ten years. Quantitative restrictions were mostly abolished on entry into force, while export duties by Poland were eliminated over five years.

The Mediterranean agreements have also seen asymmetric tariff dismantling, immediately on entry into force on the EU side, but progressively over a typical period of 10 to 12 years for the partner states.

Quantitative restrictions were eliminated upon entry into force, but exclusions remained for some agricultural products.

The EU–Chile agreement of 2002 saw commodities grouped into categories, with tariffs to be eliminated at varying speeds – some upon entry into force and others over three, four, seven and ten years.

With Ukraine the EU would presumably front-load its tariff cuts, at least to a considerable degree. It might possibly eliminate them on the day of entry into force of the agreement, given its much greater competitive strengths. Ukraine also would begin to reduce its tariffs upon entry into force, which would be close to the time when the transitional period ends for the most part under Ukraine's WTO offer. The tariff reduction schedule would normally be in a straight line of equal steps. A long transition period, up to 10 years, could be considered and has precedents in EU free trade agreements as mentioned above. The disadvantage of long transition periods, however, is that the process may lose credibility and fail to energise the private sector, so we would suggest about five years. More generally, a long transition period could be out of step with the political urgency for Ukraine to push the economy onto a new growth track.

Export duties. Ukraine's WTO offer sees the reduction but not the complete elimination of certain export duties, such as those for scrap metal, sunflower products and animal hides. For free trade with the EU these remaining export duties would be on the agenda for elimination.

Agriculture. This sector has been the main exception in the past to the general rule of eliminating tariffs in the EU's free trade agreements, as is also the case with Ukraine's free trade agreement with Russia. The pressures for at least partial exclusion of agriculture from tariff-free trade will be no less on both sides than in the past. On the EU side the current pressures on agricultural policy in the Doha Round context are very intense. On the Ukrainian side the sector has only recently been privatised and a huge agenda of modernisation lies ahead. In these circumstances the parties might identify certain commodity groups that could be liberalised first, with a schedule of tariff reductions leading to their elimination, for which the best candidates might be cereals, horticulture and vegetables. The EU has a policy for some agricultural commodities of a flexible on/off regime, i.e. switching between restrictive versus free conditions for imports depending on market conditions. Since 16 November 2005 EU imports of durum wheat and high-quality common wheat have been tariff-free[17] (while low- and medium-quality common wheat remains subject to a tariff quota regime). This market signal indicates that conditions for free trade in this important sector are relatively favourable and effectively a partial free trade regime prevails at present. For Ukraine, in the context of a possible FTA+, this tariff-free regime could be made permanent. For other products there could be extended tariff reduction schedules, for example up to 10 years, starting from the level of WTO tariff bindings.

5.2 Free trade in services

Ukraine's WTO offer for services already goes a long way towards free trade in services. Some exclusions could be brought into the present scenario, but the main ones, such as those in the transport sector, raise deeper issues of regulatory reform and possible convergence on the EU internal market acquis *(see also chapter 6).*

As reported above, Ukraine's offer to the WTO is one of the most liberal and comprehensive compared with the bound commitments of existing WTO member states. It already comes close to free trade in services. For example, Ukraine's services offer to the WTO is closer to free trade than the services content of the EU's FTA with Chile, which is itself more open than the EU's FTAs with its Mediterranean partner states.

Thus, there is a limited agenda for possibly completing sectoral coverage for omissions in Ukraine's WTO offer. The potential areas here include road and rail transport where Ukraine proposes not to make binding commitments. The case of civil aviation is generally excluded from WTO competence and would be subject to a bilateral agreement with the EU. There are restrictions on news agencies in the WTO offer, which may be reconsidered in an FTA context, while restrictions in the field of audio-visual services relating to cultural patrimony are not so different to the EU's own position in the WTO.

The main agenda for the service sectors falls beyond a narrow definition of free trade and more into deeper issues of domestic regulatory reform, where links to EU internal market laws may be appropriate to varying degrees. We return to these issues in chapter 6, section 6.2.

---

[17] See Commission Regulation (EC) No. 1865/2005 of 16 November 2005 fixing the import duties in the cereals sector, OJ L 299/58, 16.11.2005.

5.3   Free movement of capital

One scenario could involve complete liberalisation with regard to all remaining restrictions on capital movements, rights of establishment and related current payments by 2008, thus allowing time for current developments in monetary and exchange-rate policy to mature.

The European Neighbourhood Policy Action Plan already recalls the commitment in the Partnership and Cooperation Agreement (PCA) to ensure free movement of direct investments, to guarantee their protection and to hold consultations on the general goal of liberalisation. The PCA also assures the liberalisation of current payments, including payments related to direct investments, such as profits and repatriation.

Foreign direct investment has been largely liberalised as a matter of political strategy, as illustrated by the recent major cases of the re-privatisation of the steel firm Kryvorizhstal (bought by Mittal Steel) and the purchase of a major bank, Aval (by Raiffeisen International).

The key remaining restrictions on capital movements relate to government bonds with more than one year to maturity. The objective of a free trade agreement would be total liberalisation of capital movements, rights of establishment and related current payments. The timing of such moves will, however, be related to concerns about assuring macroeconomic and financial stability. In the current Ukrainian context this links to the sequencing of the move towards a flexible, floating exchange rate and inflation-targeting by monetary policy. These monetary policy reforms are ongoing and are expected to be completed in 2006 or 2007. It is generally appreciated that controls over short-term capital movements may need to be retained with fixed or semi-fixed exchange rate regimes, so as to avert de-stabilising, speculative capital movements. In view of the monetary reform timetable it might be plausible to set the year 2008 as a target for completing liberalisation of capital movements.

The current licensing system for foreign investments would then switch to just an information-reporting requirement. Current licensing and other regulatory requirements for foreign investment are considered by the business community to be unduly complicated and unpredictable in their enforcement, which links to corruption problems.

6. FROM DEEPER FREE TRADE TO DOMESTIC ECONOMIC GOVERNANCE

In this chapter we extend the agenda to the possible content of a deep free trade agreement, with priority given to policy sectors that can have an important bearing on Ukraine's economic performance. Although the list of priority sectors discussed here is already very substantial, it should be considered as more illustrative than exhaustive, and a future negotiation process would doubtless raise issues that are not covered in this study. The Commission's Strategy Paper on the European Neighbourhood Policy (ENP) of 2004 (European Commission, 2004) points the way towards progressive inclusion in the EU's internal market in the following terms:

> The implementation of the ENP itself brings with it the perspective of moving beyond cooperation to a significant degree of integration ...including through a stake for partner countries in the EU's Internal Market.

6.1 Goods sector

6.1.1 Customs procedures

The EU–Ukrainian land borders should see ambitious plans for high-tech, fast and secure passage of goods and persons, with elimination of the crass corruption that still plagues Ukraine's frontier posts.

Currently, the EU shares 778 km of its external border with Ukraine. The border consists of sections in Poland (542 km), Slovakia (99 km) and

Hungary (137 km).[18] In 2007-08, when Romania is expected to join the EU, the length of the common border will increase by 614 km. Such a long border creates significant potential for deeper integration through people-to-people contacts, cross-border investments and trade. But it also gives rise to substantial border problems such as smuggling and human trafficking. The EU should assist Ukraine in resolving these problems through technical assistance to the Ukrainian border guard and through financial assistance for modern border-related equipment. In return it should demand comprehensive customs reforms and a streamlining of border-related controls from Ukraine.

WTO accession will mean that Ukraine has to comply with requisite standards for the customs code, valuation, etc. This will not necessarily mean rapid and efficient customs services, however. In working groups with neighbouring states the European Commission has developed guidelines for best practices at border-crossing points, and made proposals for 'a simple and paperless environment for customs and trade' in the context of the integrated management of external borders. These proposals involve complex programmes for modernising and computerising trading practices, leading for example to electronic declarations made before departure and paperless procedures, with x-ray checking of goods at the border-crossing points. Such measures are looking ahead to the ideal future situation, which will involve compatible processes of technological development on both sides of the frontier.

For the immediate future there are some more basic priorities to sort out, as manifest in the huge and chronic delays for road traffic at Ukraine's frontiers with the EU. Corruption is a major part of the problem and there would be little point proceeding with ambitious plans for free trade without thorough reform. It is still the case that the traveller who wants to pass the frontier without undue delay has to pay bribes, as the article quoted in Box 6.1 vividly illustrates. This article goes on to describe crossings of Romanian and Bulgarian borders during the same journey, which were unproblematic, although the situation there was similar to that described for Ukraine only a few years earlier. These cases show that reform in this area is not at all intractable.

---

[18] These figures are from State Border Guard Services of Ukraine. The Ukrainian-Moldovan border is 1,222 km.

Box. 6.1 Corruption on Ukraine's borders – excerpt from an International Herald
Tribune *article by N. Kurlish*

I sat at a Ukrainian border station, trying to cross into Moldova. "Present? Present?" the border guard asked, holding up my CD player. I smiled and told the guard that I did not understand. He smiled back, gave the player a whack with his billy stick. Then we were inexplicably told we couldn't leave the country. In retrospect I might as well have given it to him. It could have saved me 30 hours of desperate searching for a station where the border police would let us pass without demanding a bribe higher than we were willing to pay. The asking price at the next stop was $200, a lot more than I paid for the CD player.

Entering Ukraine was as challenging as leaving. After a four hour wait in a line of cars that hadn't moved, my companion and I finally realized that we had to bribe drivers camped out ahead to get to the border station. There the agents tried to impound our car.

Source: N. Kulish, "Driving the Scenic Route to EU Membership", *International Herald Tribune*, 4 October 2005. One of the authors of the present study had a similar experience at the Ukraine–Slovak frontier in July 2005.

Measures taken by the new government in February 2005 made some improvements to reduce corruption (changes in staffing), with an increased risk of punishment. But it is reported that this translated quite quickly into rises in the price of bribes.

Eminently suitable for the FTA+ process, there should be decisive elimination of corruption of Ukraine's land border crossings with the EU. There are not that many important border crossings with Poland, Slovakia or Hungary, which employ a limited number of persons. Two of these crossings, between Poland and Ukraine, have initiated an interesting cooperative programme, where the two sets of services work together on one side of the border in close proximity to each other – at Zosin-Ustilug (near Zamosc), and at Kroscienko-Smolnica in the Bieszczady mountains, in south-eastern Poland. The Polish and Ukrainian officials check passengers and cars/trucks separately, but in sight of each other and this is reportedly helping to cut the corruption.

The EU can surely help over the medium term to build, equip and train staff for modern facilities at the border. But first there should be a real act of political will by Ukraine to install in its border services a regime of zero tolerance of corruption. The EU and Ukraine could arrange for six-monthly audits of progress towards eliminating corruption at this level.

Under FTA+ the EU–Ukraine border traffic might well come to resemble that now observed across the US–Mexican frontier, where the NAFTA has resulted in a huge expansion of bilateral trade, largely related to direct US investments in Mexico. The quality of the border crossings is also attributable to the Free and Secure Trade (FAST) programme under a bilateral Border Accord Initiative between the US and Mexico. When drivers approach a FAST lane, wireless information is transmitted to an inspection booth, displaying a digital image of the driver, biographical information, as well as cargo and carrier information. A gamma–ray imaging system displays the truck's interior on a screen, capable of detecting false compartments or cargoes not matching the associated declaration. This technology allows designated agents to instantly identify low-risk vehicles and drivers, and to expedite traffic through border crossings.[19] In 2003, a $4 million contract provided the necessary equipment for 99 FAST lanes at 22 border crossings.[20]

6.1.2 Customs union

A customs union is not a necessary next stage in the trade integration process, and even the European Economic Area (EEA) does not have this. Further, a customs union is inadvisable for an EU–Ukraine FTA+, until and unless EU–Russian free trade develops as well.

The example of the Turkish–EU customs union comes to mind as a comparator here. The advantage of a customs union is that it removes the need for complicated rules-of-origin norms and procedures governing inputs from third countries in goods traded between the two principal parties. Eliminating these complications is certainly helpful for deepening trade integration. But the disadvantage would be that it would impose on Ukraine all of the EU's trade policies with third parties, notably those including Russia and other members of the Commonwealth of Independent

---

[19] See the *FAST Reference Guide; Enhancing the Security and Safety of Trans-Border Shipments*, US Department of Homeland Security, US Customs and Border Protection, Washington, D.C., 2005.

[20] See the news release by TransCore, "TransCore's RFID Technology Selected for Extending U.S. Bureau of Customs and Border Protection's Free and Secure Trade Programme to 22 Northern and Southern Border Crossings", TransCore, Harrisburg, PA, 5 December 2003 (retrieved from http://www.transcore.com/news/news031205.htm, 10.10.2005).

States (CIS) with which Ukraine currently has a free trade agreement. This would pose multiple problems – administrative, economic and political. The customs union option thus looks implausible until and unless the EU and Russia forms a free trade area together, which is a more remote prospect as of today compared with the case of Ukraine.

A customs union is often regarded as a natural, textbook next step in the progression from free trade to deeper forms of market integration. But this should not be considered an instinctive logic. It is notable that the EEA states (Norway, etc.), in becoming totally compliant with EU internal market law, have nonetheless *not* entered into a customs union with the EU. There is already much of great importance and value for Ukraine to do in convergence on EU internal market norms without needing to enter into a customs union relationship.

6.1.3 Product standards for manufactured goods

For the Ukrainian economy it is a strategic necessity for its industrial goods to become compliant with EU technical standards. A comprehensive plan for doing so over the period 2005-10 is being prepared by the EU Commission and Ukraine.

The alignment of Ukraine with EU technical standards for industrial goods has been the policy objective of the Ukrainian government for some years. Ukraine has been making progress in this area, so far adopting 1,500 out of 8,000 EU standards. Yet progress is still slow, as illustrated by the mixed performance recently reported (Table 6.1).

Table 6.1 Ukrainian performance summary for some main EU technical norms

Technical norm	Performance
Safety of toys	Major part ok
Low voltage Directive	Partly ok
Electro-magnetic compatibility	Major part ok
Household refrigeration equipment	Major part ok
Simple pressure vessels	Not ok
Pressure equipment	Not ok
Lifts	Differences
Hot water boilers	Fully OK
Domestic gas appliances	Nearly OK
Non-automatic weighing instruments	Differences

Source: Based on a report of the Tacis project on Standards, Technical Regulations and Conformity Assessment undertaken by Afnor-Swedac-Uni consortium, November 2004.

The European Commission through the Tacis programme and the World Bank through its Programmatic Adjustment Loans have both been active with technical assistance and policy advice. For example, it is already a positive step that the State Committee for Technical Regulations has been given the authority to adopt standards, cutting out the need to pass through the Council of Ministers as before.

The ENP Action Plan contains guidelines for continuing alignment with EU standards, with supporting measures to strengthen institutional capacity on standardisation, the international accreditation of Ukrainian agencies, conformity assessment and market surveillance. Partial or full membership of leading standards bodies such as the European Committee for Standardisation, the European Committee for Electrotechnical Standardisation and the International Standardisation Organisation (ISO) is pending.

The way has very recently been opened for a decisive strategy to assure mutual recognition of products conforming to EU standards. In September 2005 the Commission presented a plan to Ukraine to work towards an Agreement on Conformity Assessment and Acceptance of Industrial Products (ACAA). The plan would be modelled on experience of the EU with accession candidate and Mediterranean partner states. A multi-stage process is proposed, from 2005 to 2011, starting with identification of priority sectors, and ending in 2001 with entry into force of the ACAA, meaning that at that time binding mutual recognition (i.e. Ukrainian products will enter the EU bearing the CE mark to show conformity with EU standards, whose validity would have been certified by Ukrainian conformity bodies and thus without needing further testing on the EU side and vice versa for EU exports to Ukraine). The ACAA would embrace both the so-called 'old' and 'new' approaches of the EU, i.e. products subject to detailed harmonised standards that Ukraine will replicate or the simpler norms of the new approach that relies more heavily on mutual recognition. The five-year plan is necessary since achieving full mutual recognition requires the full 'quality infrastructure', running the whole chain from transposition of standards into Ukrainian law to the creation or reform of the bodies required to implement the legislation and certify conformity.

To minimise adjustment costs and permit rapid transition to the new system, maximum reliance should be made on voluntary compliance with EU standards: EU norms should be simply translated into Ukrainian ones without modification, following the example of Poland before its accession.

Producers can choose to adopt these standards where they are seriously interested in export markets. Ukraine should not convert EU/international standards, which are for voluntary adoption by enterprises, into mandatory ones. Ukraine would thus be switching from the mandatory method under the old *Gosstandards* of the USSR to a mainly voluntary compliance method. Ukrainian companies could opt to continue to produce for CIS markets according to the old USSR *Gosstandards* if they wish. It is notable that Ukraine is also leading work in the CIS to switch to European and international standards, which is excellent. This work takes place in the EurAsia Council for Standardisation, Metrology and Certification, whose 2005-07 work programme is based on 29 EU directives.

The preparation and negotiation of a legally binding ACAA with wide coverage of industrial goods would thus be the strategic move in the field of technical standards. The time horizon proposed of 2005-11 is realistic in view of the extent of the in-depth reforms that will be required in the private and public sectors. However this could fit well alongside a plausible time horizon for the FTA and notably the phasing out of tariffs. These two lines of action should be mutually reinforcing, with Ukrainian industry encouraged to adopt EU standards with the prospect of tariff-free trade.

6.1.4 Agricultural and food safety standards

Recognition of standards for processed foods is going to be a long and costly process. The most plausible policy may be to focus on particular market niches and to make product- and enterprise-specific investments in production and testing facilities.

The prospects for removing non-tariff barriers between the EU and Ukraine in this second domain of technical standards, for the agriculture and food sectors, are far more difficult than for industrial goods. Discussions between the Commission and Ukrainian authorities since the adoption of the ENP Action Plan have not yet begun. This is not atypical and is even reflected in EU–US trade relations, where mutual recognition for agricultural and food products has not been possible (as exemplified in the hormone beef and other controversies associated with genetically modified food). The EU enjoys mutual recognition only with Canada and New Zealand, in addition to intra-EU and EEA trade. Moreover, the climate of political sensitivity around these issues has continued to grow in recent years, in the wake of 'mad cow' BSE episodes through to the present danger of bird flu.

The field of sanitary and phytosanitary (SPS) measures covers rules of trade in animals and animal products, animal welfare, trade in plants and plant products, and food safety. Three categories of products may be distinguished:

- cereals, which are basically free of technical standards or non-tariff barriers;
- meat products, for which trade is very heavily controlled; and
- other processed foods, which are also subject to technical standards.

The standard SPS agreement in the WTO sets out the basic rules for the application of SPS measures — in other words food safety and animal and plant health regulations. The agreement recognises that governments have the right to take SPS measures but that these should be applied only to the extent necessary to protect human, animal or plant life or health. All WTO members must base their SPS measures on international standards, guidelines and recommendations where they exist. The three international standard-setting bodies recognised by the WTO for this purpose are Codex Alimentarius, the OIE (World Organisation for Animal Health) and the IPPC (International Plant Protection Convention). Nevertheless, members may maintain or introduce measures that result in higher standards, but only if they are scientifically based. The agreement includes provisions on control, inspection and approval procedures. The main pillars of the SPS agreement are that SPS standards must comply with the principle of proportionality, non-discriminatory, be the least trade-disruptive and be based on international standards or on science. It also contains provisions on transparency, equivalence, regionalisation, special and differential treatment, and technical assistance.

At present Ukraine is only able to export cereals and a few other products such as nuts and honey to the EU, since it does not at present meet EU standards for meat products or other processed foods. The EU exports growing quantities of processed foods to Ukraine, but often finds Ukrainian standards – which are not yet bound under the WTO – difficult to meet, since sometimes they are set at a more demanding level than in the EU and implemented in a non-transparent and unpredictable manner.

The EU has adopted general principles for food safety – the General Food Law (Regulation No. 178/2002), and the Official Food and Feed Control Law (Regulation No. 882/2004) that entered into force 1 January 2006 – that Ukraine might seek to follow. For the meat sector it is instructive that Poland, for example, only reached compliance with EU standards for the majority of its abattoirs after over a decade of preparations, even with substantial financial aid from the Sapard programme. To be able to export animal products to the EU it is necessary that the exporting country has a competent authority that guarantees that the hygiene and public health requirements are met and that a monitoring system is in place to verify compliance with the maximum permitted level of residues, pesticides and contaminants. Imports are only authorised from approved establishments (e.g. slaughterhouses, cold stores and processing plants). An inspection visit by the competent EU authority is necessary to confirm compliance.

The costs of compliance are much less in this case compared with the demands made for mutual recognition, where the whole of the sector has to be compliant with EU standards (as with Norway in the EEA, for example). The total costs of EU agricultural compliance in the new member states such as Poland and Lithuania have been estimated to be 2-2.5% of GDP annually, of which the EU Sapard programme paid 75%. Lithuania alone received €205 million from Sapard in the period 2000-06 and Poland has received €172 million annually.

Therefore, the major step of reaching mutual recognition of conformity standards between the EU and Ukraine can only be a distant and costly prospect, and is less plausible as an objective for early agreement than for industrial standards. The most plausible priority would seem to be to secure conformity agreements for specific establishments and products in the foreseeable future.

6.2   Backbone service sectors

6.2.1 Financial services

Ukraine's financial services industry remains bank-dominated and is not yet suited for compliance with those parts of the EU acquis that are designed for the most advanced financial markets. The most powerful driver for deeper EU–Ukraine integration in this sector will be the greater involvement of EU banks and other financial services companies through foreign direct investment (FDI).

A dynamic financial sector is important for both the general process of economic development and for deeper regional integration. In that respect, Ukraine has a lot of catching up to do: all of the country's banks together have net assets of less than €20 billion – which is equivalent to a small EU bank. The insurance sector is even much smaller and a non-banking financial services industry barely exists. One positive implication of these weaknesses, however, is the significant growth potential in the sector, which makes it attractive for foreign investors.

Throughout Central and Eastern Europe, EU banks have driven the process of sector development and in several countries foreign bank ownership has passed the 80% mark. A handful of EU banks have established cross-border networks that cover the entire region. They not only bring capital, know-how and greater competition to the sector, but as they are supervised by their home regulator, they are also a vehicle to import better regulation and corporate governance. This aspect would be particularly beneficial for Ukraine, where most major banks are owned by oligarchs.

In recent months, EU banks have started to move into Ukraine. In August 2005, Austria's Raiffeisen International bought Aval Bank (Ukraine's second largest). This purchase brought the share of foreign ownership in the sector to over 20%. In December 2005, BNP Paribas acquired a majority share in Ukrsibbank (Ukraine's fourth largest bank) and there were rumours that a sale of Ukrsotsbank (the third largest) to foreign investors was also imminent. All three banks were owned by major financial–industrial groups (FIGs) and one positive side effect of foreign entry is their exit from the sector.

Ukraine's GATS proposals in the sector are rather comprehensive and there are few additional market-opening measures that could be included in a regional FTA. Moreover, this is one of the sectors where the adoption of EU legislation would not be appropriate for Ukraine. The main reason is that this part of the *acquis* is highly complex and geared towards sophisticated financial markets, which Ukraine does not yet have. Ukraine should thus not pursue active convergence, but rather ensure that new financial sector legislation is *acquis*-compatible (passive compliance).

Instead, deeper integration efforts should focus on facilitating cross-border consolidation at the company level (i.e. banks, insurance and financial services companies). One measure would be the sale of the two remaining state-owned banks to foreign investors through competitive tenders. Another would be the adoption and strict enforcement of the law on banks and banking. This would make related-party lending more difficult and exert pressure on the FIGs to separate their banking and non-banking activities (and thus possibly to sell further banking operations).

As far as sector regulation is concerned, banks are supervised by the National Bank of Ukraine (NBU) and financial markets by the State

Securities and Stock Market Commission (SSSMC). The NBU is a healthy institution, but the SSSMC requires considerable capacity-building. The IMF and the World Bank continue to provide significant technical assistance in the sector and the Commission could complement that work through twinning arrangements between the SSSMC and the NBU with financial market regulators in recent accession countries. These actions ought to be taken in close cooperation with other donors in the sector.

6.2.2 Transport

The strategic priorities for EU–Ukrainian cooperation in this sector are the transition towards a common civil aviation area, transport facilitation along pan-European transport corridors and a streamlining of customs and other border-related controls.

Improving the efficiency of transport and logistical flows will act as a catalyst for deeper EU–Ukrainian integration. Even though an adequate transport infrastructure is an important precondition, what ultimately matters is the speed, reliability and cost of transport services. Such qualities will require comprehensive institutional and regulatory reforms in all modes (air, road, rail and maritime). Many of these policy issues are not adequately addressed under the GATS framework and need to be tackled through unilateral reforms and EU–Ukrainian cooperation.

In air transport, the European Commission has proposed a strategy to fully integrate the ENP countries into the EU single aviation market ('common aviation area') by 2010. Negotiations with the countries of the Western Balkans have already begun. In September 2005 the Commission also requested a mandate to negotiate a common civil aviation area with Ukraine. This request followed the liberalisation of some of the bilateral agreements between Ukraine and individual member states and the signature of a 'horizontal agreement' in December 2005.

In order to enter into a common civil aviation area, Ukraine would have to adopt the full body of EU law in the sector. That includes a liberalisation of market access, routes and prices as well as the introduction of competition in ground handling, regulations on airport charges, rules on slot allocation and compliance with safety and security standards. In air traffic management, EU–Ukrainian cooperation became institutionalised, when Ukraine became a member of Eurocontrol in 2004, but it would be deepened through full integration into the Single European Sky. Cooperation with the European Aviation Safety Agency is highly desirable to facilitate the certification of Ukraine's aircraft and aviation industry production.

An important and complementary domestic reform in air transport would be the privatisation and expansion of Kyiv Boryspil International airport and possibly of some of secondary airports. At least the separation of airports from airline ownership should be assured. As in other parts of the transport sector, state-ownership remains the main obstacle to greater services trade through a commercial presence (mode 3) and privatisation would change that. Prior to full market liberalisation, the government should also try to sell its stake in the country's two main airlines to investors who can ensure fleet expansion and their integration into airline alliances.

In land transport (road and rail), the main focus of EU–Ukrainian cooperation should be to facilitate logistical flows along the three pan-European corridors that extend into Ukraine (the dual road and rail corridors III, V and IX). Along corridors III and V, the European Bank of Reconstruction and Development (EBRD) is already funding infrastructural work along the roads as well as track improvements for the rail sections. As part of that assistance, it also provides technical assistance and institutional capacity-building to the national railway company and to the institution in charge of road maintenance.

Further investments along the pan-European corridors crossing Ukraine will be needed in the future. Since many of the frictions and bottlenecks along those corridors are policy-induced, however, it will be important to combine the upgrading of the infrastructure with sector reforms and capacity-building measures. Further infrastructure funding from the Commission and the European Investment Bank (EIB) should therefore include technical assistance components and be explicitly linked to policy conditionalities (i.e. transport facilitation measures along those corridors by the government).

The third transport sector priority for EU–Ukrainian cooperation concerns border-related controls. As previously noted, customs checks particularly remain time-consuming, non-transparent and prone to corruption. Reforms to address these problems are not only needed to speed up cross-border logistics, but also to fight border-related crime such as smuggling and human trafficking. The EU should provide greater assistance in this regard, but it should demand tangible reforms by Ukraine in return.

Further measures that would improve the efficiency of transport flows between both sides include the removal of frictions at modal interfaces (including the rail-gauge change at the border), measures to increase containerisation rates, port reforms (especially those linked to corridors), Ukraine's accession to the Interbus agreement and a liberalisation of cross-border road freight.

6.2.3 Telecom and IT-enabled services

Ukraine should fully transpose the telecom acquis *by adopting missing pieces of regulation, but the main challenge will be its enforcement through a competent regulatory authority. The other key item on the reform agenda is the privatisation of UkrTelecom. This step will open up the fixed-wire segment to foreign investment and bring in the funding needed for infrastructure modernisation.*

Like other backbone services, telecommunications are a crucial connector between economies. Ukraine's outdated infrastructure and the limited competition in fixed-wire services, however, make it difficult for the sector to fulfil that function. The main priorities for deeper EU–Ukrainian integration in telecoms are thus domestic policy reforms that address those problems. Ukraine has made comprehensive GATS proposals in telecom services and as far as formal market opening is concerned, there is little more that could be inscribed into a regional free trade area.

Instead, Ukraine could commit itself to full adoption of the EU *acquis* in this sector. Given the relatively early stage of Ukraine's reform process, the country should not refer to the current telecom *acquis* (the 2002 package of legislation), but to the previous 1998 package. The latter is more detailed, but otherwise fully compatible with the current EU policy framework. Ukraine's basic telecom law is largely in line with EU requirements, but some key implementing regulations still need to be adopted (especially on fixed-wire interconnection).

One way in which the Commission could support the process of *acquis* convergence in Ukraine's telecom sector would be to use the same assistance instruments as for the non-EU countries of south-eastern Europe. For those countries, the Commission (i) prepares a detailed regulatory report once a year to monitor reform progress, (ii) it maintains an institutionalised policy dialogue (a working group meets twice a year) and (iii) it provides selected technical assistance by EU telecom experts through field trips. Extending those instruments to Ukraine could be done relatively easily.

Nevertheless, the biggest obstacles for *acquis* compliance, however, will be the enforcement of those rules. In this area Ukraine will need to significantly strengthen its nascent regulator, the National Communications Regulatory Commission. The World Bank is already providing some technical assistance, but the EU could provide complementary support through a twinning arrangement with a successful regulatory authority from one of the new Central and Eastern European member states.

So far, there is no major FDI by EU companies in the sector and the scope for greater trade in telecom services through mode 3 (commercial presence) seems considerable. The best way to promote this will be through a successful privatisation of the state-owned operator UkrTelecom. It will be critical that this major transaction is conducted in a transparent fashion (to permit major EU companies to compete on a level playing field) and that important sector reforms are launched beforehand (to reduce regulatory risk for investors). A privatisation of UkrTelecom will also mobilise the large-scale investments needed to upgrade the fixed network.

The market segment that has experienced the most rapid growth in recent years is mobile telephony. The two main providers, Kyivstar and Ukraine Mobile Communications control 95% of the market, but at least one of the smaller mobile operators under the brand name of Life:) is catching up fast. Even though there is no direct involvement by EU investors, two mobile operators have major shareholders from countries that are deeply integrated with the EU Single Market: Norway's Telenor holds a majority stake in Kyivstar and half of Life:) is owned by a Turkish investor.

The modernisation of Ukraine's telecom sector will also create the basis for future trade in IT-enabled services – one of the fastest-growing segments of international services trade. As a neighbouring country with a well-educated workforce, Ukraine has significant potential to benefit from the tendency of European firms to outsource back-office functions to low-wage countries – just as its manufacturing sector can benefit from outsourcing in EU production chains.

6.2.4 Energy

There is significant scope for greater trade in all parts of the energy sector and the inclusion of Ukraine in the Energy Treaty (signed on October 2005) concluded by the EU and the south-eastern European countries should be considered. Deeper integration with EU energy markets, however, will entail far-reaching domestic reforms in Ukraine.

Since the EU energy regulations were explicitly designed with the dual objective of cross-border integration and domestic market reform in mind, its adoption by Ukraine would also facilitate the much-needed sector reforms at the national level (e.g. unbundling and regulation of monopolistic activities). Two important measures to create a level playing field would be tariff-rebalancing (Ukraine's energy prices remain far below world market prices) and convergence towards EU environmental standards, including pollution and nuclear safety.

Acquis compliance, however, is as much about legislative approximation as it is about effective enforcement. Even more than in the other network industries, natural monopolies and anti-competitive behaviour are severe problems across the energy sector. Yet Ukraine's National Energy Regulatory Committee (NERC) is still far too weak to counter such tendencies. Hence, regulatory capacity-building will be a critical flanking measure for deeper market integration. The Commission should consider preparing a high-quality twinning arrangement between the NERC and an EU regulator, in close coordination with existing donor activities.

With over 80% of Russia's gas exports and a substantial proportion of its oil exports to Europe transiting Ukraine, pipeline issues are another important area for the bilateral energy partnership. Ukraine has already signed up to the Energy Charter Treaty, but further collaboration regarding pipeline investments and management are needed. For the EU, the main concerns in this context are security of supply and the question of who controls the pipelines, whereas Ukraine's prime interests are the lucrative transit fees and a desire to reduce its dependency on Russian energy imports.

Following the economic decline after independence, Ukraine currently uses only about half of its generation capacity domestically and has significant potential for electricity exports. Some of that potential is used for exports to Russia, but power trade with western neighbours is precluded by a lack of interconnection between the former CIS and the continental European grids. Such physical linkages would require substantial investments in infrastructure linkages and in measures required to make the two systems technically compatible. Both sides should explore possible financing strategies – including greater private sector involvement.

The inclusion of Ukraine into the European grid would also require institutional cooperation on system management and the coordination of transfers among transmission system operators. The full integration into the single electricity market would also involve cooperation among sector regulators and far-reaching domestic reforms in line with the electricity *acquis* (e.g. vertical and horizontal unbundling and open network access).

Since the *acquis* in this sector is in line with international best practice, its transposition would promote the very reforms needed to render the sector more efficient. In particular, Ukraine should reconsider its decision to vertically integrate the remaining state-owned assets into the United Energy Company of Ukraine and it should re-launch its privatisation efforts in generation and distribution. Moreover, it should move from a single-buyer model to third-party access and considerably strengthen the autonomy and institutional capacity of the energy regulator.

Other energy sector policy issues that need to be addressed for the sake of both domestic sector efficiency and deeper regional integration are the restructuring and privatisation of the vertically integrated gas company Naftogaz, the introduction of greater competition in downstream oil activities (refineries and petrol stations), a more effective exploitation of domestic oil and gas resources, the restructuring and downsizing of Ukraine's large coal industry, and trading arrangements for hot air credits under the Kyoto Protocol.

In October 2005, the EU and the south-eastern European countries (SEECs) signed a comprehensive Energy Treaty, which provides a roadmap for the integration of the region into the EU energy market within a decade.[21] All signatories commit themselves to full adoption of the energy *acquis*, including competition and environmental rules. Ukraine's inclusion in that process (it currently only has observer status) would establish a clear framework for EU–Ukrainian energy cooperation. Given the fact that the energy sector is only partially covered by the multilateral GATS framework, there would be considerable value added in such a regional approach.

---

[21] The signatories of the Energy Treaty are the EU and the countries of former Yugoslavia (Serbia, Croatia, Bosnia, Montenegro, Macedonia and Kosovo) as well as Bulgaria, Romania, Albania and Turkey.

6.2.5 Tourism and other service sectors

Other key service sectors are seriously underdeveloped and the reform of de facto market entry obstructions are an imperative part of the domestic governance agenda.

Other key service sectors to which foreign investment can make major contributions include retail distribution and tourism. The entry of European supermarket chains into Ukraine has only recently begun. Ukraine has considerable potential for international tourism, notably in the capital city Kyiv and in the Crimean and the Carpathian regions. Yet it is conspicuous that the major, internationally branded hotel chains are still almost completely absent, even in Kyiv (see Box 9.2). The reasons for this are de facto obstructions to market entry, owing to a maze of red tape, corruption and well-organised vested interests surrounding land rights and the securing of regulatory licenses.

Box 6.2 The mystery of the missing five-star hotels

A striking feature about Ukraine's largest city Kyiv is the complete lack of international-standard four- and five-star hotels – with one exception: the SAS Radisson, which opened in August 2005. Any capital city of comparable size (2.6 million inhabitants) would have at least half a dozen major hotels run by global hotel chains. The lack of such hotels is not only a major constraint for tourism and business travel, but it also implies a loss of hundreds of millions of foreign investment to the country. Research into this mysterious lack of international-standard hotels reveals some of the fundamental barriers to FDI and trade in services that also constitute major constraints for Ukraine's economic development.

During the past 15 years, about 10 global players in the hotel business – including Hyatt, Hilton and Marriot – have tried to enter the Kyiv market, but were kept out by a maze of red tape, corruption and well-organised vested interests in the hotel and real estate development industries. The main hotels in Kyiv belong to influential members of the local business elite and some aspects of the city administration are not known to be centres of integrity. The first set of problems that international hotel groups encounter pertains to land-rights: most lots are still owned by the city and development thus involves complex lease agreements with the authorities. Many attractive lots are actually controlled by local real estate developers who have struck deals with the city government.

Box 6.2 continued

Even if a lot can be secured, building permits can take years to obtain (two years in the case of the Radisson). To connect a new hotel to the electricity, water and gas networks, approvals from the utility companies are needed. Once the building is complete, an operating license is needed before the hotel can be opened, as well as various other licenses (e.g. from the local fire department). At all levels, non-transparent procedures and ample scope for arbitrary decisions create a fertile breeding ground for corruption or permit-vested interests to keep out the competition.

All hotel projects involving foreign investors have dragged on for years and all have run into massive complications. The SAS Radisson in Kyiv – Ukraine's only international-standard hotel – took more than seven years to complete and a number of empty lots and half-finished buildings are testimony to the hostile environment that foreign investors encounter. An indication of the pent up demand in this sector is the fact that the SAS Radisson has been fully booked ever since it opened. These examples from the hotel industry illustrate how corruption and administrative red tape can prevent trade in services and FDI even in markets where no official trade barriers exist. If deeper integration between Ukraine and the EU is to materialise, these problems will have to be addressed.

6.3   Economic governance

6.3.1 Corruption

Corruption as an endemic condition in post-communist societies has defied simple or rapid remedial action. Yet over the medium-term results can be achieved as other European countries have shown.

The corruption problem in all Central and Eastern European states is recognised to be extremely damaging for economic development and so pervasive that it defies simple remedial action. Business surveys, such as that conducted by the European Business Association in Kyiv, rank corruption in Ukraine as the biggest barrier to trade and investment. The most reputable international survey of corruption – that by Transparency International, which collates seven different sources – ranks Ukraine in 107th place out of the 159 countries surveyed. According to this source, in a ranking from 1 to 10, the EU-15 average is 8.0, and the 10 new EU member states average 5.0. The four current candidate states (Bulgaria, Romania, Croatia and Turkey) average 3.5, which is far closer to Ukraine's grade of 2.6. Ukraine is not alone in Europe in this position, and is in the same league as the other European CIS states and the Balkan states that do not yet have EU candidate status (Serbia and Montenegro, Albania and Macedonia). The record of the EU's new and candidate states suggests that while progress is a long and hard process, results can be achieved.

Table 6.2 Corruption ratings (2005)

Region	Rating
EU-15 member states, average	8.0
Best rating, Finland	9.6
Worst rating, Greece	5.3
EU-10 new member states, average	5.0
EU-4 candidate states, average (BG, CR, RO, TR)	3.5
Other Balkan states, average (CS, MK, AL)	2.6
European CIS six states, average	2.6
Ukraine (107th place of 159 countries)	2.6
Central Asian CIS five states, average	2.2

Source: Transparency International Corruption Perception Index (2005) (retrieved from http://www.transparency.org).

For Ukraine the will to make progress in cutting corruption has been demonstrated by the Orange Revolution at the level of the people and the leadership that it then elected. Yet so far this has not translated into a perceptible improvement across the board. While there is no simple recipe for eradicating corruption, some key actions do lead the process. It is encouraging that on 1 January 2006 Ukraine joined the 'GRECO' initiative of the Council of Europe, i.e. the Group of States against Corruption. The recent re-privatisation of the Kryvorizhstal steel firm was exemplary for its transparency, and sets a new standard in that domain. Laws on corporate governance and competition policy are other key factors, which we discuss these in the next sections. To support deep free trade a number of benchmarks could be established.

There is a vital need to eliminate corruption in Ukraine's parliament, which has become notorious for the over-representation of business interest groups. These groups are hindering legislation aimed at cleaning up economic governance. Here the role of civil society could be especially important and the initiative of civil society in Romania in preparation for its November 2004 elections deserves special mention here. In this case civil society NGOs undertook a coordinated programme to research and publish the CVs of all candidates, with details of their business interests and evidence of corrupt activities. There was massive publicity surrounding the long resulting 'black list' and the political parties became obliged to withdraw many of the initial candidates.

The experience of some EU candidate states with very serious corruption problems is not discouraging in suggesting the extent of progress that is achievable within a medium-term period, of say five years. For example, the four candidate states, Bulgaria, Croatia, Romania and Turkey, have until recently been close to where Ukraine stands today. The average for these four countries now (with a 3.5 ranking according to Transparency International) might be taken as a target for Ukraine in five-year's time. Achievement of the 3.5 ranking could be taken as a benchmark for moving on after five years of the FTA+ to a further deepening of the EU–Ukrainian relationship.

The European Business Association and other sources[22] identify a vast number of opaque administrative and technical regulations that are at best time-consuming burdens and at worst a source of corruption, such as the persistent lack of a 'one window' registration procedure for businesses, deficiencies in the databases of the Land Register and the Register of Rights to Real Estate, contradictory legal requirements related to the construction business for foreign investors, the lack of transparent procedures for foreigners to acquire non-agricultural land and the absence of a clear definition of joint ventures.

6.3.2 Competition policy

Ukraine's competition policy law is being deeply modelled on that of the EU, but a key law on state aid is still lacking, and implementation may require the executive authority to be buttressed by external institutional or jurisdictional support.

EU legal experts regard Ukrainian competition policy law as the most comprehensive case of drawing on the model of EU law by any non-candidate state (basically the laws on Protection against Unfair Competition of 1996 and on Protection of Economic Competition of 2002). The challenges of capacity-building within the Anti-Monopoly Committee and implementation are of course huge, but progress is real. This area is an example of how during the Kuchma regime there were developments in

---

[22] See the European Business Association, *Barriers to Investment in Ukraine*, Kyiv, February 2005; and the ICPS, *Improving the Business Climate*, Kyiv, 2004(a).

legal and administrative infrastructures that reflected the 'European choice', even if the regime as a whole was deeply vitiated.

Nevertheless, these laws did not cover state aid, which was the subject of a draft law that was rejected in December 2004 by the parliament. The law certainly had various legal imperfections, but its rejection was far more political. Apparently, it was voted down partly owing to concerns among business interests heavily represented in parliament that the powers of the Anti-Monopoly Committee might seriously reduce their ability to influence the allocation of state funds. This result indeed would be a major objective of the policy. Another reason was controversy over whether the head of the Anti-Monopoly Committee supported the spirit of the Orange Revolution. It is presumed that the law on state aid will be resubmitted and eventually passed, perhaps with amendments. Although the draft law is largely a copy of EU law, legal experts on the EU side tend to consider that a gradualist approach to the implementation of this important policy reform might be most feasible.

Even with this completion of the set of basic laws there remain difficult issues of leadership and implementation; indeed these will grow all the more serious given the intensely political nature of state aid. The situation bears comparison with the recent experience of the new member states of the EU, when they were building up their capacities to implement EU competition policy. The Polish experience is highly instructive. In that case the task of legal compliance was the easy part, but the task of establishing a strong enough competition authority to execute it properly, protected from political and business pressures, was found to be formidable. In fact it was judged impossible until the time of full accession, when the ultimate authority became the Competition Directorate-General of the Commission, subject to appeal to the European Court of Justice.

The comparable problem for Ukraine will presumably be more difficult still. A question therefore is whether Ukraine should consider introducing some element of external support or oversight for its competition policy authority. It is already the case that the Anti-Monopoly Committee has EU advisers from a Tacis project in-house. This could easily move on to a medium-term twinning project with an EU member state's competition authority. Yet mere advisers cannot be expected to have real leverage over heavily lobbied or disputed cases. A number of conceivable arrangements might be considered to introduce an element of supranationality to the decision-making or judicial process.

The least ambitious of these would be to have arbitration procedures for cases contested by European business interests, as for example is the case for some aspects of the EU–Chile FTA, where there are three arbitrators, one from the EU, one from Chile and one from a third party, with majority rule over decisions. This provision has never been activated, however, and in any case does not apply to competition policy. The EU and Ukraine might consider other possible mechanisms, for example for the panel of individuals constituting the Ukrainian competition policy authority to include an expert or judge from an EU member state.

More ambitious still would be to draw on the model of the European Free Trade Area (EFTA) and the EEA, which have seen the creation of the EFTA Court of Justice. The Court has jurisdiction over internal market disputes between EEA/EFTA states, and gives advisory opinions on the interpretations of EEA rules. If, for example, Ukraine deepened its relationship with the EFTA, it might be agreed to use this Court as a neutral judicial authority, possibly with addition of one Ukrainian judge and one EU judge to the panel. The European Court of Justice could be used alternatively, but Ukraine may consider this insufficiently neutral. Recourse to the external court could in a cautious variant be limited to 'prejudicial references' (i.e. where the Ukrainian authority or courts wanted an interpretation of the law). A stronger variant would be for the external court to be the court of appeal for complaints, either just for cases where European companies or governments had interests at stake, or for any Ukrainian party to appeal to.

6.3.3 Government procurement

A government procurement agreement could usefully feature in an FTA+, with or without a prior agreement between Ukraine and the WTO.

Even though reliable figures are difficult to obtain, it is reasonable to assume that procurement by public institutions and state-owned companies accounts for between 10 and 20% of Ukraine's GDP. As long as public procurement is governed by non-transparent practices (which are highly correlated with corruption), a large part of the economy remains closed to outsiders. Because of this linkage between government procurement and trade, procurement rules are an important element of the multilateral trading system and the policy framework of the European

Single Market. In 2000, Ukraine adopted the Law on Procurement of Goods, Works, and Services that is based on international model laws and on EU directives.[23] It requires open and competitive tenders and also contains the principle of non-discrimination. Since Ukraine operates a decentralised procurement system, the enforcement of these rules is patchy at best.

Ukraine is not intending to join the government procurement agreement under the auspices of WTO as part of the accession package, but is willing to open negotiations for this upon accession. Conclusion of an agreement in this sector with the EU, possibly going beyond a WTO commitment, could become a plausible part of the FTA+ package. As exemplified for example by the EU–Chile FTA the core principles are those of non-discriminatory and transparent national treatment, with explicit definition of key features of tendering procedures and a dispute-settlement procedure.

6.3.4 Corporate governance

Ukraine has yet to make internationally compliant accounting standards mandatory at least for large firms or to pass essential joint stock company legislation. Without these measures there can be no adequate reform of corporate governance.

This broad field is crucial to whether the Ukrainian economy is going to achieve the qualitative paradigm shift onto European and international standards. There are several strategic elements missing so far in Ukraine's laws and practices.

Both accounting and audit standards in the EU now converge respectively on the International Accounting Standards (IAS), and International Standards on Auditing (ISA). A key EU directive of 2002 set 2005 as the deadline for mandatory compliance in the EU with IAS for all stock-market listed companies and listed securities. For non-listed

---

[23] This law establishes a unified procurement system with open and transparent tenders that follow internationally recognised procedures (including a review of complaints). The Ukrainian Ministry of the Economy has a Department for the Coordination of Government Procurement and Government Orders, which also publishes a government procurement newsletter with all open tender invitations and tender outcomes.

companies, rules of the EU's 4th and 7th Company Law Directives apply, which, however, leave many options for national implementation. It is nonetheless expected that the rules for non-listed companies will over time converge with the IAS. Estonia has in fact done this already – first of all 25 member states. As regards audit, a 2005 directive on the statutory auditing requires compliance with ISA rules.

Since 2000, Ukraine has taked many legislative steps to converge on these European and international accounting standards. But the adoption of IAS standards has so far been largely voluntary, while Ukrainian tax law has required reporting on a different basis. This inconsistency fosters a disincentive to work with the IAS as well, unless the company has a specific motivation to do so. At some point a switch to mandatory IAS-compliant standards must come, although to follow the EU in going for listed companies alone would be inappropriate, since there are today only 11 such companies. More plausible would be a size criterion ($x million turnover or assets), which would cover all large enterprises and financial industrial groups, along with certain categories such as banks, insurance companies and public-interest entities. Some financial industrial groups are now becoming more financially transparent and have the incentive of raising capital on international markets, but more than this is needed.

Such a measure would go with a clear differentiation between IAS-compliant accounting and Ukraine's accounting standards, which might remain optional for small businesses. The auditing profession also needs huge development from its present small and weak base, apart for the major international audit/accounting/consulting firms, which are today servicing mainly international businesses. These international firms could serve as important training establishments for new generations of accountants, qualified according to international standards.

The law on joint stock companies in Ukraine is highly unsatisfactory, since there are problems of inadequate protection for shareholder interests (especially minorities) and defective corporate procedures, with numerous violations occurring constantly (asset stripping, non-disclosure of information, etc.). There has been some issuance of voluntary standards by the Securities and Stock Market Commission since 2003, but a key draft law for joint stock companies failed to be adopted by the parliament in 2003, and has remained in limbo. This law, which should also address minority shareholder rights, will be resubmitted to the parliament in the foreseeable future. The EU can only provide limited guidance in this area, as there is very limited EU legislation covering the structure and governance of corporations, although there are standards issued by international bodies such as the OECD and the World Bank.

6.3.5 Environmental standards

Any EU–Ukraine FTA needs to include a solid sustainable development and Environmental dimension drawing on existing good practice (as set out in recent OECD studies) as regards the incorporation of environmental provisions in regional free trade agreements. While Ukraine has to avoid excessively costly and premature commitments to EU environmental standards, a new factor is Ukraine's accession to the Kyoto Protocol, which could lead to cooperative implementation measures with the EU.

Over the past few years, the potential impact of planned regional and multilateral free trade agreements have attracted increasing attention. Such attention is for instance reflected in the Commission's programme of trade-related Sustainable Development Impact Assessments (SIAs) launched in 1999, which aim at looking into the economic, social and environmental aspects in an integrated way. The SIAs not only attempt to identify the key economic, social and environmental effects resulting from trade liberalisation, they also make suggestions on how these effects can be enhanced (in the case of positive ones) and prevented/mitigated (in the case of negative effects).

To help ensure that a possible EU–Ukraine FTA will make a real contribution to achieving sustainable development, such effects would need to be identified and, subsequently, appropriate enhancement and preventative/mitigation measures would have to be designed. With respect to the latter aspect, it would be important to incorporate a solid sustainable development and environmental dimension in any future EU–Ukraine FTA (e.g. taking guidance from recent comparative OECD studies on environmental provisions in regional free trade agreements).[24]

---

[24] Examples of such provisions include i) the commitment to apply common (harmonised) environmental standards; ii) the duty not to relax health, safety or environment standards to increase exports or attract foreign investment; iii) the duty to enforce existing environmental laws; and iv) environment- and health-related derogations (i.e. a general exception clause that allows for derogations to the obligations under the agreement for the protection of health, the conservation of national resources or the protection of the environment).

As regards whether, under such an FTA, Ukraine might be asked to apply the EU environmental *acquis*, it needs to be borne in mind that the investment needed to comply with all the EU's main environmental standards, notably its water and air pollution directives, would be considerable. For example, the cost of adopting the EU's environmental standards has been estimated to average around €1,000 per capita for the new member states, ranging from €760 for Romania to €1,668 for Bulgaria. This means a total of €22 billion for Romania, which might be doubled for Ukraine. In the new member states the EU has contributed substantially to paying these costs. In the case of Lithuania, half the costs were borne by EU, 20% by national budget and 30% by the private sector. Financing was also made easier by long transition periods that allowed for costs to be spread and investments to be made when old technologies needed to be replaced.

These costs also need to be put into perspective. While considerable, it was found that for the new member states the benefits were also extremely important. Modernising infrastructure and technologies has led not only to environmental benefits, but also to significant health and economic benefits as more efficient technologies were adopted by industry. In addition, protecting the environment will be necessary if Ukraine is to develop its significant tourism potential (as discussed in section 6.2.5). There is no evidence that the environmental *acquis* is harming the competitiveness of the new member states.

There are therefore good arguments for Ukraine to clean up its environment, with its energy-consuming industries needing fundamental modernisation, especially metallurgy and coal-burning power generations, but with of course the understanding that a realistic time-horizon is required. It is also essential to consider the costs of inaction, not the least in the area of public health. Such an approach is offered by the EU–Ukraine ENP Action Plan, which foresees step-by-step convergence with the aims and principles of the environmental *acquis*, particularly in the areas with cross-border impact. This policy will be backed up by a new EU financial instrument.

Furthermore, a new and potentially helpful factor is Ukraine's accession to the Kyoto Protocol. Although exact numbers are not yet known, it is sure that Ukraine will have a substantial surplus of emission credits[25] that could be sold to other countries. It is estimated that the amounts could be up to 2 billion tonnes for the period 2008-12. Ukraine could sell these credits through joint implementation (JI) projects or through emission trading under the Kyoto Protocol. The price of the Kyoto credits will be market determined. JI credits are currently priced at $5-10 per tonne.

Ukrainian and international experts held a workshop in Odessa in September and October 2005 devoted to JI projects. Ukraine is preparing emission reduction projects, which could qualify for JI (i.e. with foreign investment), with substantial opportunities in power generating, district-heating, oil, gas, cement, coal mining and in the metallurgical and forestry sectors. The Ukrainian government is expected to adopt guidelines for the approval of JI projects early in 2006.

Ukraine is also preparing a domestic emissions-trading system, which might conceivably be linked at some stage to the EU's recently activated emissions-trading system. The EU's system explicitly foresees links to the emission trading schemes of third countries that have ratified the Kyoto Protocol and have established a domestic emission-trading system that is compatible with that of the EU.

It would be a positive step for the overall EU–Ukrainian relationship for Ukraine to be deepening its energy and climate change cooperation with the EU within the Kyoto framework.

6.3.6 Movement of people and labour market regulation

The free movement of people is a natural complement to free trade, especially for trade and investment in services. A beginning has been made with Ukraine's scrapping of visas for EU citizens and the opening of negotiations over EU visa-facilitation. There is much to be done in improving working conditions in many Ukrainian industries, but little case for Ukraine to seek to become compliant with EU labour market law as part of an FTA.

Ukraine took the important step in the summer of 2005 of abolishing visa requirements for EU (and US) citizens. This step will surely be positive for Ukraine, for the tourism sector, for business connections and for people-to-people contacts in general. It is also a clear strategic signal, and a positive

---

[25] The credits are officially known in Kyoto Protocol language as 'Assigned Amount Units'.

one, for Ukraine's international reputation. An accompanying measure would be to ease the bureaucratic burden of obtaining work permits for EU nationals entering Ukraine. There are criticisms levied by members of the European Business Association in Kyiv in this regard.

The EU and Ukraine have now opened negotiations over possible visa-facilitation measures for Ukrainian citizens to travel to the EU. Negotiations over the possible lifting of visa requirements for short-term stays will for the EU side be linked to broader issues, such as illegal migration and security concerns. As the movement of persons becomes freer the policy agenda will lead on towards questions concerning the recognition of professional qualifications, provisions for 'key' personnel, coordination on social security and the supply of services in mode 4 (presence of natural persons).

The area of occupational health and safety (OHS) of the working population is a matter of very serious concern in Ukraine. The rate of fatal industrial accidents is twice as high as in developed countries, and the percentage of related fatalities mortalities increased from 2.1% in 1993 to 4.9% in 2003.[26] The root causes of this distressing record are obsolete production facilities that do not match European OHS standards (70% in metallurgy, 90% in agriculture) and to societal disorders (one-third of industrial accidents are due to drunkenness). The Law on Labour Protection of 2002 (No. 229-IV), however, was a landmark act, bringing Ukrainian law in line with European OHS law. Of course the task of implementation remains huge and will take a long time and large renewal of investments. To induce Ukrainian enterprises to improve safety standards it might be more helpful at this stage to introduce a system of liability insurance, binding upon companies, rather than adopt many new laws.

Other areas of EU labour market law are far less plausible for approximation by Ukraine, e.g. the detailed and onerous regulation of part-time and temporary work, working time, hiring and firing regulations and parental leave provisions. The EU is itself in the middle of a period of reflection on where regulatory burdens have become unduly heavy and whether they could be rolled back in parts. This climate makes it all the more inappropriate for Ukraine to anchor on the EU *acquis* in this area.

---

[26] See UEPLAC, *Ukrainian Law Review*, No. 5, Kyiv, 2004.

6.4   The human capital factor

Ukraine's human capital is strong in the mathematical and natural sciences, which is a good basis for the expansion of knowledge-intensive industries. Yet the social sciences still need radical modernisation and EU education programmes should make a major contribution here, for which the resources are available with the foreseen expansion of Tacis/European Neighbourhood Policy Instrument (ENPI).

In common with most of Central and Eastern Europe, Ukraine inherited from the communist period advanced levels of general education by comparison with Western countries. The European transition countries are evidently in a completely different category compared with the standards achieved in the southern (Arab–Mediterranean) neighbourhood states, which are much more poorly placed. Although detailed and comparable data for Ukraine are not available, there is little doubt that Ukraine finds itself broadly in the same category as Russia and some of the new EU member states, and considerably higher than the weakest of the EU-15 member states such as Portugal and Greece. The overall picture is that on some basic quantitative measures schooling is comparable to that between the European transition countries and the advanced Western countries, while the level of achievement in completing university education may be somewhat lower (Table 6.3).

Table 6.3 Educational indicators

Regions	Average years of schooling	Population completing higher education (%)
Advanced countries	9.8	13.0
European transition countries	9.7	9.9
North Africa, Middle East	5.4	3.4

Notes: Covers the total population aged 25 and over; indicator takes into account typical duration of each level of schooling within countries.

Source: Barro & Lee (2000).

More qualitative studies of the levels of educational achievement suggest that the European transition countries actually exceed the levels observed in much of Western Europe in the fields of mathematics and the physical sciences (Table 6.4). In these fields there is no problem of political obsolescence. These deep strengths in the mathematical sciences provide a good human capital base for the growth of new electronic and technological sectors of industry.

Table 6.4 Educational performance

Groups of countries	Performance index*
EU – average of France, Germany, Italy, Spain and UK	511
EU – average of Greece and Portugal	450
EU new member states – average of Czech Republic, Hungary, Latvia, Lithuania, Slovakia, Slovenia	530
Russia	539
North Africa – average of Morocco, Tunisia, Jordan	415

* These ratings are derived from the Third International Mathematics and Science Study (TIMSS) conducted in 1995 by the International Association for the Evaluation of the Educational Achievement and the TIMSS-Repeat study conducted in 1999. Mean performance: TIMSS-95/TIMSS-Repeat Study, re-scaled, weighted by sampling probabilities.

Source: Schuetz et al. (2005).

By contrast, in the social sciences – especially economics, politics, management studies, international relations and the new field of European studies – the problem has indeed been one of the total obsolescence of Marxist-Leninist political economy theory, textbooks and knowledge of a large proportion of teachers. Here there is a huge task of modernisation still to be achieved, even 15 years after the start of the post-communist period. Indeed this is a task for one or two generations.

The EU and the member states have opened their educational programmes to Ukraine, yet on a scale that is not yet up to the task. The EU Tempus programme and the bilateral programmes of some EU member states have been active, but the number scholarships awarded to Ukrainians to study in the EU has only been in the order of dozens. The new Erasmus Mundus programme is an important global initiative for the EU, but Ukraine's allocation is for 23 students out of the global total of 808 for the year 2005-06. As a further example, the London School of Economics, which is one of the largest and most internationalised universities in the social sciences, has about 5,000 non-British students, of which 6 are from Ukraine.

Thus at present the scale of the EU's educational effort for Ukraine is only a small beginning. The most relevant comparison could be made with neighbouring Poland, which has the same population size. Under the Erasmus programme the annual number of incoming Polish students studying elsewhere in the EU has risen from 200 in 1998-99 to 1,400 in 2003-04, with the number of Polish teachers having risen to 750 in 2003-04. The

EU plans to raise the level of its grant aid to Ukraine from €50 million in 2003 to €100 million in 2006. This resource is a very precious one, since grant funds on this scale are hardly available from any other source. Correspondingly there has to be a major effort to define the most cost-effective ways of using these funds, given that many projects of the Tacis programme have also been extremely difficult to execute. We would recommend that a high percentage of this increase be devoted to the strengthening of Ukrainian human capital, for example by a transfer of funds from Tacis (or the future ENPI) for execution by the Erasmus programme. The unit cost of a year's university studies in the EU may be about €30,000. On this scale a budget of €30 million would buy 1,000 scholarships. We suspect that a programme on this scale would be getting closer to the needs of Ukraine to create a new elite professional group, capable of driving the country's transformative modernisation during the next generation, in line with the objectives of the Orange Revolution.

7. INTERNATIONAL ASPECTS

7.1 Role of the international financial institutions

In support of an FTA+ there is important scope for the coordination of incentives and conditionalities used by the EU and international financial institutions (IFIs) in their financial instruments. Such coordination can enhance the overall incentives for Ukraine and mitigate the absence of EU membership prospects.

The World Bank, the International Monetary Fund (IMF) and the European Bank for Reconstruction and Development (EBRD) are already significant players in Ukraine and there are important opportunities for donor coordination with the EU. The EU is revising its grant aid instrument, Tacis, which will become the European Neighbourhood Instrument according to proposals of the European Commission. Tacis commitments are set to rise from €50 million in 2003 to €100 million in 2006. The EU is also extending its role as financier through the European Investment Bank (EIB). A mandate was agreed in December 2004 for the EIB to invest €500 million in Ukraine until mid-2007 in trans-European networks and corridors for transport, energy, telecoms and the environment.

The IFIs are actively seeking to coordinate their work with the EU in the wider European area, for which they gained notable experience during the pre-accession period with the Central and Eastern European states. The World Bank in particular has clearly been supporting reform efforts within the framework of convergence on EU economic standards and regulatory policies. While the EIB is a newcomer to Ukraine, it is already signalling its willingness to co-finance projects with the EBRD and World Bank. It is highly desirable that these intentions be given the opportunity to fully develop. For example, the policy adjustment loans of the World Bank entail detailed technical assistance and financial incentives for Ukraine to adopt reforms in the broad field of economic governance. These efforts are currently being framed to support objectives of the European Neighbourhood Policy (ENP) Action Plan and they work could be amplified further for supporting an FTA+. Major bilateral suppliers of assistance, including EU member states and the US, can reinforce these policy thrusts.

7.2 EFTA & EEA connections

An EU–Ukraine FTA+ would presumably lead to at least a simple free trade agreement between Ukraine and the members of the European Free Trade Area (EFTA). The EFTA-Ukraine agreement might be further deepened with some special roles for the EFTA Surveillance Authority and EFTA Court of Justice.

The prospect of free trade between the EU and Ukraine prompts the question of whether there should be a link to the EFTA states as well (Iceland, Liechtenstein, Norway and Switzerland). The parties have already signed a Declaration on Cooperation (2000), providing for technical assistance. In the context of a free trade agreement between Ukraine and the EU a first scenario would be for Ukraine to make simple free trade agreements with the EFTA states, as has been the normal pattern when the EU makes a new FTA with a third party.

Consideration might then be given to deeper links with EFTA. Accession to the EFTA is not as simple as it might sound. That is because the EFTA has transformed itself beyond its original free trade formula into a virtual merger with the EEA. The Vaduz Convention of 2002 updated the earlier EFTA Convention to take account of the fact that all the EFTA states except Switzerland had acceded to the EEA. This means that the EFTA states are now trading with each other on a basis analogous to the EEA, although with some special provisions for Switzerland given that is not part of the EEA.

There are nonetheless several EFTA links that could be considered. The EFTA states and Ukraine might discuss the idea of an associate-membership relationship. This relationship might not only define the rules for trade between the parties, but provide additional technical assistance and even some institutional anchorage for Ukraine. An alternative might be for Ukraine to become associated with the EEA – not to make premature moves towards total compliance with the EU's internal market law as is the case for EEA members, but to profit from a mentoring relationship on the complex issue of choosing how far and fast to go towards EU compliance. The EFTA Surveillance Authority might take on Ukrainian staff for training purposes and assume the role of mentor for Ukraine in helping it to plan and execute a progressive course for EU *acquis* compliance.

The EEA has also seen the creation of the EFTA Court of Justice, which has jurisdiction over issues of compliance by the EEA states with the EU *acquis*. The Court has interesting features in the present context. While it is located in Luxembourg, the judges are all from EEA states, an arrangement intended to make the institutional structure less asymmetrical. The EU could accept this degree of external jurisdiction because of the high level of trust in the competence and professional integrity of the EEA judges. For Ukraine, at least for an initial period, the EFTA Court might be mandated with responsibility for ruling on EU–Ukraine disputes, possibly with the addition of one EU and one Ukrainian judge. Such a mechanism could have the qualities of both professional competence and neutrality with respect to the EU and Ukraine.

Of course all such ideas would be for the EFTA states and Ukraine to consider, rather than the EU.

8. POLITICAL ECONOMY
FROM SENSITIVE SECTORS TO A REBRANDED UKRAINIAN ECONOMY

8.1 General interests

The Ukrainian business community has in the last decade come to be dominated by a number of powerful financial–industrial groups (FIGs). During the Kuchma period, these interests sought to secure various economic privileges, such as favourable conditions for acquiring privatised assets, tax advantages for individual firms, or regional special economic zones. At the last election, the parliament became notoriously over-represented by these business leaders, the oligarchs. A recent World Bank report claims that this 'insider economy' threatens to become a primary obstacle to Ukraine's economic development.[27] The new government has already taken bold measures to reduce these corruption-prone 'insider privileges', swiftly eliminating hundreds of them in early 2005. But the new government has not been able to assure parliamentary majorities for the various laws required for WTO accession, nor for other laws vital for a correctly functioning market economy (e.g. the refusal of parliament to pass laws for joint stock companies and the protection of minority rights or EU-compliant competition policy).

It is therefore still an open question as to whether the Ukrainian leadership can gather sufficient support for the transformation of its economic model along the lines implied by an FTA+. In part this question

---

[27] See World Bank, "Ukraine – Country Economic Memorandum'', Washington, D.C., 2004(b).

has to be resolved by the March 2006 parliamentary elections, after which it will become clearer whether a stable majority can be found for a real convergence on European standards of economic governance.

On the positive side there is an evolution of the perceived interests of the new business leaders of Ukraine. Having acquired valuable economic assets in the first phase of the post-communist transition, the second stage in the last five years has seen fast economic growth based on exports. The metal boom is over, however, and these same interests now need to find more diversified and sustainable business strategies. Such strategies will require investment (especially since many existing industrial assets are heavily depreciated) and access to international financial and capital markets, which in turn necessitates convergence on EU and international standards of corporate governance. Tendencies in this direction are now being amplified by the willingness of both the government and business interests to sell strategic assets to foreign investors (such as in the re-privatisation of the Kryvorizhstal steel company and the Raiffeisen International acquisition of Aval bank). These seminal steps may lead on to the formation of a political majority in favour of a change of economic paradigm, away from the insider economy and towards an open economy obeying international standards of corporate governance. Such a change is without doubt in line with the long-term interests of the Ukrainian population in order to help them achieve better living standards.

The European business community has a broad interest in expanding the EU's Single Market into neighbouring non-member states. This would not only mean openness for trade and investment, but also a favourable business climate and regulatory framework based on European standards. While Russia is clearly the biggest neighbouring market, Ukraine perhaps presents itself as a more willing partner to converge on EU standards, as signalled politically by its 'European choice'. The European Round Table, a powerful group of 45 leading EU companies (with a combined turnover of €1,500 billion and 4.5 million employees), produced a monograph in 2004 on the *ERT's Vision of a Bigger Single Market*, which advocates a step-by-step progression from WTO accession to free trade for all neighbourhood countries and ultimately full inclusion in the Single Market in the long term.[28] With the EU's recent enlargement up to the Ukrainian frontier and

---

[28] See the European Round Table, *ERT's Vision of a Bigger Single Market*, Brussels, 2004.

Ukraine's fast economic growth in recent years, awareness of Ukraine's potential interest as an economic partner is growing.

There is currently a major political debate in the EU over how to face up to the growing challenge of globalisation and Asian competition in particular. This debate is cast in rather general terms over the optimal degree of trade policy openness, and even if the most acute concerns are over Chinese competition there is a tendency for this to also colour the debate about other trade liberalisation initiatives. Additionally, there is also sensitivity in some EU countries, especially France and Germany, over the transfer of jobs to the new member states. Yet the proposition of deep free trade with Ukraine should objectively be seen as a potential advantage in relation to these concerns, rather than an additional threat. Given the proximity of Ukraine and its political will to converge on EU standards, a plausible strategy for EU business interests is to regard Ukraine as a potentially important part of the European value-added chain, in due course and in many industries. European enterprises that bear high labour costs in any case can regard outsourcing to neighbours with lower labour costs as a way of improving or defending their competitiveness in the global market. Nevertheless, the complexity of modern supply-chain management means that Ukraine would have to become an extremely reliable and open partner for the EU, hence the need for deep free trade with a strong emphasis on Ukraine's convergence on EU technical standards and regulatory policies.

8.2   Sectoral interests

Defensive anxieties on the EU side are typically concentrated in the agricultural, steel and textile sectors. In agriculture and steel Ukraine has significant capacities, actual or potential. Ukrainian defensive interests are most apparent in agriculture, but also in automobiles. These several sectors are now briefly discussed (and in more detail in the annexes), since they are sectors in which the greatest protectionist resistances might be expected. Yet it turns out that in some of these cases the problems may be less severe than initial apprehensions.

Agriculture. Ukrainian agriculture has a natural comparative advantage with its huge endowment of high quality soils for agriculture (see annex 1). But the competitive condition of the sector is for the time being seriously handicapped by the lack of an advanced market economy system and the absence of capabilities to meet EU technical sanitary and phytosanitary standards (SPS). As a result, Ukraine is not currently able to export virtually any animal products or processed foods to the EU. The Ukrainian agricultural producers association would like technical assistance from the EU to achieve EU standards, but Ukraine's own standards are sometimes even more demanding. Ukrainian agriculture is now privatised, but it will take time for the management culture to change. For example, the farm sector is strongly represented in parliament by a large contingent of former collective-farm managers. Farm interests have secured very high levels of tariff protection, even if these have been reduced in Ukraine's offer to the WTO.

COPA, the EU's farm lobby, is not against moving towards free trade, but would press for several conditions, such as gradualism to prevent sudden market disruption with long transitions (there was a noticed surge in Ukrainian cereal exports in 2002), the maintenance of SPS, the recognition of exclusive marks for geographical origin and progress towards meeting animal welfare and environmental standards.

Overall, there will be great caution on both sides over a rapid move to free trade in agriculture. The sugar industry on both sides has managed to maintain highly protective support systems, even if the EU sugar policy now seems set for serious reform. In due course there would be good long-term prospects for trade and complementarity in food produce. EU processed food manufacturers can see a growing future market in Ukraine for high value-added foods and could use competitive Ukrainian commodity exports. Moreover, as income increases in Ukraine, imports of high-quality EU products will likely increase more than proportionally (as for Poland in the last decade).

Steel. For steel, the prospects for trade expansion with the EU are very considerable, since the EU's present steel quota system will have to end when Ukraine joins the WTO (see annex 2). This is already understood on the EU side in both official and private-sector circles, and has prompted steel enterprises to begin thinking about cooperative schemes for market integration, for instance through mutual foreign investment projects. Thus the largest EU steel group, Arcelor, made a major bid for the re-privatisation of Krivorizhstahl, and even if they were outbid in this, it signals a new direction for European steel interests in Ukraine and is unlikely to be the last attempt of its kind. A major Ukrainian industrial group has already made significant investments in the Polish and Hungarian steel sectors, signaling that Ukrainian interests are also looking towards an integrated European business strategy. EU steel companies see the increasing diversity of steel products, which are very far from being a simple commodity. This trend means that much of the sector's production is in specialised market niches, which gives plenty of scope for two-way trade expansion. The EU steel industry is looking for growth abroad (given the slow growth of its home market) and for investment opportunities that will lead to partnerships of industry interests. Elimination of Ukraine's export duty on scrap metals, which give Ukrainian producers a competitive advantage, will surely feature among the EU's conditions for free trade.

Textiles. Trade in textile products between the EU and Ukraine was completely liberalised in March 2005.[29] The recent agreement removes export and import licences – some of the remaining restrictions on trade in textiles and clothing products. Both sides are also to maintain customs tariffs on each other's textile exports at low levels.[30] An earlier agreement of 2000 provided for the reciprocal liberalisation of textile and clothing trade from 1 January 2001. In accordance with the terms of the agreement, Ukraine implemented tariff reductions for EU exports of textile products from 23 February 2001 and the EC lifted all quantitative import restrictions on 26 March 2001. Ukraine then continued to reduce its maximum tariff rates until they were fully aligned with EU tariffs in 2004.

The EU is a major textiles trading partner for Ukraine. In 2004 Ukraine exported $500 million[31] worth of goods to the EU or 60% of total textile exports. Still, Ukraine remains a relatively small supplier to the European market as its share in textile imports amounted to 0.7% in 2004. Moreover, the clothing industry itself is quite small in Ukraine; its share in total industrial output is a mere 1.1%.

The trade volumes between the EU and Ukraine are rapidly increasing. Ukraine's proximity to the EU and its comparatively low labour costs makes for good opportunities for the intra-industry trade. Currently, about 80% of the Ukrainian clothing industry relies on the imported inputs recorded as goods made on commission (textiles and knitted fabric) coming largely from the EU.

---

[29] The description of the bilateral agreements' chronology is taken from the website of the European Delegation to Ukraine, Ukraine–EU Trade Relations (retrieved from http://www.delukr.cec.eu.int/site/page36088.html).

[30] Ukraine and the EU apply the same tariff levels, which do not exceed 4% for yarns, 8% for fabrics or 12% for clothing.

[31] Data derived from the EU. Trade in textiles is one of the areas where there are large discrepancies between Ukrainian and EU statistics.

Investment in the sector will grow as the EU manufacturers move further east from the new member states and accession countries, where there are upward wage pressures and labour shortages.[32] Total foreign direct investment (FDI) in the industry was estimated to be $120 million in 2004. Competition from China, Turkey and India – the EU's major suppliers – will significantly increase because of the Multi-Fibre Agreement. But the short order-to-delivery cycles in the textile industry[33] enable Ukraine to exploit its geographical advantage. Hence, if the country's transport and logistical inefficiencies are reduced, FDI and clothing exports to the EU can be expected to grow rapidly.

Automobiles. Car-making in Ukraine is one of the major industrial sectors enjoying a number of substantial breaks. Thus, over 2003-04,[34] the fact that the highest growth in the machinery sector was in vehicle output is owing to both domestic demand for durable goods and protectionist government policy. The industry traditionally has had strong lobbyists in parliament, which provided a range of privileges to the car-makers such as exempting individual enterprises from customs duties, reducing tax rates or even removing tax obligations. Some of the privileges have contradicted WTO terms and certain clauses in the Partnership and Cooperation Agreement that require equal conditions for both domestic and foreign manufacturers.

The government will likely liberalise the industry by 2009, if a three-year transition period with the WTO is negotiated. The government also

---

[32] The textile companies producing in Bulgaria, for example, estimate a 10% annual increase in labour costs. The average annual wage in Bulgaria's textile sector is €1,400 (€900 in Ukraine). (See Oxford Business Group, *Emerging Bulgaria 2005*, London, 2005.) Increased labour costs and shortages caused a big Lithuanian knitwear firm, Utenos Trikotazas, to shift production to Ukraine. See also the 28 September 2005 issue of the *Economist*, p. 89.

[33] EU retailers have to adapt quickly to the seasonal and fashion changes in the market. Hence, traditional up-front ordering to China (five months prior to the selling season) is often more expensive for the retailers in terms of demand-forecasting errors than the in-season replenishments from the nearby higher-cost producers (see D. Muller-Jentsch, *Deeper Integration and Trade in Services in the Euro-Mediterranean Region*, World Bank, Washington, D.C. and the European Commission, Brussels, 2004).

[34] In 2004, car-making output grew by 63.3% and by 78.1% for passenger cars. The Ukrainian market for new cars is estimated to equal $1.5 billion.

has legally binding obligations with investors to maintain certain preferences until 2008,[35] although in 2005 some of the most contradictory privileges were removed.[36] Further legal amendments remain likely since both importers and producers have responded negatively to the changes.

Support for the car-making industry has been largely through an inefficient allocation of public money in Ukraine. Although investment in the industry is growing fast,[37] as privileges are lifted Ukraine's industry will not be able to effectively compete with Chinese, Central European or Russian car-makers. These countries have attracted far greater investment into this sector from the top international car-makers.[38] The largest foreign investor in Ukraine's car industry, the South Korean company Daewoo, went bankrupt in 2000.

Despite the failures of the protectionist policy, Ukraine still could effectively participate in the global car production chain. Ukraine's major car-makers are often major car importers as well, along with the assembling sites for the Russian, Japanese, Chinese and European companies. Domestic car-makers will likely continue to increase the level of localisation and move away from the SKD (semi-knocked down parts) operation as is carried out at the Skoda assembly plant in western Ukraine. Low labour costs and proximity to the European markets have already attracted some of the big car parts manufacturers like Leoni and Yazaki.

---

[35] Investment programmes and related breaks for a number of large enterprises in the sector, such as for ZAT Lviv Car Plant and ZAT Zaporizhzhia Car Plant, were enshrined in law in the 1990s and are valid until 2008.

[36] The government amended the laws several times over 2003-05. With the 18 March 2004 Law on the Development of the Car-Making Industry in Ukraine, the government cancelled some privileges and reduced the base of beneficiaries. In 2005, among others, the country-of-origin criterion and related duty exemptions were lifted, but the import duties for new cars have also been increased to 20%.

[37] Capital investments in the industry grew by 46% and amounted to $63 million in 2004. A case of outward investment was reported in 2005. The Ukrainian owner of the country's major car manufacturer, ZAT Zaporizhzhia Car Plant, acquired the Daewoo-FSO (with a line capacity of 200,000) production site in Poland. The Polish company is a major supplier of the components to its Ukrainian counterpart.

[38] Slovakia and Russia have been the destination of big investments from Volkswagen, Toyota, Renault and other leading car-makers.

More generally, Ukraine has the potential to become the location for a massive expansion of industrial and service-sector investment with deep intra-industry linkages with the EU. The example of Mexico under the impact of the NAFTA points to the scale of this potential. Arguably Ukraine is even better poised for such a development, given its combination of high educational levels and very low wage costs, as well as geographical proximity (see Box 8.1).

Box 8.1 How Ukraine might become a Mexico for Europe

The deeper integration of Ukraine into the EU's Single Market could considerably enhance EU competitiveness in the global economy. Monthly wages in Ukraine are about 10% of the EU average and less than half of those in Romania and Bulgaria.* If Ukraine and Turkey are brought into the wider European market, they will create, together with Romania and Bulgaria, a low-wage industrial powerhouse in Europe's back yard – a zone of 150 million people even able to compete with China and India.

That thought might frighten highly paid workers in Germany or France. But it is better for all of Europe if new investment goes to Eastern Europe and not faraway China or Brazil. More investment and more growth in low-wage Europe generate more demand for goods and services from high-wage Europe...Enlargement is globalization in miniature. If the EU holds its neighbours at bay, it is putting off a shock of adjustment that will get bigger and bigger the longer it is delayed.**

Ukraine could become a low-cost production site for Europe and a key regional leader in attracting hi-tech investment during the next decade. The Eastern European Working Group (which encompasses major electronics manufacturing companies and whose combined global revenues in 2004 stood at $100 billion) announced their plans to develop an alternative to Asia by expanding R&D and manufacturing capacities in Eastern Europe.† Initial production sites in Ukraine have already been launched by such electronics manufacturing companies as Flextronics International and Jabil Circuit. These companies provide manufacturing and design services for Ericsson, Nokia, Alcatel, Philips and other leading brands. Other multinational companies (e.g. Intel and Foxconn) are considering starting production in Ukraine.

With its highly qualified, competitive workforce and borders with the EU, Ukraine merits their consideration. Ukraine has a strong network of schools and universities, which is why it is known for having a generally better-educated population than even some developed countries. Today, some 30% of Ukrainian students major in engineering, mathematics and information science. The labour costs in the country are some of the lowest in southern and Central Europe.

Ukraine is also quite attractive for export-oriented, full-scale electronics production. Placing some of a company's manufacturing facilities in Ukraine and gaining access to pan-European Transport Corridor V (which runs Venice–Ljubljana–Budapest–Uzhorod–Lviv), would make it possible for transnational companies that currently manufacture in China to cut delivery times to the European market by 20-25 days and to reduce dependence on China. For example, Hewlett Packard expects Ukraine-manufactured PC prices to be around $40–100 less than those manufactured in Europe because of lower costs related to logistics and labour.††

The majority of the above-mentioned companies use imported components to assemble their products and export most of them to the EU. At present, Ukraine presents several problems for such companies. First, Ukraine lacks a supplier base, although the country has the necessary raw materials and components to develop a strong supply network to start full-scale production. Second, Ukraine applies import duties of 5 to 10%, which makes it very costly since most components are imported. As discussed elsewhere in this study, the third major problem is the complicated customs procedures.††† The reform of customs and logistical systems is key to fostering Ukraine's integration with the global production networks, despite the fact that it will require time and significant effort. Meanwhile, establishing industrial parks and granting a customs-free status to those investors who manufacture in Ukraine and export 100% of their products could compensate for the cancellation of various exemptions connected with special economic zones. The recent statements made by the president and other high-ranking officials may indicate that some form of compromise can be reached.

Ukraine might develop a deep industrial and trading relationship with the EU comparable to that of Mexico in relation to the US – enabling the EU and Ukraine together to compete more effectively with China.

---

* See Deutsche Bank Research, "Ukraine: The Long Road West", *Current Issues*, Frankfurt, 27 May 2005.

** Quoted from "Meet the Neighbours – A Survey of the EU's Eastern Borders", *Economist*, 25 June 2005.

† It is estimated that in 2005 Eastern Europe will account for 54% of total European EMS production (worth $45.4 billion), while in 1997 the figure was a mere 15% (out of $12.5 billion). See "Ten new member countries join the EU this month with far reaching implications for the future of electronics manufacturing", *Electronics Supply & Manufacturing*, 15 August 2004 (retrieved from http://www.my-esm.com/print/showArticle.jhtml?articleID=19205595).

†† HP started the production of PCs in Ukraine (100,000 line capacity) in 2005. See the Interfax-Ukraine newswire of 18 October 2005.

††† In the EU, the only organisation normally involved in clearing goods across borders is customs, while other organisations carry out post-clearance audits. In Ukraine, the border process is more time-consuming and complex because of the multiplicity of organisations involved: customs, quarantine services, the national sanitary and medical agency, the ecological department and certification authorities. Owing to the difficult import process in Ukraine, international companies like Leoni, Yazaki or Jabil Circuit are consolidating all their raw materials outside the country before importing them.

Source: Much of the text in this box draws extensively from ICPS, 2005(b), along with materials provided by Intel and Jabil Circuit.

9. SUMMARY OF SOME OPTIONS, THEIR FEASIBILITY AND COST BENEFITS

The preceding chapters have shown that the contents of conceivable packages for free trade and deeper integration have many possible variables, which could make for numerous alternative packages. But for the policy-maker, these possibilities have to be concentrated and organised into a manageable number of well-identified options, to facilitate evaluation of their feasibility and likely cost/benefit qualities. For focus we therefore highlight four categorical options:

1. Simple free trade

2. Customs union

3. Deep free trade

4. European Economic Area (EEA) market integration

Each are summarised for its possible content, feasibility and cost benefits.

1.   Simple free trade package (FTA)

Content. This package would comprise, beyond the conditions for WTO membership, the elimination of customs tariffs over a short- or medium-term period, some additions to the already the very extensive list of services to be liberalised in the WTO offer, completion of capital market liberalisation and some visa-facilitation measures by the EU for the movement of persons to complement the scrapping of visas by Ukraine.

Feasibility. This approach is feasible in terms of Ukrainian administrative capacity, since it either frees public bodies from various burdens of regulatory or executive activity (e.g. for the licensing of service-sector activity and capital movements) or at least does not increase regulatory burdens (for customs). In terms of political economy feasibility it has to be observed that obtaining parliamentary support even for WTO accession is still proving difficult. With the WTO accession completed the building of support for simple free trade with the EU might be easier, especially if its political implications at that time are considered as positive.

Impact and cost/benefits. The economic impact of the steps that would need to be taken in additional to WTO membership will not be great, and there are even some risks of negative effects if liberalisation is not accompanied by adequate complementary measures for improving the domestic business climate.

2.   Customs union

Content. This strategy would mean adding to the simple free-trade scenario the alignment of Ukraine's external customs tariffs with those of the EU, as well as convergence on various other EU trade policy measures such as anti-dumping rules and exceptional quantitative restrictions.

Feasibility. The technical and administrative burden of full alignment on the EU's external tariffs and other trade policy measures has already been seen (in the case of Turkey) to be heavy. To which has to be added the political tensions that can arise in having to adopt new EU trade policy measures. For Ukraine these burdens would be as heavy if not more so.

Impact and cost/benefits. From an economic cost/benefit standpoint, a customs union is problematic when a partner state has an important trade relationship with a third party, since it leads to trade-diversion effects. For Ukraine this would be all the more applicable since it already has a free trade relationship with Russia, which would have to be scrapped unless the EU also forms a free trade area with Russia, and that is not on the horizon.

3.   Deep free trade package (FTA+)

Content. In addition to the free trade in goods and services and free capital movements arising from option 1, the deep free trade package would consist of a large but still selective set of priority actions, many of which already feature in the ENP Action Plan for Ukraine in some formulation. An illustrative but non-exhaustive priority list might include:

- the reform of customs services;
- product standards, with a medium-term programme for harmonisation/mutual recognition;

- the adoption of agri-food standards (sanitary and phytosanitary rules), in the context of a medium-term action programme;

- convergence on regulatory policies;

- financial services, with complete openness but a staged process for regulatory approximation (Basel I);

- civil aviation, with full *acquis* compliance and inclusion in a common aviation area;

- road transport, with liberalisation and *acquis* compliance, plus investment in pan-European corridors;

- telecommunications, complete with openness and compliance with the 1998 *acquis*;

- the energy sector, with extensive *acquis* compliance for regulatory norms;

- electricity, if grid linkage is sought, then full *acquis* compliance would be necessary;

- competition policy, with staged convergence on EU practices;

- corporate governance, for which basic measures of best international practices are needed; and

- the environment, with a start on a long-term process of gradual *acquis* compliance and links to Kyoto measures.

Feasibility. The feasibility of deep free trade is surely much more difficult than for simple free trade as regards administrative capacity, which is why a heavy investment in institution- and capacity-building would be needed. As regards political economy feasibility this is surely a somewhat fluid matter in the current political climate, and in the period ahead will depend on the broad political-will factor, which will stem from political leadership, public understanding of the issues and perceptions of sectoral and national priorities on the part of different business and civil society interest groups. In an unsettled political situation, typical of a mid-way stage in the transition process, there is a special need and value for external anchorage for the reform process. But in the Ukrainian case there is also a vital need for the authorities to engage in stakeholder consultations, in order to prepare business interest groups and the parliament to support the reform process. The difficulties in even passing WTO-compliant legislation have illustrated the obstacles that can arise when basic processes of information and consultation are neglected. These needs will surely be on a larger scale with a deep free trade agreement.

Impact and cost/benefits. The evidence from contemporary experiences of the post-communist transition in Europe is suggesting that the benefits to Ukraine from an effectively implemented and well-designed FTA+ package could be of major importance for inducing rapid and sustainable economic growth. Its relevance is enhanced by the now evident need for Ukraine to restructure as quickly as possible into an energy-efficient, rather than energy-wasteful economy. There are also many synergies between the individual elements of the deep free trade package and the credibility of the whole, which together acquire a holistic quality and constitute a strong reason not to reduce the level of ambition by taking only sub-sets of the package. For the EU, the economic impact will in any case be rather minor, but not without interest for industries confronting the challenges of globalisation. Furthermore, the EU has a major political interest in seeing a prosperous, stable and democratic Ukraine, to which a deep free trade strategy could make an important contribution.

4.   Complete market integration (EEA)

Content. This theoretical case would consist of full compliance with the entire EU Single Market *acquis* for goods, services, capital and labour at the level of commitments made by Norway and other members of the EEA. The EEA commitment is also dynamic in the sense of the automatic obligation to comply with new EU legislation.

Feasibility. This approach would not be feasible within a medium-term period, although it could become feasible in the long run. The initial problems of feasibility would certainly be those of the implementation capacity for the Ukrainian private sector to adopt many of the most complex parts of the *acquis,* for the Ukrainian executive branch to regulate the application of EU directives and for the judiciary to enforce them. A major question of political feasibility is whether the Ukrainian parliament would be willing to cede so much sovereignty to the EU without membership.

Impact and cost/benefits. This strategy would in theory be superior to the deep free trade package in terms of the ultimate benefits to Ukraine's economy, but since it is not feasible over at least a medium-term period further discussion is not necessary.

The model of the EU-Swiss agreements is sometimes suggested as a more realistic variant of the EEA for Ukraine. Its selectivity is a consideration, but its content is dependent on a very high mutual-recognition factor, which reduces its relevance for Ukraine.

Yet some kind of association between Ukraine and the EEA could be both feasible and beneficial. With independent technical assistance on how Ukraine might best converge progressively on the EU *acquis*, this element could be added to the deep free trade scenario.

5.   Intermediate packages

Between the simple and deep free trade packages above it would in principle be possible to construct a continuum of sub-options, adopting or setting aside some areas of action or selecting different sequencing paths. To test this idea one may consider breaking the deep free trade package up into the following four modules, each of which has internal coherence, and looking at the case for a more selective approach:

a)   *Deepened free trade in goods.* This module would take the first three headings in the above list for customs and product standards.

b)   *Deepened free trade in services.* This aspect would encompass the headings listed for the main service sectors – financial, transport, telecommunications and energy distribution.

c)   *Deepened investment in infrastructures.* The focus here would be on the pan-European corridors and related regulatory policies.

d)   *Deepened reforms of corporate and public economic governance.* These reforms would concern competition policy and basic elements of corporate governance.

Would there be a case for prioritising one or another or a sub-set of these options? One could argue in favour of a traditional free trade model, with deepened free trade just for goods (a). But this would be to ignore (b) and the strong argument that free trade in services is at least as important for both external trade and internal reform. One could draw the line there, but already under (c) substantial arrangements are underway for investment in pan-European transport infrastructures, which would be in support of (a) and (b) and in which it would make no sense to exclude Ukraine. One might then draw the line by saying that under (d) there are items far removed from the trade policy agenda. But these items are also major prerequisites for obtaining the full benefits from trade liberalisation, especially for a country such as Ukraine with weak corporate and public economic governance.

Overall the case for advocating a more limited agenda does not seem persuasive. It would be possible to make purely semantic distinctions, by saying that (a) and (b) are about free trade, whereas (c) and (d) are about other economic policies and are covered by the ENP. From an economic perspective, however, and a diagnosis of the needs of the Ukrainian economy, the quantitative economic analysis shows evidence of synergies to be derived from a holistic approach, which would mean embracing all four modules together. It is no coincidence that the ENP Action Plan also follows a comprehensive and holistic approach. The deep free trade proposition could be seen as giving the plan backbone and a stronger focus.

Of course there would be many variables, such as the speed and intensity of undertaking the individual components of deep free trade, offering opportunities for alternative ways of fine-tuning the content of an agreement. Yet this degree of detail is beyond the scope of the present study and would in any case become subject matter for the official negotiation process.

As an example of an intermediate scenario between the simple and deep free trade packages, the EU–Chile FTA has quite rich content, but the absence of the European neighbourhood factor makes it a less relevant model for Ukraine.

6.   Overall assessment

A summary of these four main scenarios for free trade between the EU and Ukraine is:

- Option 1 – simple free trade is the most easily feasible, but its impact is weak and the cost/benefits less impressive.

- Option 2 – a customs union is rejected because of its serious disadvantages in terms of both feasibility and cost/benefits.

- Option 3 – deep free trade is complex and demanding in terms of feasibility, but offers the prospect of large economic advantages of strategic value.

- Option 4 – complete market integration is not feasible at least for the medium term.

A persuasive logic does not emerge for identifying specific intermediate packages lying somewhere between the options of simple and deep free trade. Therefore, option 3 is the scenario that invites special consideration, by virtue of both its coverage and potential interest for Ukraine. There could be many ways of fine-tuning the content and the sequencing of individual measures, some of which are discussed in some detail in this study (in chapter 5 and annex 3).

GLOSSARY LIST OF ABBREVIATIONS

ACAA	Agreement on Conformity Assessment and Acceptance of Industrial Products
ASAs	Air service agreements
CEECs	Central and Eastern European countries
CGE	Computable general equilibrium (model)
CIS	Commonwealth of Independent States
COPA	Committee of Agricultural Organisations in the European Union
EASA	European Aviation Safety Agency
EBRD	European Bank for Reconstruction and Development
EEA	European Economic Area
EFTA	European Free Trade Area
EIB	European Investment Bank
ENP	European Neighbourhood Policy
ENPI	European Neighbourhood and Partnership Instrument
Eurofer	European Confederation of Iron and Steel Industries
FDI	Foreign direct investment
FIGS	Financial–industrial groups
FTA	Free trade agreement
FTA+	A 'deep' free trade agreement
GATS	General Agreement on Trade in Services
GSP	Generalised System of Preferences
IAS	International Accounting Standards
IBRD	International Bank of Reconstruction and Development
IFI	International financial institution
IMF	International Monetary Fund
ISA	International Standards for Auditing
ISO	International Standards Organisation
JI	Joint implementation (projects)
MES	Market economy status
MFN	Most-favoured nation
MoU	Memorandum of Understanding
Mt	Million tonnes
NAFTA	North American Free Trade Agreement

NBU	National Bank of Ukraine
NCRC	National Communications Regulatory Commission
NERC	National Energy Regulatory Committee
NGOs	Non-governmental organisations
OECD	Organisation for Economic Cooperation and Development
OHS	Occupational health and safety
PCA	Partnership and Cooperation Agreement
SEECs	South-Eastern European countries
SES	Single Economic Space
SIAs	Sustainable Development Impact Assessments
SPS	Sanitary and phytosanitary standards
SSSMC	State Securities and Stock Market Commission
t/ha	Tonnes/hectare
TBT	Technical barriers to trade
UAH	Ukrainian *hryvnya*
UEPLAC	Ukrainian–European Policy and Legal Advice Centre
UNDP	United Nations Development Programme
UNICE	Union of Enterprises of the European Community
WTO	World Trade Organisation

BIBLIOGRAPHY[*]

Åslund, A. (2005), "The Economic Policy of Ukraine after the Orange Revolution", *Eurasian Geography and Economics*, Vol. 46, No. 5, pp. 327-53.

Barro, R. and J.-W. Lee (2000), *International Data on Educational Attainment: Updates and Implications*, Working Paper No. 42, Centre for International Development, Harvard University, Cambridge, MA.

Bilan, O. (2004), "In Search of the Liquidity Effect in Ukraine", *Journal of Comparative Economics*, Vol. 33, No. 3.

Blue Ribbon Commission for Ukraine (BRC) (2005), *Proposals for the President – A New Wave of Reform*, BRC and the United Nations Development Programme, Kyiv.

Boratynski, J., G. Gromadzki and O. Sushko (2005), *How to Make a Difference? EU–Ukrainian Negotiations on Facilitation of Visa Regime*, Stefan Batory Foundation, Warsaw-Kyiv, October.

Brenton, P. (1999), "Executive Summary", *Study on Evaluating the Economic Feasibility, General Impact and Implications of a Free Trade Agreement between the European Union and Ukraine according to the Partnership and Cooperation Agreement*, CEPS, Brussels.

Brenton, P. and J. Whalley (1999), *Evaluating a Ukraine–EU Free Trade Agreement using a Numerical General Equilibrium Model*, CEPS, Brussels.

Concorde Capital (2005), *Ukraine's Gas Issue: The Way Out*, Concorde Capital, Kyiv, September.

Debruxelles, J.-P. (2005), "The Greenhouse Gas Challenge: How the EU Steel Industry Competitiveness Could be Affected", Presentation at the OECD "Special Meeting at High-Level on Steel Issues: The Outlook for Steel", held in Paris, 12-13 January 2005.

DekaBank (2005), *Developing Country Risk Indicators*, DekaBank, Frankfurt/Main.

Deutsche Bank Research (2005), "Ukraine: The Long Road West", *Current Issues*, Deutsche Bank, Frankfurt, 27 May.

---

[*] A comprehensive list of the references on economic modelling is given in annex 4.

Diehl, M. and R. Schweickert (2005), *Monetary Management of Transition in China: Balancing Short-Run Risks and Long-Run Optimality*, Kiel Economic Policy Paper No. 1, Institute for the World Economy, Kiel.

Economist Intelligence Unit (EIU) (2005), *Ukraine Country Profile 2005*, EIU, London.

Edwards, T. Huw (2005), *Implicit Trade Costs and European Single Market*, Loughborough University and the Centre for the Study of Globalisation and Regionalisation, Warwick.

Esanov, A., C. Merkl and L. Vinhas de Souza (2004), *Monetary Policy Rules for Russia*, Discussion Paper Series 11/2004, Bank of Finland Institute of Transition, Helsinki.

European Business Association (EBA) (2005), *Barriers to Investment in Ukraine*, EBA, Kyiv, February.

European Commission (2004), European Neighbourhood Policy, Strategy Paper, COM(2004) 373, final, Brussels, 12.5.2004.

————— (2005a), Joint Statement, EU–Ukraine Summit held in Kyiv on 1 December 2005, 15222/05 (Presse 337), Brussels, 1.12.2005.

————— (2005b), *Networks for Peace and Development – Extension of the Major Trans-European Transport Axes to the Neighbouring Countries and Regions*, Report from the High-Level Group chaired by Loyola Palacio, Brussels, November (retrieved from http://europa.eu.int/comm/ten/transport/external_dimension/doc/2005_12_07_ten_t_final_report_en.pdf.)

————— (2005c), Communication on developing the agenda for the Community's external aviation policy, COM(2005) 79 final, Brussels, 27.6.2005.

————— (2005d), Communication on developing a common aviation area with Ukraine, COM(2005) 451 final, Brussels, 27.9.2005.

European Round Table (2004), *ERT's Vision of a Bigger Single Market*, European Round Table, Brussels.

Fernandez-Arias, E. and M. Spiegel (1998), "North-South customs unions and international capital mobility", *Journal of International Economics*, Vol. 46, No. 2, pp. 229-51.

François, J. and L. Schuknecht (1999), "International Trade in Financial Services, Competition and Growth Performance." Center for Economic Policy Research, London, October.

Golodniuk, I. (2004), "Evidence on the Bank Lending Channel in Ukraine", Mimeo, Department of Economics, Simon Fraser University, Vancouver.

Hammermann, F. and R. Schweickert (2005), "How Far Away are the EU's Balkan and Black Sea Neighbors?", Mimeo, EU Enlargement and Institutional Development, UACES, Zagreb, 5-9 September.

Harrison, G.W., T.F. Rutherford and D.G. Tarr (2003), *Rules of Thumb for Evaluating Preferential Trading Arrangements: Evidence from Computable General Equilibrium Assessments*, Policy Research Working Paper Series No. 3149, World Bank, Washington, D.C.

International Centre for Policy Studies (ICPS) (2003), "Policy memo to the draft Law of Ukraine 'On telecoms'", ICPS, Kyiv, February.

——————— (2004a), *Improving the Business Climate*, ICPS, Kyiv.

——————— (2004b), *How to Make Small and Medium Businesses More Effective in Ukraine?*, ICPS, Kyiv.

——————— (2005a), *Quarterly Predictions*, No. 32, Third Quarter, ICPS, Kyiv.

——————— (2005b), "Government policy to support electronics manufacturing in Ukraine", Mimeo, ICPS, Kyiv.

——————— (2005c), *Problems and prospects for developing the air passenger carrier market in Ukraine*, ICPS, Kyiv.

International Monetary Fund (IMF) (2005), *Ukraine: Article IV Consultation – Staff Report; Staff Supplement; and Public Information Notice on the Executive Board Discussion*, IMF Country Report 05/15, IMF, Washington, D.C.

Kaufmann, D., A. Kraay and M. Mastruzzi (2005), *Governance Matters IV, Governance Indicators for 1996–2004*, World Bank, Washington, D.C.

Kulish, N. (2005), "Driving the Scenic Route to EU Membership", *International Herald Tribune*, 4 October.

Le Jour, A.M., R. De Mooij and R. Nahuis (2001), *EU Enlargement: Implications for Countries and Industries*, CPB Netherlands Bureau for Economic Analysis, The Hague.

Leheyda, N. (2004), "Determinants of Inflation in Ukraine: A Cointegration Approach", Mimeo, University of Mannheim.

Lienemeyer, M. (2005), "State aid for restructuring the steel industry in the new member states", *Competition Policy Newsletter*, No. 1, spring.

Lücke, M. and A. Szalavetz (1999), "Export Reorientation and Transfer of Know-how and Technology – The Case of Hungarian Manufactured Exports", in M. Fritsch and H. Brezinski (eds), *Innovation and Technological Change in Eastern Europe*, Cheltenham: Edward Elgar.

Lücke, M. and D. Spinanger (2004), *Liberalizing International Trade in Services: Challenges and Opportunities for Developing Countries*, Discussion Paper

No. 412, Kiel Institute for the World Economy, Kiel (retrieved from http://www.uni-kiel.de/ifw/pub/kd/2004/kd412.pdf).

Mattoo, A.; Rathindran, R.; Subramanian, A. (2001), "Measuring Services Trade Liberalization and its Impact on Economic Growth: An Illustration" (see http://www.sice.oas.org/geograph/services/mattoor.pdf).

McKinsey Global Institute (1999), *Unlocking economic growth in Russia*, McKinsey Global Institute, Washington, D.C.

Müller-Jentsch, D. (2001), *The Development of Electricity Markets in the Euro-Mediterranean Area – Trends and Prospects for Liberalization and Regional Integration*, World Bank, Washington, D.C. and European Commission, Brussels.

————— (2002), *Transport Policies for the Euro-Mediterranean Free-Trade Area – An Agenda for Multimodal Reform in the Southern Mediterranean*, World Bank, Washington, D.C. and European Commission, Brussels.

————— (2004), *Deeper Integration and Trade in Services in the Euro-Mediterranean Region – Southern Dimensions of the European Neighbourhood Policy*, World Bank, Washington, D.C. and European Commission, Brussels.

Newman, J. (2005), "Policies to reduce greenhouse gas emissions in industry: Implications for steel", paper presented at the OECD Special Meeting at High-Level on the Outlook for Steel, held in Paris on 12-13 January.

OECD (2001), *The Development Dimensions of Trade*, OECD, Paris.

————— (2005), *Capacity Expansion in the Global Steel Industry*, Report from the OECD Special Meeting at High-Level on Steel Issues, "The Outlook for Steel", OECD held in Paris on 12-13 January.

OECD and the World Bank (2004), *Achieving Ukraine's Agricultural Potential*, OECD, Paris and World Bank, Washington, D.C.

Oxford Business Group (2005), *Emerging Bulgaria 2005*, London.

Pavel, F., I. Burakovsky, N. Selitska and V. Movchan, (2004), *Economic Impacts of Ukraine's WTO Accession: First Results from a Computable General Equilibrium Model*, Working Paper No. 30, Institute for Economic Research and Policy Consulting, Kyiv.

Piazolo, D. (2001), *The integration process between Eastern and Western Europe*, Kieler Studien No. 310, Berlin: Springer-Verlag.

Purdue University, GTAP Project Database, Department of Agricultural Economics, West Lafayette, IN (project website https://www.gtap.agecon.purdue.edu).

Schuetz, G., H. Ursprung and L. Woessmann (2005), *Educational Policy and Equality of Opportunity*, Working Paper No. 1515, CESifo, Munich.

Schweickert, R. (2004), "How Far Away is Europe? Institutional Development in Europe's Balkan and Black Sea Neighbours", *Intereconomics*, Vol. 39, No. 6, pp. 305-09.

TransCore (2003), "TransCore's RFID Technology Selected for Extending U.S. Bureau of Customs and Border Protection's Free and Secure Trade Programme to 22 Northern and Southern Border Crossings", News Release, TransCore, Harrisburg, PA, 5 December (retrieved from http://www.transcore.com/news/news031205.htm, 10.10.2005).

Ukrainian–European Policy and Legal Advice Centre (UEPLAC) (2004), *Ukrainian Law Review*, No. 5, UEPLAC, Kyiv, May.

US Department of Homeland Security (2005), *FAST Reference Guide: Enhancing the Security and Safety of Trans-Border Shipments*, US Customs and Border Protection, Washington, D.C.

Van Aarle, B., E. de Jong and R. Sosoian (2004), "Macroeconomic Stabilization in Ukraine: Is It Sustainable?" Mimeo, Katholieke Universiteit Leuven.

Vinhas de Souza, L., R. Schweickert, V. Movchan, O. Bilan and I. Burakovsky (2005), *Now So Near, and Yet Still So Far: Economic Relations between Ukraine and the European Union*, Discussion Paper No. 419, Kiel Institute for World Economics, Kiel.

World Bank (2003), *Country Assistance Strategy for Ukraine for 2004-07*, World Bank, Washington, D.C.

———— (2004a), *Ukraine Trade Policy Study*, Report No. 29684, World Bank, Washington, D.C.

———— (2004b), "Ukraine – Country Economic Memorandum", World Bank, Washington, D.C.

———— (2004c), *Ukraine – Building Foundations for Sustainable Growth: A Country Economic Memorandum*, Vol. 1, World Bank, Washington, D.C., December.

———— (2004d), *Steel Sector Development*, World Bank, Washington D.C.

———— (2005a), "Ukraine: FY2006 Unified Survey", Office Memorandum, World Bank, Washington, D.C.

———— (2005b), *Electronic Communications in Ukraine: The Bottleneck to Sustainable Development*, World Bank, Washington, D.C.

———— (2005c), *A Strategy for Modernising Ukraine*, World Bank, Washington, D.C., March.

Yushchenko, V. (2000), "Monetary Policy in the Transition to a Market Economy", *Russian and East European Finance and Trade*, Vol. 36, No. 1, pp. 78-96.

ANNEX 1. AGRICULTURE[*]

1.1 Background and policy developments

As the traditional 'bread basket' of the former USSR, Ukrainian agriculture holds serious advantages for competing in the world market, with large-scale fields and good soils. Yet for the time being these are underexploited assets. Employment in agriculture amounts to 5.7 million people (19.8% of the active population). Nevertheless, during 1990-99 agricultural output dropped by nearly half and around 40% of rural residents are living in poverty, with average monthly agricultural wages below $40.

Important reform measures were introduced at the end of 1999, when collective farms were transformed into private enterprises and former collective-farm members started receiving properly issued titles to their land. This move was followed by the abolition of state orders, farm debt relief and protection against arbitrary state intervention.

The years 2000-04 saw a major recovery in Ukrainian grain production and exports. By 2002-03, Ukraine had become the world's third largest exporter of wheat and its fifth largest exporter of grain. Agricultural production began to cover its costs.

The situation has been more favourable in food processing, where privatisation occurred earlier, and in contrast to crop production and animal husbandry, has since 1997 witnessed significant capital inflows and technological modernisation. Positive developments are observed in the food industry. Its output in 2004 was double that of 1999. Substantial increases took place in the following products:[1] fat cheeses (4.2 times), vegetable oil (2.3 times), margarine products (2.6 times), sausage products and alcoholic beverages (2 times), mineral water (3.3 times), confectionery (1.7 times) and granulated sugar (by 15%).

Regrettably, anti-reform trends in some areas have returned since 2004. Poor grain yields (mostly owing to weather conditions) in 2003-04 served as an official argument for reinstating government intervention in

---

[*] This annex was prepared by Olexandr Shevtsov and Andreas Schneider.

[1] These increases are noted in physical terms.

agricultural markets, mainly in the form of administered pricing and restrictions on the free movement and sale of commodities. Ukraine's foreign trade policy for agricultural products suffers unjustified protectionism on the imports side, given the competitiveness of its major products. The concept of 'food security' in Ukraine is still widely misunderstood to mean achieving self-sufficiency in food production. This autarkic approach is difficult to reconcile with Ukraine's aspirations for international trade integration.

Regardless of official policies, foreign trade in agriculture and foods has been developing and diversifying quite well, with exports growing in recent years despite fluctuations in grain yields. Trade with the EU has increased significantly, especially in cereals, animal feeds and processed vegetables and oils. The lack of compliance with EU food safety regulations means that Ukraine finds it harder, if not impossible, to export value-added food products to the EU (see discussion below).

The potential of Ukraine's agrarian sector is high but to a great extent underutilised. For example, the yield capacity of the main grain crops grown in Ukraine is currently 3-6 t/ha less than in neighbouring countries, while this figure for sugar beets is 20-50 t/ha lower (see Table A.1).

Table A1.1 Comparable yielding capacity of some product types

Country	Maize (t/ha)		Barley (t/ha)		Sunflower (t/ha)		Wheat (t/ha)		Sugar beets (t/ha)	
	1999	2004	1999	2004	1999	2004	1999	2004	1999	2004
Germany	8.8	9.1	6.0	5.8	1.4	1.4	7.5	8.2	56.4	61.6
France	9.0	9.0	6.3	6.8	2.3	2.4	7.2	7.6	74.2	79.1
Czech Rep.	6.6	6.4	3.9	5.0	2.2	2.2	4.7	5.8	45.6	50.3
Hungary	6.4	4.2	3.1	4.3	1.5	2.5	3.6	5.1	44.6	51.3
Poland	5.8	6.1	3.1	2.5	–	–	3.5	3.9	33.8	39.3
Ukraine	2.5	3.0	1.9	1.9	1.0	0.9	2.3	3.2	15.6	23.8

Note: t/ha = tonnes/hectare
Source: FAO.

The major change in the structure of agricultural production after 1999 was the reduction of the share of animal products, from 45.6% down to 35.7% of the total, whereas the share of plant products (especially grain crops) increased notably. Favourable weather conditions, the profitability and expansion of grain exports, some progress in farm restructuring and improved access of farms to credit resources contributed to the growth of grain production.

Production of sugar beets was unstable during the same period. Tariff quotas for preferential imports of raw cane sugar allowed a replenishment of supplies with sugar made of cheaper, imported raw cane material. There is a large surplus of sugar-producing capacities, but they are not competitive, mainly because of obsolete technology. Policies in the sugar sub-sector continue to be mostly focused on helping existing refineries to survive, rather than pursuing long-term restructuring objectives.

The share of potatoes, vegetables and sunflower seeds in the structure of agricultural production increased from 19% to 23%. Potatoes and vegetables are mainly produced by private farmers or on private plots, where manual labour-intensive production technologies are used. Growth of sunflower seed production was stimulated by favourable export markets.

So far, however, technologies, crop rotations and farm specialisation remain mostly as inherited from traditional Soviet-style practices, thereby continuing an inefficient use of resources. Although progress in land reform and the restructuring of agricultural enterprises after 1999 has contributed to the development of agricultural production, the growth has been more of an extensive nature, and only limited qualitative change has taken place.

There are various assessments of the potential for Ukraine's agricultural production. The weather and climatic conditions are exceptionally favourable for growing of all kinds of cereals, especially wheat for food consumption. For instance, in the most favourable 1990 crop year, the average yield of winter wheat was 4 t/ha, which was 76% higher than in Canada and 50% more than in the US. Experts judge that with improvements in technology, even without expanding the cultivated area the gross output of grains might be increased by 20%, or to about 52 Mt. This level of output would enable the doubling of grain exports to the level of 14-15 Mt (7.6 Mt in 2004).

Because of its low competitiveness and the shrinkage of the domestic market, it is more difficult to assess the potential of the animal husbandry sub-sector, but physically Ukraine should be capable of producing at least 18 Mt of milk (13.8 in 2004) and 2.5 Mt of all types of meat (1.6 in 2004).

1.2 Foreign trade in agricultural goods

In 1999-2000, the trade surplus for agricultural and food industry products was as low as $0.5 billion, because of a temporary loss of demand from Russia following the 1998 financial crisis and a cut-back of grain supply for export. Since 2000, however, the average year-on-year growth of exports (in monetary terms) was around 30%. As a result, exports of agricultural and food industry products reached $3.5 billion in 2004, with net exports of $1.5 billion.

In the overall structure of agricultural foreign trade, members of the Commonwealth of Independent States (CIS) import the largest share of Ukrainian exports – about 47% (based on nine months in 2005). The CIS consumes 99% of Ukraine's exports of meat products, 80% of dairy produce, 89% of alcoholic beverages, 92% of cocoa and products thereof, 75% of sugar and confectionary. Yet for plant products a geographical redistribution of Ukrainian agricultural exports has taken place, with major supplies going to Asia (45%), the EU (26%) and Africa (23%).

In 2004, the share of the EU-25 in Ukraine's overall agri-food exports was about 20%, of which a little under half is accounted for by the new member states. Ukraine's trade balance with the EU-25 remains positive.

Since 1999, significant liberalisation of agricultural imports has taken place in Ukraine. In particular, the application of the minimum customs values was phased out during 1999-2000; previously, they were applied to an extensive list of goods, including meat, milk products, grain crops, flour, fruit and vegetables. In 2000, the list of excised goods was cut dramatically: coffee, sea and fish products, and other foodstuffs were withdrawn, while import duty rates were decreased for some goods. Excise tax is now paid only on importation of ethyl alcohol, alcoholic beverages, raw tobacco materials and tobacco products. The recent adoption of Law No. 2775 concerning changes to import duty rates for agricultural products substantially liberalised access to Ukraine's market. The Law sets zero or low *ad valorem* rates for some commodities (5-10%), which correspond to Ukraine's tariff offer at the WTO accession negotiations. For sensitive commodities (e.g. ch. 02 – meat and edible meat offal; ch. 04 – dairy produce; ch. 11 – milling products; and ch. 17 – sugars), combined tariffs remain in force. While their *ad valorem* part has been reduced, the high specific rates have been preserved. But as soon as Ukraine joins the WTO, all tariffs for these goods should be converted to *ad valorem* alone and be no higher than 10-12%.

Major obstacles to exports. There are both internal and external factors restraining Ukrainian agricultural exports. Domestic obstacles include obsolete grain storage systems, a costly transport infrastructure, over-regulated and time-consuming export procedures, underdeveloped market-information systems and the poor access of producers to information, as well as a low supply of high quality products, especially grain. All risks and costs associated with these factors are ultimately paid by farms, with farm gate prices being traditionally depressed. In as much as primary agricultural producers cannot obtain a better price for their output, they are not properly stimulated to improve technology, diversify or make long-term investments. Obviously, this does not add to the development of export potential or the proper utilisation of land.

Another important domestic factor is non-reimbursement of VAT on exports (as of September 2005, the state's arrears on VAT reimbursement to exporters of grain were as high as UAH 400 million). This situation actually means that farm's gate prices are further depressed and that farmers (not exporters or traders) are subject to this additional tax. Ukraine also continues to administer export duties for raw hides and skins and for oilseeds (further discussed in the WTO section below).

External factors include unstable access to foreign markets, both in the form of unpredictable tariff changes (which has happened frequently with the EU and Russia), and many cases where Ukrainian goods are subject to sudden veterinary and sanitary inspections from various countries. The extensive application of non-tariff barriers by the EU is described below.

Entry into the WTO. In its WTO accession negotiations, Ukraine committed to reduce the average tariff for agriculture and food products (chs. 1-24) down to 12% in 2007. The only exceptions will be sugar (with a 50% rate) and sunflower oil (with 30%). Ukraine has also committed to the sole use of *ad valorem* rates upon accession, with combined and specific rates applied only to excised goods until 2009. The schedule of Ukraine's market access commitments has already been agreed with most of the working party members (38 out of 48 bilateral protocols have been signed).

To complete the WTO negotiations, a number of outstanding issues have to be resolved. One of them is the tariff rate quota for raw cane sugar, for which the quantity and distribution mechanism must be agreed. Ukraine's previous position (annual tariff quota of 260,000 tonnes at 2% duty, with 50% duty above the quota) was changed in 2005 to 15% within the quota and 50% (but no less than €300/tonne) beyond the quota. The volume of this tariff quota (of 260,000 tonnes) has been agreed in bilateral protocols with Brazil, Cuba, India, Paraguay and the EU. Nevertheless, based on information about the expansion of legal and illegal imports of raw sugar and white sugar into Ukraine, Australia is demanding that the tariff quota be increased to 408,000 tonnes. Australia also insists on the abolition of the compulsory re-export of sugar made using imported raw materials.

Ukraine was requested to cancel export duties for agricultural goods before the accession. The 23% export duty for sunflower seeds and other oil crops was reduced to 17% in 2001. When Ukraine becomes a WTO member the export duty rates for seeds of flax, sunflower and rape will be set at 16% of their customs value, with further reductions by 1 percentage point annually down to 10% from 1 January 2007.

Ukraine has a draft law that would abolish the export duty for live animals and reduce them for raw hides and skins starting from 1 January 2006. It is proposed that there be a 15% export duty for raw hides in 2006, with subsequent annual 1% reductions starting from 1 January 2007 down to the 10% level. But this draft law has failed so far to win enough votes in the parliament.

1.3 Foreign trade with and foreign direct investment from the EU

Formally, Ukraine benefits from the EU Generalised System of Preferences (GSP). Most agricultural and food industry products are in the 'sensitive' goods category, however, where the margin of preference is small and procedures are complicated (particularly by rules of origin). Also, information about GSP advantages has not been efficiently delivered to Ukrainian producers and exporters; hence the level of GSP usage by Ukraine remains low.

One of the major restrictive factors for Ukrainian agricultural exports to the EU was the introduction of quotas for low- and medium-quality wheat starting 1 January 2003 (2.98 Mt of low- and medium-quality wheat at a duty rate of €12/tonne, €95/tonne above the quota). Only the US and Canada obtained bilateral shares in the quota, while the rest, 2.37 Mt, was open to all other countries, including Ukraine. For comparison, Ukraine exported 3 Mt of grain to the EU in 2001-02, and about 5 Mt in 2002-03. This measure was painful for Ukrainian exporters and producers through depressed farm gate prices, during these years of grain surplus. Yet EU policy for some agricultural commodities is a flexible on/off regime, i.e. switching between restrictive versus free conditions for imports depending on market conditions. Since 16 November 2005, EU imports of wheat have been tariff-free.[2] This condition signals that the market for free trade in this important sector is relatively favourable, and effectively a temporary free trade regime prevails at present. For Ukraine, in the context of a possible FTA+, this tariff-free regime could be made permanent.

Table A1.2 Exports and imports of selected agricultural commodities between the EU and Ukraine in € millions (for commodities exceeding €10 million) (2000-04 annual averages)

Commodity	EU-25 imports from Ukraine	EU-25 exports to Ukraine
Milk/cream concentrate	11	–
Meat	–	26
Dried vegetables	11	–
Coconuts, brazil nuts	11	1
Fruit/nuts – uncooked	14	1
Coffee	–	24
Wheat	145	17
Rye	10	–
Barley	29	4
Maize or corn	11	8
Malt	–	11
Sunflower seeds	171	3
Cane/beet sugar	–	25
Food preparations	–	20
Oilcake	51	3
Unmanufactured tobacco	–	16
Mixes of onions, etc., substances	–	31
Casein	25	–
Raw hides – bovine	38	3
Total	**594**	**370**

Source: Eurostat.

---

[2] See European Commission, Regulation (EC) No. 1865/2005 of 16 November 2005 fixing the import duties in the cereals sector, OJ L 299/58, 16.11.2005.

In the structure of Ukraine's agricultural exports to the EU-25, the share of milk and dairy produce is very small, at only 2%. The low competitiveness of Ukraine's dairy sector is further aggravated by the non-conformity of Ukrainian dairy products with EU requirements on safety and quality. A similar situation is observed for meat and edible meat offal, which Ukraine does not export to the EU at all, while the share of these products in total agricultural imports from the EU-25 amounts to 40%.

In January 2004 the EU amended the list of countries from which it can import live animals and meat products. The import of such categories as the fresh meat of domestic animals and meat products, the fresh meat of wild animals, live cattle, live swine and live poultry from Ukraine to the EU is not allowed. Permission to import from Ukraine to the EU is given to only one category, namely live horses and donkeys.

Investment from the EU-25 accounts for 57% of total foreign direct investment (FDI) in agricultural production ($129 million) and 70% for the food industry ($777 million). EU investment in the agri-food sector accounts for 10% of total FDI in Ukraine. While these absolute numbers are still extremely low given the size of Ukraine, the potential of its agriculture and its geographical proximity to the EU, the relative figures suggest that FDI in agri-food sectors could become important with a free trade area.

Table A1.3 FDI in agricultural and food production (US$ '000s)

Agricultural production	01.01.2001	31.12.2001	01.01.2002	31.12.2002	01.01.2004	31.12.2004
Total	35,893	45,133	45,908	60,663	205,994	227,125
CIS	587	947	949	1,342	7,860	11,853
EU-15	11,854	18,408	18,587	22,702	73,692	100,357
CEEC-10	4,584	6,042	5,949	7,688	20,973	29,034
Other	18,868	19,735	20,424	28,930	103,469	85,881

Food industry	01.01.2001	31.12.2001	01.01.2002	31.12.2002	01.01.2004	31.12.2004
Total	615,309	600,346	633,281	654,795	1,006,458	1,123,684
CIS	3,030	3,416	4,564	5,360	12,128	19,307
EU-15	431,761	414,466	422,038	432,695	593,946	667,339
CEEC-10	42,474	46,116	60,388	59,661	111,481	110,584
Other	138,044	136,349	146,291	157,079	288,901	326,454

Note: CEEC-10 refers to the 10 EU accession countries from Central and Eastern Europe.

Source: State Statistics Committee of Ukraine.

1.4   Technical barriers to trade, sanitary and phytosanitary measures

Based on the Agreement on Technical Barriers to Trade (TBT) and on Art. 51 of the EU–Ukraine Partnership and Cooperation Agreement, Ukraine undertook to introduce in its national legislation the international and European standards for health and safety, while ensuring product competitiveness and removing unnecessary barriers to trade. Ukraine reaffirmed at the negotiations its intention of reviewing and replacing all of its national standards with international standards or technical regulations based on them, in accordance with the Action Plan of full harmonisation of standards and technical rules for 2005-11 developed by the State Committee for Technical Regulation and Consumer Policy.

Yet only 52% of the total number of Ukraine's state standards (DSTU) for agricultural products is harmonised with international standards; for the food industry this indicator is only 29%.

Table A1.4   Extent of introduction of international and European standards (ISO, IEC, EN) in Ukraine

Sector	Standards harmonised with international and European ones			Percentage of harmonised DSTU standards
	DSTU	**GOST**	**Total**	
Agriculture	122	77	199	52
Food industry	196	62	258	29

Note: GOST refers to Russian standards, ISO to the International Standards Organisation, IEC to the International Electrotechnical Commission and EN to European standards.

Source: The State Committee for Technical Regulation and Consumer Policy of Ukraine as of 1 July 2005.

Ukraine's draft law on the development and application of standards, technical regulations and conformity assessment procedures has been prepared and should be passed. The draft defines legal and organisational principles surrounding these activities and the granting of the right of conformity signs usage for all goods, processes and services. The draft also contains provisions about the recognition of equivalence of foreign and Ukrainian technical regulations and about the creation of a centre for inquiry processing and messaging.

Steps are also being undertaken to ensure the compliance of the sanitary and phytosanitary standards (SPS) system with all provisions of the SPS agreement. Laws amending legislation on the quality and safety of foodstuffs and raw food materials have been passed and draft laws on amending legislation on veterinary medicine and plant quarantine

have been developed. In May 2005, the SPS reference and message centre was established, and will start working as soon as Ukraine has joined the WTO.

For cereals and vegetable products major exporters from Ukraine do not regard current SPS and TBT standards as a significant factor restraining international sales, since indeed there are few technical requirements for these products. Most of Ukraine's primary agricultural output has a considerable price-competitive advantage, owing to low production costs, and the potential for further export growth is high.

By contrast, for animal products and processed foods improved compliance is vital. The need to meet up-to-date international and European requirements would also greatly contribute to the introduction of new technologies, the restructuring of the animal breeding sub-sector and advances in the quality to the level required for import substitution and promotion on foreign markets.

For Ukrainian dairy products, the hygienic quality in particular prevents their access to the EU market. Only the top quality milk in Ukraine meets European standards for somatic cell count. For bacterial plate count, the European ceiling is $100,000/cm^3$, while the Ukrainian maximum is $300,000/cm^3$ for top quality milk and 3,000 for other types.

Residues of veterinary preparations and other substances not allowed for use in the EU have been found in Ukrainian dairy products. Widely discussed was the presence of antibiotics banned by the EU in Ukrainian dry non-fat milk, as well as certain pollutants (for instance, chloramphenicol) in 2002.

With regard to meat and meat products, this lack of compliance is even greater, starting with requirements for the maintenance of live animals and the personal hygiene of workers, and ending with standards of processing and transporting ready products. This situation further complicates the low competitiveness of Ukrainian meat production and makes any exports to the EU impossible.

The biggest obstacle for Ukraine's agriculture will not only be to comply with SPS rules, but also with EU food safety regulations. The entire range of EU food safety regulations, in particular Council Regulation (EU) No. 178/2002, exceeds the SPS standards set by the WTO. The food safety regulations/directives are set over and above trade agreements, meaning that despite an expected FTA, certain agricultural products that are non-compliant with food law regulations will be stopped at borders.

The regulatory impact on Ukrainian agriculture could be costly. This has been observed in the 10 new accession countries, which despite being member states of the EU were not allowed to export certain agricultural products into the EU-15 without meeting EU food safety standards. Although a transitional period allowing imports for some products was implemented, a huge restructuring of food processing plants took place to meet these regulations. The strict application of these EU food laws is also evident intra-EU, where at times internal cross-border trade is hindered because of food safety standards.

Also, there are no legislative acts to regulate relations in the field of genetic engineering or define principles for using genetically modified organisms in Ukraine. Some of Ukraine's immediate neighbouring countries permit genetically modified organisms and products containing such organisms, thus almost certainly cause their unauthorised and uncontrolled distribution in the territory of Ukraine. Hence, a relevant legal framework needs to be created as soon as possible.

1.5   Interest groups and the political environment

So far, the recent democratic changes in Ukraine have not directly resulted in more reasoned and market-oriented agricultural policies. Discussions on the need for greater subsidisation and the perceived danger of liberalisation are not surprising in a country where one-third of the population is dependent on agriculture, and whose main neighbours and trade partners also tend to protect their market and subsidise. Moreover, agriculture keeps playing an important social role by employing excess manpower in subsidiary plot farms and by restraining great social difficulties through the deceleration of migrations between urban and rural areas.

Interest groups in Ukraine's agrarian sector include large agricultural enterprises established on the basis of former collective farms, farmers (small enterprises), exporters and traders of agricultural products and industrial-agrarian holdings. All of them are represented through a large number of public professional associations (more than 50).

These interest groups are rather active and successful in advocating and promoting the interests of their members. They take part in the policy discussion and formulation process, including the development of regulatory and legal acts. Since 2002, a regular practice has been the signing of annual memoranda on the coordination of actions between the government and leading public associations of the agro-industrial complex in the markets of grain, sugar, milk, meat, bread and bakery products.

The first group of public associations includes *producers and processors of agricultural products by sectoral specialisation:* the Union of Dairy Enterprises of Ukraine, the Union of Grain Processors, the Ukrainian Grain Association, the Ukroliyarpom Association, the National Association of Meat Product Manufacturers of Ukraine and the National Association of Sugar Producers of Ukraine, etc.

The second group includes representatives of *service providers and suppliers of inputs:* the Association of Agricultural Equipment Producers, the Association of Insurers in the Agrarian Sector of Ukraine, the Ukrainian Association of Seed Producers and Distributors, the Ukrainian Association of Plant Protection and the Union of Ukrainian Breeders, etc.

The third group includes associations by *form of economic management and ownership in agriculture:* the Association of Farmers and Private Land Owners of Ukraine, the All-Ukrainian Association of Lessors, the All-Ukrainian Public Organisation 'Council of Female Farmers of Ukraine', the All-Ukrainian Union of Agricultural Enterprises, the National Union of Agricultural Cooperatives and the Peasants' Union of Ukraine, etc.

ANNEX 2. STEEL*

Ukraine is a major player in the world steel industry, yet one that has been largely kept out of the EU market so far. It therefore merits special attention in this study. The basic economics of the Ukrainian steel industry have been analysed well in a recent World Bank study on Ukraine's trade policy. The outstanding issues are those of clarifying the extent of possible trade expansion as and when quota restrictions might be lifted, and the policy options that Ukraine may negotiate in the framework of its WTO membership.

1.   Overview of the steel sector

Steel has been the leading growth sector in the recovery of the Ukrainian economy over the last five years. In 2004 the sector accounted for 27% of the country's industrial output. Of the 33 Mt of rolled steel production in 2004, 26 Mt were exported, which amounts to 7.5% of the world steel trade. Ukraine entered the world steel markets in 1992 to compensate for the fall in domestic demand. The competitiveness of Ukrainian steel was the result of available iron ore and coking coal deposits, a favourable location and competitive energy supplies and labour costs. From 1994 to 2004 steel exports more than doubled and Ukraine became the third largest exporter of steel in the world.

Currently, semi-finished steel products take up around a quarter or more of Ukraine's metal product mix.[1] Yet the low value added of Ukrainian steel exports is compensated by the robust external demand for the semi-finished products, given the dominance of mini-mills across the world and the aim of developed countries to outsource environmentally unfriendly stages of the production process. (The low presence of mini-

---

* This annex was prepared by Ildar Gazizullin.

[1] In 2004 the share of semi-finished steel products in Ukrainian exports was 32%, down from 47% in 1999. The world's average share of this production is 12-15%. See World Bank, *Steel Sector Development*, Washington, D.C., 2004(c).

mills in Ukraine is explained by the former USSR's concentration on integrated mills, with almost no investment made in mini-mills there).[2]

Ukrainian steel exports surged in 2002-04 when the world prices for this commodity increased dramatically. Steel export revenues[3] in 2004 grew by 60% to $10.76 billion, accounting for one-third of all merchandise exports. Countries in Asia, Africa and the Middle East account for the lion's share of the exports, while the access of the finished steel products to the markets of the EU and the US is restricted by quotas and duties. In 2004, half of the rolled steel exports went to Asian countries, with only 10.1% (2.59 Mt) to the EU and another 6.6% to other European non-members of the Commonwealth of Independent States (CIS) countries. The noticeable slowdown in export activity in the first half of 2005 was in part the result of a drastic reduction (by 76% from January to June 2005) in the exports of Ukrainian steel to China, since that country has changed into a net exporter of metals. Despite this, Ukraine's steel exports continue to grow, given high world steel prices and a well-diversified exports structure.[4]

2. Sector restructuring

The dramatic fall in production in 1990-95 was not matched by an adequate reduction in employment or by any significant shut down of capacity. This resulted in an average capacity utilisation of about 50% in the mid-1990s. The industry enjoyed the soft budget constraints. By 1998 the enterprises were burdened with debts and making losses. The impact of the unfavourable situation in the world markets and a series of anti-dumping investigations became significant. To remedy the situation, in 1999 the

---

[2] The development of mini-mills was not a priority for the former USSR as the country had abundant resources of the ore, coal and natural gas needed to power the integrated mills and capacity satisfied the internal demand. The presence of very few mini-mills explains most of the capital productivity gap between the CIS and other countries and the low share of high value-added products in the product mix, especially coated sheets and specialty products. See the McKinsey Global Institute, *Unlocking economic growth in Russia*, Washington, D.C., 1999.

[3] These relate only to revenues for Code 72 projects.

[4] In January-September 2005 the structure of the metallurgy exports (in tonnes) from Ukraine was the following: Middle East (22.4%), the EU-25 (15.4%), other Europe (5.2%), Asia (19.2%), Turkey (11.7%), the CIS (12.9%), Africa (9.8%) and the Americas (3.3%).

government launched an 'economic experiment' in the sector, entailing debt restructuring, loans and reduced taxes. The experiment ended in 2002 as the financial standing of the enterprises had improved and world steel prices started to pick up.[5]

Indirect subsidies to the steel sector are of limited scope and are decreasing. A major benefit to the metalworking sector has consisted of subsidies to the coal industry and the resulting low prices for coking coal. State aid to the coal sector is decreasing, however, as the private sector is becoming dominant in coke mining and in the by-product coke industry. The government intends to completely stop subsidies to the private mines, which will reduce instances of transfer pricing.

Government intervention in the steel sector sought to protect the internal market, but for the most part was not effective. For instance, to soften the effect of the rapidly rising domestic prices for iron ore and steel and resulting shortages of resources in 2003-04, the government undertook the following actions and policies: administering the assignment of the resources among the enterprises; introducing temporary price controls in the metals sector;[6] imposing a €30/tonne export duty on ferrous scrap and the licensing of the iron ore exports. The first two initiatives were largely ignored, as about 93% of the industry is in private hands and the government does not have much leverage on the industry participants.

The steel industry has been privatised to domestic investors, with foreign companies largely kept out at first. Four Ukrainian financial–industrial groups (FIGs) own the key companies in the industry and also control the assets connected with the steel sector – the ore-mining and

---

[5] During the time of the experiment, the profits of the 10 major enterprises in the sector more than doubled. Barter operations along with wage and debt arrears were significantly reduced while the tax payments increased. For an economic analysis of the experiment, see World Bank (2004c), op. cit.

[6] Cabinet Instruction No. 179-r of 26 March 2004 set volumes for metal product deliveries to the domestic market at 1 January 2004 prices for a number of sectors, including machine-building and piping companies, as well as for deliveries of coke, iron ore, steel alloys and fired products to metalworks.

enrichment plants and by-product coke plants.[7] Western investors were represented by the ISTIL mini-mill, which only has a 1.2 Mt capacity.

The 2004 sale of a 93% stake in Kryvorizhstal, Ukraine's largest steel works was the most substantial privatisation transaction ($0.8 billion) in the history of modern Ukraine. Yet the privatisation was not carried out to benefit society in the long run, but to serve the short-term interests of those in power and certain oligarchs by redistributing property.[8] Given the favourable situation on steel markets and the plant's launch of profitable performance and investment programmes, a company like this could have been sold for a much higher price. Instead, a speedy sale before an election meant that the privatisation revenues could go mostly to increasing social outlays rather than to investing. The conditions of the tender largely predetermined the winner, which is why foreign participants complained about them as being clearly unfair. This kind of treatment negatively affected Ukraine's investment image.

Nevertheless, the Orange Revolution has arguably begun to bring this 'insider economy' system of Ukraine to an end. In August 2005, the state property fund announced a tender for the repeat sale of Kryvorizhstal, with a starting price of $2 billion.[9] As the result of fair tender and auction,

---

[7] These FIGs are: 1) ZAT System Capital Management (the AzovStal steel works, the Enakeevo steel mill, the Khartsysky pipe mill and 56% of Kryvorizhstal); 2) the Industrial Union of Donbass (the Alchevsk steel works, the Dzerzhinsky steel mill and the Lenisnky pipe mill); 3) Interpipe Corporation (44% of Kryvorizhstal, the Nikopol ferroalloys plant, the Nizhnedneprovsky pipe plant, the Novo-Moskovsky pipe plant and the Nikopol seamless pipe mill); and 4) Privat Holding (the Petrovka steel mill, the Zaporizhzhe ferroalloys plant and the Stakhanov ferroalloys plant).

[8] The winner of the tender was Investytsiyniy Metalurgiyniy Soyuz [Steel Investment Union], an industrial and financial consortium that includes: 1) the Interpipe Corporation (Viktor Pinchuk) and the affiliated Nyzhniodniprovsk Piping, Bipe, a Ukrainian-Cypriot company, Kredyt-Dnipro Bank, and Aura, an insurance company; 2) ZAT UkrInvest, a shareholder in UkrSibBank; and 3) AzovStal, a Mariupol-based steel works, Avdiyivka Coking Plant, MarkoKhim Coking Facility – all controlled by ZAT System Capital Management (Donetsk-based Rynat Akhmetov).

[9] It is likely, however, that further revisiting of privatisation tenders will stop with the dismissal of the Tymoshenko government, as ex-Premier Yulia Tymoshenko largely initiated all revisions.

the winner, the world's largest steel producing group Mittal Steel,[10] paid $4.84 billion for the company.

The oligarchs' influence in securing state protectionism in certain sectors is thus being reduced. This trend can also be seen with regard to another problem, namely the notoriously low degree of financial transparency of the steel industry. Ukraine's FIGs were actively practicing transfer pricing and showed very little if any taxable profits. A recent tendency for more financial openness is driven by both an increased pressure from the new government and active attempts of the major FIGs themselves to improve their access to international capital markets and increase the capitalisation of their assets. Initial public offerings still have a long way to go in the steel industry, but they have certainly become an objective for some companies.

3.   EU–Ukrainian trade policy in steel

In spite of various trade restrictions, steel is an important commodity in EU–Ukrainian trade. In 2004 Ukraine exported 2.6 Mt of rolled steel ($1.91 billion) to the EU, with steel replacing energy as the largest export commodity.[11] Ukraine is among the top three steel exporters to the EU,[12] with Italy, Germany and the Netherlands being the major importers of Ukrainian steel in 2004. The key steel products imported by the EU include semi-finished steel products, hot rolled coil, wire rod, galvanised sheet, hot rolled plates and cold rolled sheet. Figures for the EU's steel imports in

---

[10] Other main bidders at the tender were the consortium of Arcelor SA and the Industrial Union of Donbass, and the Ukrainian Smart Group.

[11] In 2003, iron and steel accounted for 15.2% of merchandise exports, while energy led with a 22.2% share of Ukraine's exports to the EU.

[12] In the first four months of 2005 the EU-25's key import sources included Russia (2.2 Mt), Turkey (1.2 Mt), Ukraine (1.1 Mt), China (0.9 Mt), India (0.6 Mt) and Brazil (0.5 Mt). In the first half of 2005, Germany's largest supplier outside of the EU was Russia, supplying 5% of the total, followed by Mexico, Romania, Ukraine and Brazil. Italy's major suppliers were Russia and the Ukraine, both supplying 9% each, followed by China (7%), Turkey, Bulgaria and Romania (see ISSB Ltd, at http://www.issb.co.uk/).

2005 indicate that those from Ukraine further increased, especially semi-finished steel products that face no quantitative trade restrictions.[13]

The trade of steel between the EU and Ukraine is restricted by the EU's steel quota system and anti-dumping duties.[14] In 1996-2002 the quota amounted to an average of 250,000 tonnes for certain steel categories.[15] In addition, the EU maintains anti-dumping duties in the range of 38-52% against a number of steel products in Ukraine, such as seamless and welded pipes, steel cables and wires. Import tariffs for the metals are hardly restrictive to trade, reaching on average 2.6% in the EU[16] and 4% in Ukraine.

In 2001 the EU and Ukraine reached an agreement for 2002-04 that anticipated an increase of quotas by 35% to 355,000 tonnes, provided Ukraine eliminated restrictions on the ferrous scrap exports to the EU. The EU did not sign the agreement because of the dilatory VAT refunds to the ferrous scrap exporters in Ukraine. After Ukraine introduced an export duty on ferrous scrap, the EU retaliated by reducing the steel quota in 2003 by 30%. The impact of the fixed €30 export duty has diminished, however, as the scrap prices reached $220-230 by the end of 2004. Exports of scrap to the EU have also been channelled through Moldova, which has an FTA with Ukraine.

---

[13] Imports by the EU-25 in the first six months of 2005 increased by 33% to 16.3 Mt. The EU-25 has been a net importer of steel since August 2004, although in June 2005 imports fell significantly, making it a net exporter. In both Germany and Italy, the major steel-importing countries, about half the increase were in slabs, blooms and billets (see *World Steel Review*, September 2005 retrieved from http://www.steelonthenet.com/production.html).

[14] In the early 1990s, the former USSR countries became major exporters of metals, which created a supply shock in the world markets. In response, the EU imposed trade barriers against imports of steel from Kazakhstan, Russia and Ukraine.

[15] The quota covers about 20% of all Ukraine's exports of metal products to the EU. These are hot-rolled coils (SA1), heavy plate (SA2), other flat-rolled products (SA3), beams (SB1), wire rod (SB2) and other long products (SB3). Detailed information on the quota volumes is provided by the on-line source, SIGL (at http://sigl.cec.eu.int/querysteel.html).

[16] All tariffs were expected to disappear in 2004 in line with the EU's commitments in the Uruguay Round.

The expansion of the EU in 2004 had mixed results for Ukraine's exports of steel. As a result of negotiations to ease the negative impact of EU expansion, some anti-dumping probes[17] have been postponed and the quota for metal products to the EU-25 was set at 606,800 tonnes in 2004. This figure was not the increase Ukrainian producers had expected, since in 2003 Ukraine exported nearly 800,000 tonnes of metal products to the EU-10 alone. On the other hand, the import tariffs for steel have decreased, e.g. from 10% (in Poland) to 2.6%[18] in the EU.

The import quotas in 1997-2004 were used by the Ukrainian side by an average of 60%. This level is explained by low demand in the EU for some of the steel categories and problems with licensing and distribution in Ukraine. Since the quotas are given directly to the firms (and not to the traders), large transaction costs make it unattractive for the metalwork's' management to negotiate small steel export volumes with EU buyers.

In March 2005, the EU and Ukraine reached an agreement that the quota for 2005 will be increased to 980,000 and 1,004,500 tonnes in 2005 and 2006 respectively. The agreement also stipulates that the quotas could be increased for the Ukrainian companies that open new steel wholesale centres in the EU.

The quota system will be cancelled when Ukraine becomes a WTO member, which is expected in 2006. Other issues such as the anti-dumping investigations and EU concerns with regard to the dubious accounting standards, state-interference in pricing in the metal sector and non-operating bankruptcy laws have yet to be dealt with by Ukraine.

4. EU–Ukrainian trade outlook

The trade in steel between the EU and Ukraine has great potential for growth as Ukraine joins the WTO. Total steel imports from Ukraine could more than double to 6 Mt or 4% of the EU market. As the quotas are removed, the exports of flat-rolled and long products might grow threefold

---

[17] After joining the EU, new member states were supposed to automatically launch the same anti-dumping probes against Ukraine that had earlier been initiated by the EU-15. As a result of negotiations, three probes into Ukrainian chemicals were postponed until May 2005. The remaining three probes into chemicals and steel products have been pursued in full since 1 May 2004.

[18] Some sources quote 4% and 1.7%.

to about 2-2.5 Mt a year. Ukraine is interested in the diversification of its exports to European markets from its present heavy reliance on Asian markets. Strong demand in the EU for semi-finished steel products will also drive up exports of slabs, blooms and billets. Despite a recent increase in the share of the high value-added steel products in Ukraine's exports, the share of semis will continue to be significant in the country's exports in the next 5–10 years, given the current structure Ukrainian steel production capacities and the expected strong demand for semis in the EU.

Ukraine will, however, face strong competition from both EU companies and other major exporters to the EU market. The EU steel industry has obvious technological advantages and better access to the large European buyers of steel. Moreover, the EU will intensify its efforts to achieve fair competition or a level playing field at a time when trade liberalisation will enable Ukrainian firms to fully utilise their cost advantages over their EU counterparts. It is very likely that the anti-dumping investigations against certain Ukrainian steel products (e.g. pipes) will continue and possible cases of indirect state aid (e.g. to support unprofitable production capacities) will be carefully monitored;[19] These issues will compel the Ukraine's government to liberalise the steel industry.

Integration of the EU and Ukrainian steel companies would be beneficial to both. The metal works in the accession countries have traditionally been relying on Ukrainian supplies of iron ore, coke and semi-finished steel. The outsourcing of production and some high value-added products to the CIS, in particular to Ukraine, is being considered by some

---

[19] Since the expiry of the ECSC Treaty in 2002, the general EC state aid rules apply to the steel sector. Yet instead of these EC restructuring guidelines, the Commission issued a Communication on rescue and restructuring aid and closure for the steel sector (OJ C 70/21 of 19.3.2002), which stipulates that such aid is not permitted. Only closure aid, as an exception from the prohibition to grant restructuring aid, is exceptionally allowed. Such closure aid may be used to help redundant employees who are laid off or to support companies in the closure of their facilities. But the latter is only acceptable if the entire legal entity is closed (see M. Lienemeyer, "State aid for restructuring the steel industry in the new member states", *Competition Policy Newsletter*, No. 1, spring, 2005).

of the European steel-makers.[20] Ukrainian companies are already actively acquiring mills and steel traders in the EU to overcome current trade restrictions and expand the customer base.[21]

Ukraine will also face fierce competition both from the traditional exporters to the EU (Turkey and Russia) and some emerging ones, such as China and India. Russia is currently the main competitor to Ukraine in the EU market. Russian companies have the following advantages over Ukrainian ones: 1) lower energy prices; 2) more up-to-date steel production capacity; 3) greater political leverage on EU policy; and 4) common steel production projects between EU and Russian companies. Russia's major disadvantages, however, are: 1) greater transportation costs; 2) the likelihood of later accession to the WTO; and 3) more conspicuous state support for steel expansion.[22] Another major exporter of steel to the EU, Turkey, is very closely integrated with the EU. Turkish steel companies and their national association are associate members of Eurofer. But the fact that Turkey is the largest importer of ferrous scrap in the world makes it a high-cost producer.[23] Therefore, unless Ukraine takes steps to compete more effectively with both low cost and high-tech steel-makers, it will not be able

---

[20] In 2005, Arcelor announced its plans to move some of its production to the low-cost countries, in particular to the CIS. At present, the company has a common production project with the Russian Severstal Group. The partnership formed by Arcelor and the Industrial Union of Donbass to tender for Kryvorizhstal during its privatisation may signal future expansion of EU–Ukrainian cooperation in steel production and trade.

[21] This issue is a relevant issue for the Ukrainian manufacturers as the semi-finished products often cannot be sold directly to end-users because they require further processing.

[22] A 2005 OECD report on steel capacity expansion claims that Russian producers benefit from domestic scrap prices that are below Russian export prices and world market prices. Since 1999, Russia has imposed a tax of 15% (currently – 12%), with a minimum tax of €15/tonne, on exports of ferrous scrap. Russia also retains high levels of government subsidisation for energy and electricity. See OECD, *Capacity Expansion in the Global Steel Industry*, Report from the OECD Special Meeting at High-Level on Steel Issues, "The Outlook for Steel", held in Paris on 12-13 January 2005.

[23] Being Ukraine's major importer of ferrous scrap, Turkey was most interested in abolishing the export duty on scrap.

to increase its share of the European market and in the medium run could even lose some of its share to China, which is both a low-cost and high-tech steel-maker.

5. Overall outlook for the Ukrainian steel industry

In 2004, Ukraine's steel industry reached one of highest levels of capacity utilisation – 95.4%, up from 52.1% in 1998. A major reduction of inefficient steel production capacity – from 47 to 40.9 Mt – was achieved in 1998-2000. As world prices started to rise in 2003, firms responded with higher existing capacity utilisation and some investment into new capacity (1.5 Mt). Capital investment was insufficient over the period, however, with the depreciation of the steel-making investments reaching 60-70%.

It very likely that the steel industry will pursue better utilisation of the existing steel-making capacity rather than its expansion. Replacing the outdated capacity to increase its efficiency will become a main goal of investment, given the expected fall in world prices after 2008 and rapidly rising domestic transportation and energy costs.

State plans for the steel sector's development do not envisage any significant capacity expansion or reduction.[24] The output of crude steel for 2011 is expected to reach 40 Mt, 1 Mt above the 2004 figure. The share of the domestic market for steel is expected to increase twofold to almost 40% of total production. The government's policy objectives for the steel sector are to close down excessive and inefficient capacities and introduce modern and environmentally friendly technologies. In the coming five to six years the mining and metalworking sectors are forecast to attract $10 billion, most of it coming from the private sector.

Private sector investment and development plans seem to fit well with the state's intentions of modernising the sector assets. Fixed investment in the steel sector in 2004 grew by 43% to $620 million. Despite the government's decision to revise certain privatisations, thus reducing incentives for investment in related companies, the growth of investment in the steel sector during January-June 2005 stood high at 56%. The total volume of announced investment in the metalworking sector is estimated

---

[24] See the 28 July 2004 Cabinet Resolution, "On the State programme for developing and reforming the mining and metalworking for the period until 2011", Kyiv.

to be $6 billion for 2005-08.[25] Yet typical investment projects only encompass the modernisation of the existing capacity and the rehabilitation of open-hearth production, and green field projects tend to be rare.[26] Hence Ukraine's steel industry attracts less investment per tonne of steel produced than Russia or EU countries.

Moderate local investment plans are compensated by an active global expansion of Ukrainian companies. Ukrainian FIGs own four metalworks/mills and a number of wholesale and retail metal traders in Europe (in Hungary, Italy, Poland and Switzerland).

6.   Steel and the environment

Ukraine dramatically cut the volume of its environmental pollution after 1990, because of the economic recession. But with the recovery in 2000-04, its pollution performance deteriorated again, although the current level of emissions remains well below the 1990 level.[27] The steel industry is the second largest air polluter in the country, responsible for 28% of all air pollution.

The current policy regarding harmful emissions does not encourage the reduction of pollution in Ukraine, since fines and fees for polluting above the established limits are financially insignificant for businesses. For example, the total amount of ecological payments owed by the steel industry in 2003 was a mere $13 million. Further, the proportion of environmental fines levied against polluters in the country that were actually paid into the budget fund was well under 100%. Emission reductions are achieved mainly as a result of the current trend in the steel

---

[25] See the interview of Mr V. Grishchenko, Deputy Minister, Ministry of Industrial Policy, in the Interfax-Ukraine newswire of 29 September 2005.

[26] A number of such projects were announced by some domestic investors. One example is a company in the ferrous scrap business that intends to build a 2 Mt capacity, electric arc furnace steel mill in 2006-07.

[27] The inflow of hazardous substances into the atmosphere from stationary sources and road traffic amounted to 15.6 Mt in 1990, which fell to 6.1 Mt in 2003.

industry towards increasing capital investment.[28] The improvements are not dramatic though, as open-hearth furnace technology still dominates the industry technology mix.[29]

Meanwhile, the environmental burden on the EU's steel industry is increasing. EU member states each have differentiated targets that collectively amount to an 8% reduction in greenhouse gas emissions over period 2008-12 compared with 1990. Eurofer claims that the reduction of CO_2 emissions can be achieved only by reducing production, given that actual CO_2 emissions in the industry are almost down to the theoretical limit and the margin for future improvement is small for technological and economic reasons.[30]

The international trading of emissions therefore provides promising opportunities for both the EU and Ukraine, in particular under the Kyoto Protocol.[31] According to the Kyoto Protocol, participating countries have the right to trade quotas for greenhouse gas emissions and to carry out joint projects to reduce such emissions. Ukraine can use both options: its current emissions are below the norm, set at the 1990 level, while the inefficiency of its economy (particularly its steel industry), makes investment into state-of-the-art, energy-saving technologies profitable. EU steel companies could thus use Ukraine's untapped potential to meet the emission targets using

---

[28] According to MetalurgProm, a production association, the proportion of environmental costs in the gross investment made in metalworks and steel plants more than doubled, from 6% in 2003 to 15% in the first half of 2004 (see the Interfax-Ukraine newswire of 15 October 2004). While in the overall economic investment in environmental projects increased by 2.3 times during 2000-03, its share of all capital investments remained unchanged at 1.4-1.7%.

[29] Ukraine has the largest share of the open-hearth production of steel in the world – 43.4% compared with the world's 3.2% (figures derived from the IISI).

[30] See J.-P. Debruxelles, "The Greenhouse Gas Challenge: How the EU Steel Industry Competitiveness Could be Affected", Presentation at the OECD Special Meeting at High-Level on Steel Issues: "The Outlook for Steel" held in Paris, 12-13 January 2005.

[31] In 2005, the Kyoto Protocol came into force, which Ukraine signed on 23 February 2004.

the Kyoto Protocol's project-based mechanisms.[32] The gap between the Kyoto target for Ukraine and the current levels also allows a moderate outsourcing of steel-producing capacity to Ukraine.[33]

A number of factors hinder the cooperation of the EU and Ukraine in the environmental sphere. Unlike the EU, Ukraine does not have a domestic emissions trading programme and therefore lacks the institutional and technical means to introduce and utilise the necessary instruments. Moreover, until recently, the international carbon trade market was not yet functioning. With the Kyoto Protocol coming into force, active emissions trading is expected to take place in 2007-08. In general, EU member countries are interested in investing in Ukraine to benefit from the Kyoto mechanisms, with electricity generation for the moment as one of the priority areas.

---

[32] The Council of Ministers and the European Parliament agreed (in April 2004) on a text for the EU Directive (2004/101/EC) Linking Joint Implementation and the Clean Development Mechanism, which will allow entities covered by the EU Emissions Trading Scheme to use emission units from the Kyoto Protocol's project-based mechanisms towards meeting their emissions targets. The use of the mechanisms is to be supplemental to domestic action, in accordance with the relevant provisions of the Kyoto Protocol and the Marrakech Accords. The EU Directive does not include recognition of assigned amount units (i.e. governments' overall emissions allocation under the Kyoto Protocol). (See J. Newman, *Policies to reduce greenhouse gas emissions in industry: Implications for steel*, Paper presented at the OECD Special Meeting at High-Level on Steel Issues, "The Outlook for Steel" held in Paris on 12-13 January 2005.)

[33] As Newman (2005, ibid.) notes, the EU countries could, "along with energy taxes and related measures, create incentives for producers to source increasing quantities of semi-finished steel (i.e., slabs and billets) from countries which are not taking aggressive measures to limit GHG emissions. They could alter the market for semi-finished products, and would effectively shift emissions to the semi-finished steel exporting areas."

ANNEX 3. SERVICE SECTORS*

1. Banking and financial services

1.1 Banking

Even though Ukraine's financial sector is very much bank-dominated, its banks remain small by international standards. All of the 156 licensed banks together have less than €20 billion in assets – the equivalent of a small bank in the EU.[1] Ukraine's 10 largest banks account for about 60% of total assets, while many of the smaller banks remain 'pocket banks' of enterprise groups and are too small to survive on their own. The positive implication of the low banking penetration of the economy, however, is an enormous growth potential that makes the Ukrainian market attractive for multinational banks. For instance, the credit-to-GDP ratio was only 30% in late 2004, even though it had already doubled since 2000. The ratio of mortgage credits to GDP is less than 1%, compared with 40-60% in more developed economies. The same holds for credit card ownership, consumer credit, etc.

In the Central and Eastern Europe countries (CEECs) that have acceded to the EU, international banks play a critical role in the modernisation of the banking sector. They have brought foreign direct investment (FDI) to recapitalise banks and expand their operations, introduced modern management and technology to improve efficiency, and rolled out new financial products such as mortgages and leasing. In Hungary, Slovakia and the Czech Republic, for instance, multinational banks now own over 80% of banking assets and they compete fiercely to the benefit of the host countries. A handful of major European banks own

---

* This annex was prepared by Daniel Müller-Jentsch.

[1] According to the National Bank of Ukraine (NBU), banking sector assets in Ukraine have grown from the equivalent of 20% of GDP in 1999 to 43% of GDP in 2003. (See World Bank, *A Strategy for Modernising Ukraine*, Washington, D.C., March 2005(c)).

subsidiaries across the CEECs (e.g. Bank Austria or Societé Générale) and they are driving the process of regional integration in this sector.[2]

The most promising strategy for Ukraine to develop its financial services industry and to integrate it more deeply with that of the EU would be to attract some of these regional players. The easiest way to do so would be to privatise the remaining state-owned banks and to increase regulatory pressure regarding the separation of banking from non-banking activities. Currently, most major banks are owned by oligarchs and are integrated into the financial–industrial groups (FIGs) that control large segments of the economy. An important regulatory instrument in this regard will be the proposed law on banks and banking, which will make related-party lending much more difficult.[3] It is a precondition for WTO accession, but its adoption has been obstructed for several years.

Until recently, the presence of Western banks in Ukraine was limited to small operations serving corporate clients. The first substantial entry of a major EU bank came in August 2005, when Austria's Raiffeisen International bought 94% of Aval Bank for over €500 million. This move gives Raiffeisen over 12% of the market share, as Aval is Ukraine's second largest bank with 18,000 employees, 1,400 branches and net assets of UAH 14.8 billion.[4] The IMF estimates that this takeover will bring the percentage of foreign ownership in Ukrainian banking from the low teens to the mid-20% range in terms of net assets.

---

[2] The largest regional player is Italy's Unicredit (including subsidiaries Hypo-Vereinsbank and Bank Austria-Creditanstalt) with 2,300 branches and 48,000 employees in a dozen CEECs. The other main players are Austria's Erste Bank, Belgium's KBC Group and Austria's Raiffeisen International (see *Financial Times Deutschland*, 13 June 2005).

[3] As banking crises in Turkey and other countries have shown, related-party lending poses a major threat to the stability of the financial sector and thus its prevention is an important part of prudential regulation. The main practical problem in enforcing related-party lending restrictions is the need to reveal the ultimate ownership of the banks and their clients – a severe problem in a country with FIGs and non-transparent business practices. Ukraine's legislation on related-party lending is fine, but legislation on ownership transparency still needs to be passed.

[4] The bank serves 3 million private and 210,000 corporate clients (*Financial Times Deutschland*, 22 August 2005). Raiffeisen International plans to combine Aval together with a small existing operation, and to buy out the minority shareholders.

In December 2005, BNP Paribas announced the purchase of a 51% stake in Ukrsibbank for an undisclosed price. With 760 branches, a market share of 5% and UAH 7.6 billion in net assets, Ukrsibbank is the fourth largest player in the market. The current owners are businessmen Alexander Yaroslavsky and Ernest Galiev, who were close to the previous government. They plan to retain their remaining shares, but are granting the buyer the option to expand its stake to 60% at a later stage. In addition, several international banks were also said to explore a possible purchase of Ukrsotsbank – Ukraine's third largest bank with net assets of UAH 9.2 billion. The majority owner of Ukrsotsbank is tycoon Viktor Pinchuk, the son-in-law of former President Leonid Kuchma. If those takeovers actually materialise, this could mark the exit of some notorious oligarchs from Ukraine's banking sector. The country's largest bank, Privatbank, with net assets of $18.4 billion, is also owned by tycoons.[5]

Less than 20% of Ukraine's banking sector remains government owned. The main public bank is the savings bank, Oschadbank.[6] With 40,000 staff, it accounts for almost half of Ukraine's banking sector employees and controls more than half of the market for individual deposits. Its large network of 530 branches with several million clients covers the entire country and constitutes a potentially attractive asset. Oschadbank has been in need of some significant restructuring, however, and received technical assistance from the World Bank. The sale of Oschadbank to an international strategic investor would considerably increase the share of foreign ownership in the market. In mid-2005, Erste Bank of Austria expressed its interest in Oschadbank and met with government officials to explore options.

---

[5] The three owners are the Dnipropetrovsk-based Ihor Kolomojsky, Hennady Bogolubov and Oleksy Martynov (*Wall Street Journal*, 8 September 2005). According to the annual ranking of Eastern Europe's richest persons by the Polish business weekly *Wprost*, Mr Kolomojsky had a net worth of $2.8 billion, Mr Pinchuk $1.5 billion and Mr Yaroslavsky $650 million. Businessman Fedir Shpig, who sold his controlling stake in Aval to Raiffeisen International, was valued at $800 million.

[6] The second state-owned bank is the export-import bank of Ukraine, UkrEximBank, with 29 branches and 2,900 employees. UkrEximBank provides trade-related banking products and handles intergovernmental credit lines. It has 31,000 corporate and 91,000 individual clients.

A key benefit of FDI in the financial sector is that it helps to import better regulation and corporate governance – as long as the foreign bank comes from well-regulated countries. The reason is that foreign banks are being supervised by their home regulators. This feature could provide an important external anchor for the development of a sound financial sector in Ukraine. Better corporate governance in financial services would also spill over into the rest of the economy, as private banks will demand high levels of transparency and good corporate governance from their clients as a means to reduce their own lending risks.

The regulatory framework and the prudential regulation exercised by the central bank (National Bank of Ukraine or NBU) are generally considered sound. Compliance with Basel capital ratio requirements is reasonably good and overall the financial system appears stable. As part of their joint Financial Sector Assessment Programme, the World Bank and the IMF analysed the structure and stability of Ukraine's financial sector in 2003. The IMF continues to provide advice and technical assistance to the NBU. As part of its assistance to Ukraine, the EU should fund a twinning arrangement with counterpart institutions in a recent accession country for both the NBU and for the financial market regulator (as discussed below).

As far as trade liberalisation is concerned, market access to the banking sector is largely open to foreign players and Ukraine's GATS proposal in this area is very liberal. The main restriction is that foreign banks can only operate through subsidiaries (supervised by the Ukrainian regulator) and not through branches (supervised by the home regulator). Nevertheless, this does not create any major constraints for the industry.[7] Overall, there appears little need for additional liberalisation measures as part of an EU–Ukraine FTA.

1.2 Financial markets

Non-banking financial services, including securities and insurance, are at a very early stage of development and total assets in these sub-sectors are

---

[7] In practical terms, a more binding constraint for market access thus far has been the fact that most Ukrainian banks are controlled by local oligarchs. After all, the way to enter a market is normally through the purchase of an existing bank, since the establishment of a country-wide network from scratch tends to be very difficult.

equivalent to around 5% of the assets in the rather small banking sub-sector (this figure includes a small third pillar of the pension system).

Given the critical importance of modern capital markets for cross-border investment flows, comprehensive reforms in this area will be required for deeper integration between the EU and Ukraine. But Ukraine's capital markets remain illiquid and shallow. According to the IMF, total stock market capitalisation is equivalent to a mere 20% of GDP. With several licensed stock exchanges but very few listed companies, Ukraine's securities markets are in need of consolidation. It is estimated that more than 90% of securities-related deals are settled outside the trading floor and the regulator is lobbying for legislation that would require trades to be conducted through the exchange. Two measures that could help to develop financial markets are the new Pension Law of 2004 (which will encourage the establishment of pension funds) and the framework Law on Mutual Funds of 2001. The State Securities and Stock Market Commission, which regulates the industry, is a young and relatively immature institution. The recent replacement of its head is hoped to improve matters, but significant capacity-building will be needed in the future.

Severe constraints on the development of securities markets are the low levels of transparency and poor standards of corporate governance. This is not only a hindrance to the development of financial markets, but also a major deterrent for foreign investment. Investors often simply do not know what they are buying into or how to control their interests. A key priority in that context is the protection of minority shareholders. To address these problems, the Ukrainian government needs to adopt the joint stock company law that has been under discussion for several years and it needs to ensure greater transparency and the rule of law.

In the development of its financial markets, Ukraine could also benefit from the activities of EU companies that are expanding their activities across the CEECs. An example is the Vienna stock exchange, which is in the process of establishing a regional network. In 2004, it bought 68% of the Budapest stock exchange and it plans to bid for the Warsaw stock exchange, which is to be privatised in 2006. Negotiations have also been launched to draw the Czech, Slovak and Slovenian counterparts into a holding company under which the national exchanges would retain a high degree of autonomy.[8] In the medium term, the participation of the Ukrainian stock exchange in this network should be considered as a means to transfer know-how and to help develop Ukraine's limited financial markets.

Two key donors supporting financial sector development are the European Bank of Reconstruction and Development (EBRD) and the World Bank. As in other countries of the region, the EBRD is playing an important role in the development of the Ukrainian financial sector. Its projects to date include several credit lines to small and medium enterprises, the establishment of a venture capital fund and a credit line for mortgage lending. The EBRD is trying to extend its credit lines through local banks to help them build capacity and develop new financial instruments. The EU institutions, which have a good working relationship with the EBRD, should encourage the latter to expand its financial sector activities in Ukraine, possibly including equity participation in local banks or privatisation assistance to the government. The World Bank has provided technical assistance to the financial sector for several key pieces of financial legislation as part of a Sector and Structural Adjustment Loan and is currently helping to establish a market for mortgages, among other activities.[9]

The only segment of the financial sector where Ukraine's GATS proposal contains a significant restriction is the insurance market. For a five-year period after accession to the WTO, foreign insurance companies will be prohibited from entering the market. As part of a possible FTA, the EU should seek more liberal market access for its companies. As the domestic sector is in need of significant investment and development, this should also be in the interest of Ukraine. Many of the 340 insurance companies are owned by enterprises and mainly used as tax-saving vehicles. The largest formerly state-owned insurance company, Orata, was transferred to a group of investors that were associated with the son-in-law

---

[8] See the *Financial Times Deutschland,* 19 January and 17 June 2005. On a global scale, all these stock exchanges are very small. All CEEC exchanges together (including Vienna) have a market capitalisation of only €200 billion – about a third of Germany's 30 largest quoted companies. Romania, Bulgaria and Croatia could also become part of the regional network.

[9] See World Bank, *Country Assistance Strategy for Ukraine for 2004-07,* Washington, D.C., 2003.

of former President Leonid Kuchma through a dirty privatisation deal and there have been some rumours about a possible re-privatisation.

Ukraine's currency, the *hryvnya*, is pegged against the US dollar as part of a fixed exchange rate regime. As the $/UAH rate has remained stable since mid-2001 and the euro has appreciated against the dollar, the *hryvnya* has thus depreciated against the euro and is now undervalued. If a fixed exchange-rate regime were to be maintained, it would be preferable to peg the hryvnya against a basket that reflects Ukraine's trading patterns (about a third of Ukraine's trade is with the EU). Notably, however, the IMF is advising the government to move towards a more flexible exchange rate, for which it provides technical assistance to prepare for such a move.[10] A flexible exchange rate would also facilitate trade with the EU in the longer term.[11]

In financial services, the EU *acquis* does not seem an appropriate template for Ukraine at this stage of its development. First, the *acquis* in this sector is still evolving to a great extent and thus remains a moving target. Second, it is extremely complex and geared towards developed financial markets, instead of a banking-dominated financial services industry like the one in Ukraine. Third, one of the potential benefits of *acquis* compliance – simplified access for Ukrainian banks to EU markets above and beyond access gained through GATS – would not just require some regulatory convergence, but 100% compliance with all existing and future EU rules, acceptance of existing and future jurisprudence in this area as well as effective application of existing and future EU rules and jurisprudence on competition and state aid. The reason for this is that the EU's 'single passport system', which allows banks to open branches across the EU once they obtain a license in one member state, requires full compliance. Yet such a passport would bring few additional benefits to Ukraine.

---

[10] The main technical challenge of the transition is that inflation will have to be controlled through a domestic inflation target instead of the exchange rate. For that, the NBU will need to upgrade its institutional capacity.

[11] The reason is that a $/UAH peg makes the €/UAH exchange rate subject to $/€ fluctuations. A peg of the *hryvnya* against the euro does not seem a plausible alternative, as the majority of Ukraine's trade is denominated in dollars.

2. Transport

Transport is not only an important sector in its own right, but the efficient flow of goods and people is crucial for deeper integration between the EU and Ukraine. Current transport sector inefficiencies thus constitute an important non-tariff barrier. Even though a sufficient physical infrastructure is a necessary condition, many frictions and bottlenecks are policy-induced (e.g. the state ownership of airports, limited competition for port services and border-related red tape).[12]

Despite the fact that transport services themselves constitute one of Ukraine's main services exports, important aspects of the sector are excluded from the WTO/GATS framework.[13] The investment decisions and policy reforms required to render regional transport flows more efficient thus need to be addressed through domestic policy reforms in Ukraine or bilaterally between the EU and Ukraine. From the perspective of deeper integration, the three main priorities should be: i) the negotiation of an open skies arrangement with a gradual inclusion of Ukraine in the EU's common civil aviation area; ii) facilitation measures along major land corridors; and iii) a elimination of border-related frictions, with a specific emphasis on customs reforms.

Currently, trade in transport services mainly takes place through mode 1 (cross-border supply) and mode 2 (consumption abroad). Trade and transport facilitation could unlock growth potential in both of these modes, but the main unexploited opportunity for deeper integration in the sector appears to be trade through mode 3 (commercial presence). Even if market access for foreign companies might not be formally prohibited, the natural monopoly nature of many transport facilities (e.g. ports, airports,

---

[12] For a detailed review of international best practice and EU policies in the transport sector, see D. Müller-Jentsch, *Transport Policies for the Euro-Mediterranean Free Trade Area – An Agenda for Multimodal Transport Reforms in the Southern Mediterranean,* World Bank, Washington, D.C. and European Commission, Brussels, 2002.

[13] The reasons underlying that exclusion are that: air transport is governed by a separate multilateral regime (the Chicago Convention); cross-border land transport via road and rail mainly takes place between immediate neighbours (and is therefore not of much relevance for a multilateral regime); and the main policy issues arising in maritime transport relate to ports, which are largely considered a domestic policy issue.

roads and railways) and widespread state ownership imply that FDI will require privatisation (e.g. of port services and logistics companies) and the issuing of concessions (for airport terminals, container port terminals, major roads, etc.).

Although EU–Ukrainian cooperation on transport should focus on a few priorities, cross-border transport flows are also a function of the general performance of Ukraine's multimodal system. Broader domestic transport reforms that enhance efficiency across modes will also promote deeper integration. Particularly important are measures that improve the efficiency of modal interfaces, increase the degree of containerisation in general cargo (essential for modal exchanges) and promote the development of the third-party logistics industry (which packages different transport services into multimodal logistics solutions).

A major bottleneck for transport flows between Ukraine and the EU are border-related frictions. The main problems are the red tape and delays associated with customs controls. Consequently, comprehensive customs reforms in Ukraine should receive priority attention in the European Neighbourhood Policy (ENP) Action Plan. Reform needs to include a subordination of the customs authority to the Ukrainian Ministry of Finance (it is currently reporting directly to the president), the computerisation and streamlining of procedures (there are many superfluous requirements), more transparency for traders and a campaign to root out smuggling and human trafficking.[14] Juxtaposed controls between the border guards of Ukraine and its EU neighbours – as those introduced on the joint border with Poland in 2005 – are also important. As part of the EU's effort to secure its external border, more technical assistance should be provided to Ukraine's border guards.

2.1 Air transport

Deeper integration of Ukraine's air transport sector into the EU's common civil aviation area would be a powerful catalyst for the expansion of

---

[14] Customs-related corruption and smuggling are widespread. Its prevalence is illustrated by this example: according to an official interviewed by the mission, only 200,000 mobile phones were officially imported into Ukraine in a year in which the number of mobile phone subscriptions in the country increased by 2 million.

people-to-people contacts, business travel and tourism.[15] It should be treated as a key priority for the EU–Ukrainian partnership and seems feasible over the course of the next five years. In September 2005, the European Commission proposed to open negotiations with Ukraine towards that goal, but is yet to receive a negotiation mandate from EU member states.[16] Previously, in March 2005, the Commission started negotiations on a common European aviation area with the Western Balkans (Serbia-Montenegro, Albania, Croatia, Macedonia, Kosovo and Bosnia).[17] As with the EU's Energy Treaty, which was signed by the EU and south-eastern European countries and was extended to Ukraine (see the section on energy), so too could a common aviation area in principle be expanded to Ukraine. Alternatively, a bilateral agreement along similar lines should be negotiated.

The core of the air transport sector – international traffic rights – is excluded from the WTO–GATS framework and is generally not covered by a free trade agreement. Instead, traffic rights are regulated by the multilateral Chicago Convention and by bilateral air service agreements (ASAs) between governments. Other key policy issues for the sector – such as the regulation of ground handling and airport services – remain in the domain of domestic policy. Because of this, there would be considerable value added in a regional agreement.

While there has been an international proliferation of open skies agreements in recent years (i.e. ASAs with liberal market access provisions), the EU has the most deeply integrated air transport market of any group of sovereign countries in the world. The policy framework for the Single Market in air transport includes several key elements. On the one

---

[15] In 2004, 1.5 million passengers travelled between the EU and Ukraine – a 25% increase within a year.

[16] The European Commission's Communication on developing the agenda for the Community's external aviation policy (COM(2005) 79 final, Brussels) proposed a strategy that was endorsed by the European Council on 27 June 2005. It foresees the creation of a wider European common aviation area with ENP countries by 2010. A more specific strategy for Ukraine was proposed in September 2005 in the Communication on developing a common aviation area with Ukraine (COM(2005) 451 final, Brussels, 27.9.2005).

[17] There are separate negotiations between the EU and Russia on a horizontal open skies agreement.

hand it abolishes all ASAs among member states and fully liberalises traffic rights and market access. On the other hand, it addresses domestic policy issues such as the liberalisation of ground handling services, the transparent regulation of airport charges and slot allocation as well as common standards and institutional cooperation on air traffic control and safety/security issues. Neighbouring countries Norway and Switzerland have already been integrated into the EU's civil aviation area, through bilateral agreements and the adoption of the relevant *acquis*. Air transport is a sector where *acquis* compliance could also be highly beneficial for Ukraine.

A first step towards deeper integration into the EU's common civil aviation area has been the 'horizontal agreement' between Ukraine and the Commission, which was signed in June 2005 but has yet to be ratified. It will modify the bilateral agreements that Ukraine has with all 25 EU member states, by permitting EU airlines to fly to Ukraine from any country in the Union. This step will lead to a moderate liberalisation of cross-border traffic.[18] A more ambitious option would be the negotiation of a 'global aviation agreement' between the EU and Ukraine, which should be launched as soon as the Commission receives the mandate.

A key element in any deeper integration package for air transport should be cooperation on air traffic management and on safety/security issues. In 2004, Ukraine became a full member of Eurocontrol, which coordinates air traffic control across Europe. A more ambitious strategy would be the adoption of the Single European Sky legislative package by Ukraine. As far as safety and security are concerned, Ukraine is still to become a full member of the Joint Aviation Authorities (JAA), which has 39 member states and whose functions are to be integrated into the European Aviation Safety Agency (EASA).[19] Ukraine should join the JAA and seek technical assistance from the US Federal Aviation Administration (FAA), the International Civil Aviation Organisation and EASA for its aviation safety agency (DerzhAviaSluzhba), since low safety standards reduce the

---

[18] In addition, the bilateral agreements between Ukraine and several EU countries became more liberal in 2005.

[19] The EASA is still evolving: in November 2005, the Commission called on EU member states to expand EASA's mandate to include the monitoring of compliance by non-EU airlines with EU safety and security rules and the institution could also be put in charge of airport security.

competitiveness of its airlines: in 2005, the FAA downgraded Ukraine from category 1 to category 2, which restricts the access of Ukrainian airlines to international destinations.

After the country's separation from Russia, Ukraine was left without a flagship carrier.[20] As the example of Slovakia (which separated from the Czech Republic in 1993) shows, however, the absence of an entrenched incumbent lobbying for protectionism can facilitate the transition towards a liberal air transport regime. Sky Europe, Central Europe's leading low-budget carrier, has its hub in Slovakia's capital Bratislava and is expanding rapidly. Since September 2005, the airline has been quoted on the Vienna stock exchange and it plans to use its initial public offering receipts to triple the size of its fleet from 15 to 47 planes by 2009, while increasing the number of passengers from 1 to 6 million annually. Thriving in an open skies environment, the stock market value of the young airline is almost as high as that of Austrian Airlines.[21]

A major objection against open skies is the argument that Ukraine's domestic airlines are too small and too weak to compete internationally. The two largest domestic airlines, AeroSvit and Ukrainian International Airlines (UIA), are very small by EU standards (i.e. each of them has no more than a dozen airplanes). The government has stakes in both of them (23% and 62% respectively) and is contemplating a merger of them in order to create a national flagship carrier.[22] For the development of the sector, it

---

[20] A good overview of air transport policies in Ukraine can be found in ICPS, *Problems and Prospects for Developing the Air Passenger Carrier Market in Ukraine*, Kyiv, 2005(c).

[21] See the *Financial Times Deutschland* (13 September 2005) and the *Economist* (15 May 2005). A similar example comes from Lebanon, where the government was long reluctant to open aviation markets to protect the small flagship carrier MEA. In 2001 Lebanon adopted an open skies policy and within a year, tourism grew by 14% in a globally stagnant market. MEA also benefited from this growth and recorded its first profit in 16 years.

[22] Among Ukraine's 60 commercial airlines, 3 are partly state-owned. AeroSvits has four other private investors. The other main shareholders in UIA are Austrian Airlines (23%) and the EBRD (10%). AeroSvit, UIA and the other two largest players (Ukrainian Mediterranean Airlines and Donbassaero) accounted for 80% of passenger traffic. One argument for a possible merger is the fact that both airlines have complementary route networks: UIA mainly flies to Western Europe and AeroSvit to south-east Europe, the US and the Far East.

might be better to sell the state-owned shares in both airlines separately to leading international airlines, under the condition of further investments and their integration into international airline alliances. If this was done three or four years prior to a full opening of the market, it would grant those international investors a head start in the local market. A commitment to market opening after a relatively short transition period would create an incentive to expand operations quickly.

It should be stressed, however, that the notion of a flagship carrier is somewhat outdated. In Europe several countries no longer have a national airline: Belgium's Sabena went bankrupt, Switzerland's Swiss Air was taken over by Lufthansa and the Netherlands' KLM was taken over by Air France. In other EU countries, the importance of flagship carriers has significantly diminished, as low-budget airlines have rapidly grown. In Eastern and Central Europe, budget airlines have also become important players (e.g. Air Polonia in Poland, Wizz Air in Hungary or Sky Europe in Slovakia). Yet to create regional hubs and to expand their networks, these airlines need an open skies environment. In another sign that budget carriers are ready to expand into markets like Ukraine, the CEO of Ryanair (Europe's leading low-budget airline) recently appealed to policy-makers to expand the EU's open skies policies to neighbouring countries.

A major constraint for the development of domestic airlines is the VAT charged on imported planes, in an effort to induce airlines to purchase aircraft from the local aircraft manufacturer Antonov. This policy should be changed. Instead, Ukraine should seek cooperation with the EU for the restructuring of its local aircraft manufacturing industry. Appropriate measures could be included in a deeper integration package. Moreover, the government should transfer the responsibility for civil aviation from the Ministry for Industrial Policy to the Ministry for Transport and elaborate a development strategy for the sector.[23]

Of Ukraine's 30 airports, 18 handle international traffic, with Boryspil International in Kyiv being the major one. Transforming the capital's

---

[23] This strategy should cover the following: convergence with the EU *acquis*, a transition towards open skies, the development of domestic routes, the privatisation of stakes in airlines and airports, the regulation of airport services, the upgrading of air traffic control and security, and the development of the country's airports (e.g. the division of labour and allocation of investment among them and the coordination of flight schedules).

airport into a transport hub is a priority for the government and will require the modernisation of the airport. The airport is reaching its limit with regard to transfer capacity and will need significant investment in its infrastructure. Such investment has repeatedly been postponed, however. The best way to improve operational efficiency and to finance infrastructure expansion would be to concession the airport to a leading international airport operator. In the EU, most major airports are already privately owned and this trend is spreading to Eastern Europe. In December 2005, Hungary privatised its capital airport in Budapest (sold to Britain's BAA) and Slovakia sold its two largest airports (to Austria's Vienna Airport) after competitive biddings. Ukraine should try to benefit from the significant investor interest in the region's airport. An interesting model for Boryspil International could be the case of Albania's main airport in Tirana, which was sold to a consortium involving the EBRD and Hochtief, a leading private airport operator.

2.2 Land-based transport

Most freight and passenger traffic between the EU and Ukraine is transported by road and rail. As a large share of that traffic moves through a few major corridors, the facilitation of transport along these arteries is a natural priority for deeper integration efforts. In fact, four of the pan-European corridors between the EU and its Eastern neighbours, identified at the 1994 Pan-European Transport Conference in Crete, extend into Ukraine: Corridors III, V, VII and IX. Corridor VII is an inland waterway corridor (the Danube) and only touches Ukraine's southern border. The other three corridors are multimodal and comprise both rail and road:

- Corridor III runs from the Polish/Hungarian border to Lviv and then on to Kyiv.

- Corridor V extends from the Hungarian/Slovak border to Lviv, where it meets Corridor III.

- Corridor IX runs from Finland to Greece. After branching out in St Petersburg (to Moscow and Pskov respectively) both legs meet again in Kyiv. In Ljubashevka, the corridor splits again, with one branch going to Odessa and the main branch to the Moldovan border.

In the 1990s, a Memorandum of Understanding (MoU) was signed for each corridor between the countries concerned and the European Commission. On the basis of each MoU, steering committees were established to monitor and coordinate the development of the respective corridor. The progress achieved through these instruments has been mixed.

After the recent EU enlargement, most of the pan-European corridors are now within the EU. In the context of the ENP, a High-Level Group was established on the issue to make proposals for the extension of the existing corridors to neighbouring countries. The report of the group, presented in late 2005, identified five priority corridors for the ENP regions. For one of them, the 'central axis', Ukraine plays a major role:[24] three legs of this axis basically correspond to Corridors III, V and IX. Of the newly included sections, three cross Ukraine. These are the inland waterway Belarus–Kyiv–Odessa (i.e. the Dnepr), the road/rail connection Minsk–Kyiv and the road/rail link from Kyiv to Kharkiv and to the trans-Siberian/Caucasus. Two additional branches, propagated by the concerned governments but not officially included, are the road/rail link between Warsaw and Kyiv and the road/rail link from the Ukrainian border to the industrial town of Zilina.

All these routes should receive priority attention in future EU–Ukrainian cooperation. While the High-Level Group has stressed the need for further studies, it has already identified a number of key projects along the central axis. For rail transport, the most important projects in Ukraine are the Beskyd tunnel (already in preparation) and a new logistics centre and infrastructure in Chop. For roads, the priorities are an upgrading of the road between the Polish border and Lviv as well as two sections on the Kyiv–Odessa route. For multimodal transport, three logistics centres are planned in different areas of the country.

Infrastructure improvement projects along the road corridors have begun, especially along Corridor III: the EBRD has funded the rehabilitation of the first section west of Kyiv and recently signed a loan agreement for the expansion of the eastern section through the Carpathian mountains; it is now about to start negotiations for funding the middle section (with co-financing from the European Investment Bank or EIB). The

---

[24] See European Commission, *Networks for Peace and Development – Extension of the Major Trans-European Transport Axes to the Neighbouring Countries and Regions*, Report from the High-Level Group chaired by Loyola Palacio, Brussels, November 2005(b). In addition to the central axis, another of the five priority corridors marginally touches Ukraine: the Motorways of the Sea project, which includes the port of Odessa/Illyiehevsk. The other priority axes relate to other ENP regions.

entire upgrade of the corridor should be completed by 2010. Along Corridor IX, the Ukrainian government has also removed some bottlenecks along the Kyiv–Odessa section in recent years. Along Corridor III, the section between the border and Lviv is a single-carriageway trunk road that still needs to be upgraded.

Three pan-European rail corridors extend into Ukraine:

- the rail section of Corridor III runs from Mistiska at the Polish border to Lviv and then to Kyiv. Since the change between the European and the Russian gauges poses a fundamental problem for cross-border rail transport, Ukraine Railways has proposed an 84 km extension of the European gauge from the border to Lviv and estimates that this would reduce waiting times by three to four hours.

- Rail Corridor V extends from Chop at the Hungarian border to Batewo and Lviv, where it meets Corridor III. Except for a 1.8 km tunnel at Beskyd, the 264 km line is double track and electrified. The expansion of the tunnel is being facilitated through an EBRD project.

- The Ukrainian rail section of Corridor IX is 871 km long – 722 km of which are double track and 789 km are electrified. Automatic signalling has been installed along the entire corridor and container trains and shuttle trains are being operated. With the Odessa port being an end-point of the corridor, modal interfaces and port-related bottlenecks will also have to be addressed.

The focus of the development of pan-European corridors has long been on infrastructure investments. But as goods and people are transported through a corridor, they encounter both physical and 'software' bottlenecks. In other words, infrastructure investments need to be accompanied by complementary regulatory and institutional reforms that facilitate transport flows along these corridors. The most pressing issue in this regard are the frictions at border crossings as a result of customs and other border-related controls. European exporters and traders frequently cite the inefficiency of border controls and high levels of corruption as a major concern. A streamlining of border controls and comprehensive customs reforms between Ukraine and its western neighbours should thus be one of the top priorities in any strategy for deeper EU–Ukrainian integration. The EU should provide technical assistance for customs reforms and a streamlining of border controls. Moreover, both sides should agree on a set of concrete reform measures and clear progress indicators (e.g. customs clearance times) that could be included in the EU–Ukraine ENP Action Plan.[25] They should also establish a complaint and dispute-settlement mechanism so traders can voice their concerns on border control issues.

The work of the EBRD along the pan-European corridors shows how infrastructure projects can be designed to also promote the institutional reforms and capacity-building that are needed to render transport flows more efficient.[26] The EBRD loans for road Corridor III not only fund rehabilitation work between Kyiv and Chop, but the EBRD (in cooperation with the EU's Tacis programme) is helping Ukravtodor[27] to restructure its road financing and administration functions and to introduce competitive tendering for civil works contracts. These efforts should reduce the costs of future infrastructure investment and ensure that what is currently in place is maintained more efficiently. In rail transport, the EBRD is also packaging infrastructure project funding with technical assistance. As part of a loan for track maintenance on the section between Lviv and Kyiv, the EBRD (with Tacis co-financing) helped UZ, the railway transport of Ukraine, to modernise its maintenance procedures (to reduce life-cycle costs) and develop a commercialisation programme (i.e. the phasing out of cross subsidies and the establishment of a five-year business plan). A follow-up loan, approved in mid-2004, will also mix infrastructure financing and technical assistance. The infrastructure component includes the removal of a key bottleneck in Corridor V through the construction of the Beskyd tunnel, the continuation of the track rehabilitation programme and new rolling stock to speed up intercity passenger traffic. Technical assistance will help with the conversion of UZ into a joint stock company and the introduction of more efficient procurement methods.

If transport costs and frictions are to be further reduced along the EU–Ukrainian corridors, physical infrastructure investments and policy reforms will need to go hand-in-hand. The work of the EBRD provides a

---

[25] For instance, both sides could agree that waiting times at border crossings between the EU and Ukraine should be reduced by half over a two-year period. For this to occur, however, reliable waiting-time statistics would be needed.

[26] Project fact-sheets can be downloaded from the EBRD website (www.ebrd.org).

[27] Ukravtodor is the Ukrainian state corporation for road construction, maintenance and repair.

good model for such a dual-track approach and should be extended to other areas. EU contributions to infrastructure investments along key transport corridors should be channelled through the EBRD, and the Tacis co-funding of technical assistance packaged with EBRD investments provides a good model. Another option would be for the EU to offer Ukraine additional funding for corridor investments (e.g. through an expansion of EIB lending to Ukraine), in return for explicit conditionalities regarding progress on customs reforms and the reduction of frictions at border crossings.

If Ukraine wants to exploit its full potential for transit traffic between Europe and the CIS countries and between its northern neighbours and the Black Sea, intermodal traffic will be the key for a simple reason: Ukraine stretches about 800 km from north to south and about 1,600 km from east to west. Hence, any transit will have to be of a long-distance nature. As a rule of thumb, rail freight has a competitive edge over road transport from 500 km onwards. As most rail freight does not have a door-to-door advantage, however, the rail transit routes would have to involve multimodal traffic – either through containers or through the transfer of trucks/trailers onto trains. Both types of intermodal traffic require special equipment and transfer facilities as well as reliable shuttle train services. Ukraine and the European Commission should develop a strategy to increase containerisation rates and facilitate modal transfers along the pan-European transport corridors.

In addition, convergence towards EU policies in road and rail could help improve the efficiency of Ukraine's transport sector. Some examples for the selected adoption of EU norms and standards include: the European rail traffic management system (to harmonise signalling and data communication); a mutual recognition of rolling stock maintenance standards in rail or vehicle safety standards in road freight; the extension of EU rules for competitive access of private operators to rail tracks along key routes; and Ukraine's adoption of the EU *acquis* for the liberalisation of road freight. An interesting model for the extension of EU rules to neighbouring countries through regional agreements could be the Interbus Agreement.

In 2000, the EU and 13 accession candidates (including Turkey) signed the Interbus Agreement to liberalise coach operations among the signatories. It provides for the harmonisation of national legislation and fiscal regimes, mutual recognition of documentation as well as common standards for vehicles and employment conditions on the basis of the EU *acquis* in this specific market segment. It does not extend to regular services (i.e. coach lines) or liberalisation measures such as cabotage.[28] Other parties have since signed up to the Interbus Agreement. Of Ukraine's non-EU neighbours, Bulgaria and Romania have acceded to the agreement, while Moldova has signed but not yet ratified it. As a member of the European Conference of Ministers of Trade, Ukraine is eligible to join the Agreement, but it has not yet applied. Accession to the Interbus Agreement would entail a concrete integration measure that could be implemented prior to a more comprehensive FTA.

2.3   Other transport modes

Even though maritime transport is not such an important mode for EU–Ukrainian trade, it is critical for transit trade and the efficiency of the overall multimodal system. Ukraine should elaborate an integrated port strategy, including plans for infrastructure development, improved linkages with land modes as well as regulatory and institutional reforms. The twin ports of Odessa/Illyiehevsk (the country's largest) were declared a priority for the Motorways of the Sea project by the High-Level Group and it constitutes an important nodal point for the central axis (i.e. for corridor IX). Comprehensive reforms concerning this port should be anchored in the EU–Ukraine ENP Action Plan. More specifically, the new container port at Illyiehevsk, identified as an important project by the High-Level Group, should be concessioned to a private investor. A more general liberalisation of port services and concessions for other key terminals would open the sector to foreign investors (and thus to trade through mode 3) and thus should also be a priority. The European Commission has recently proposed its Port Package II measures, which would introduce a much greater degree of competition in port services across the EU. Its rules could provide guidance for similar reforms in Ukraine. Last but not least, Ukraine is one of the countries with the greatest

---

[28] Regular services need to be negotiated on a bilateral basis (i.e. between Ukraine and individual EU member states), but accession to the Interbus Agreement would facilitate the negotiation of such bilateral agreements. As long as Ukraine remains outside the Interbus Agreement, tour operators need an authorisation for each trip. The number of privately-owned busses in Ukraine trebled between 1995 and 2000 to more than 45,000.

number of seafarers worldwide (about 50,000) and the EU would like to see the country tighten its labour laws and their enforcement.

Ukraine's 4,400 km of inland waterways play only a marginal role for EU–Ukrainian traffic. The country has limited access to Europe's most important inland waterway: the Rhine–Main–Danube corridor, which runs about 3,500 km from Rotterdam on the North Sea to Sulina (Romania) on the Black Sea. Ukraine has signed an MoU for the development of pan-European Corridor VII (the Danube) and is a member of the steering committee.[29] Yet the river merely skirts Ukraine's territory along the southern border with Romania and only a small section of the delta lies on the Ukrainian side.[30] Most of the traffic actually bypasses Ukraine via the Danube–Black Sea Canal in Romania. Plans of the Ukrainian Ministry of Transport to re-open the silted Prorva Canal from the Danube to the Ukrainian Black Sea coast would violate Ukraine's international commitments to preserve the Danube delta – a fragile biosphere that was declared a UNESCO World Heritage Site in 1991. Another important cross-border inland waterway is the Dnepr between Belarus and Ukraine, which is also part of the central axis that has been identified by the High-Level Group.

A very specific transport mode that is important for the long-distance transport of oil and gas are pipelines. About three-quarters of Russia's gas exports to the EU are transported through Ukraine via transit pipelines. Since the policy issues related to pipelines are more intertwined with energy sector issues, however, they are discussed in the energy section of this report.

---

[29] There are no important bottlenecks along Corridor VII within Ukraine, such as water depth, channel width or free air draft under bridges. Other transport issues addressed by the steering committee include interoperability and border-crossing frictions.

[30] Ukraine also participates in the Danube cooperation process among the 10 countries through which the river runs. This process covers various policy areas, including transport. Ocean-going vessels can only enter the lower part of the Danube and inland waterway vessels cannot reach the Ukrainian port of Odessa, which is 150 km away from the Danube delta. As a result, the Danube is not really an integral part of Ukraine's transport system.

3. Telecom and IT-enabled services

A comprehensive reform of Ukraine's telecom sector will be needed for the development of a knowledge-based economy and for deeper integration with the global economy (including the EU). Fixed and mobile penetration rates remain low, only a small percentage of the population has access to the Internet and service quality in most parts of the sector are far below European standards. To solve these problems, a number of key issues will have to be addressed: the development of the Communications Regulatory Commission into an effective regulator, the privatisation of fixed-wire operator UkrTelecom and the encouragement of more effective competition and private investment in fixed-line services. To ensure that these reforms are embedded in a coherent strategy, the EU–Ukraine ENP Action Plan should include a provision that the government elaborates and publicly endorses a national strategy for the development of the information and communications technology sector.[31]

As part of its WTO/GATS proposal, Ukraine committed itself to the comprehensive opening of all forms of electronic communication: voice telephony, mobile voice and data, circuit-switched data, private leased circuits, electronic and voice mail, online information, etc. Ukraine is also subscribing to the Telecom Reference Paper, which codifies key principles of sector regulation. The main barrier to trade in telecom services, however, is the effective enforcement of these principles as well as in the opening of the core of the sector to private investors (i.e. the fixed-wire network) through the privatisation of UkrTelecom. To conduct this important and technically complex transaction, the government would be well advised to seek the assistance of an international finance institution that has the appropriate expertise, such as the EBRD or the World Bank.

The legal and regulatory framework for the telecom sector is still a work in progress. The 2003 Law on Telecommunications is in line with the GATS commitments, but many of the detailed regulations (which are also foreseen by the basic telecom law) still need to be developed – especially with regard to licensing, interconnection rules, spectrum management and tariff regulation. Most important will be the facilitation of network access for competing operators through interconnection rules that provide for non-discriminatory and transparent access at prices that are cost-related, as

---

[31] This section draws on World Bank, *Electronic Communications in Ukraine: The Bottleneck to Sustainable Development*, Washington, D.C., 2005.

well as for an effective dispute-settlement mechanism. This item is in fact among those listed in the EU–Ukraine ENP Action Plan. In mobile telephony, appropriate rules on the sharing of physical infrastructure or roaming could help the smaller providers catch up with the two dominant market players.

The National Communications Regulatory Commission (NCRC) was only recently established and needs considerable institutional strengthening before it can fulfil its functions. To date, only the eight commissioners of the NCRC have been appointed. Its statute and institutional structure still need to be elaborated, its employees still need to be hired and trained, and its working practices still need to be established. In terms of budgetary resources, the regulator is still not sufficiently independent and public sector staffing rules make it difficult to hire qualified staff. The World Bank provided advice on the telecom sector law and is helping with capacity-building at the NCRC. This important assistance needs to continue and the EU should complement it through a twinning arrangement between the NCRC and a telecom regulator from one of the recent accession countries.

In the telecom sector, full *acquis* compliance is feasible and it would be desirable from the perspective of domestic economic development. The *acquis* in this area reflects international best practice and is in line with both GATS rules and with the needed regulatory reforms outlined above. *Acquis* convergence in this specific sector, however, will not require the adoption of the current set of EU rules (which came into effect in 2002), but of the previous set of rules that date from 1998. The 1998 *acquis* was much more detailed and specific. As the telecom market in the EU matured and as competition unfolded, however, the EU streamlined its *acquis* and increasingly relied on national regulators for the enforcement of some rather general principles.[32] Given the relatively early state of development of Ukraine's telecom sector, the 1998 *acquis* would be more appropriate for the time being. In fact, Ukraine's telecom law is largely based on the 1998 package of EU rules and thus the country is in formal compliance with the

---

[32] The 2002 *acquis* is not in contradiction with the 1998 *acquis*, it is just more general. It actually refers back to the 1998 *acquis* for those countries that are not yet advanced enough to comply with the 2002 version.

acquis.[33] But in practical terms, *acquis* compliance would require the passing of detailed regulations and especially the effective enforcement of these rules through a capable and independent regulator, which is yet to occur.

One way in which the European Commission could support the process of *acquis* convergence in the telecom sector would be to use the same assistance instruments as for the non-EU countries of south-eastern Europe. For those countries, the Commission 1) prepares a detailed regulatory report once a year to monitor reform progress; 2) maintains an institutionalised policy dialogue (a working group meets twice a year); and 3) provides technical assistance by EU telecom experts through field trips and capacity-building.

With 22 telephone connections per 100 persons in 2003, Ukraine's fixed-line penetration rate is considerably lower than that of its EU neighbours Slovakia (41), Hungary (35) or Poland (31). In recent years, the number of connections has grown by 6% annually and the government plans to double teledensity by 2010.[34] In 2004, however, about 2 million applications for fixed-wire connections were still outstanding. Infrastructure deficiencies are particularly pronounced in rural areas and with regard to broadband access.[35] To address these problems, large-scale investments will be required, which can only be mobilised through greater private participation and a privatisation of UkrTelecom.

The privatisation of UkrTelecom has been on the agenda for a number of years, but in 2004 the government postponed the scheduled sale of a 43% stake in the operator. The privatisation of UkrTelecom will not only be crucial to increase sector efficiency and FDI, but also to allow for greater trade in telecom services through mode 3.[36] But the government must ensure that the transaction is fully transparent and structured in a way that will attract an international strategic investor with the appropriate

---

[33] For a comparison between the Ukrainian law with the EU *acquis* and with the WTO/GATS requirements in this sector, see ICPS, "Policy memo to the draft Law of Ukraine 'On telecoms'", Kyiv, February 2003.

[34] See the Economist Intelligence Unit, *Ukraine Country Profile 2005*, London, 2005.

[35] One measure of the availability of broadband access is bps per inhabitant. According to ITU data for 2003, Ukraine had 19 bps per capita, compared with 1,850 in Slovakia and 1,000 in Hungary.

[36] According to efficiency indicators (e.g. lines per employee), the company's performance lies considerably below that of comparators from other CEECs.

know-how and resources for network expansion. The weaknesses of the regulatory framework need to be addressed prior to privatisation.

The fastest growing market segment is mobile telephony. Ukraine had 16 million subscribers in early 2005, but the penetration rate of 33% still remains one of the lowest in Europe. Neighbouring Slovakia has 81%, Hungary has 80% and Romania has 49%. Competition in this sub-sector – which is fully privately owned – has lowered tariffs and has led to improved services. The two largest providers, Kyivstar and Ukraine Mobile Communications (UMC), control 95% of the market. UMC is owned by Russia's Mobile Telesystems, whereas the two main shareholders of Kyivstar are Norway's Telenor (56.5%) and Russia's Alfa Group (43.5%).[37] In addition, there are four small providers: Golden Telecom, Ukrainian Radio Systems and Digital Cellular Communications (DCC). Golden Telecom is Russian-owned, whereas DCC belongs to Turkey's Turkcell and the private Ukrainian company System Capital Management. The new provider under the brand name of Life:), which is owned by a Turkish investor, only entered the market in 2005, but is expanding aggressively and might establish itself as a third force next to the two market leaders.

According to a survey published in October 2005, the number of Internet users in Ukraine is rising rapidly, albeit from a low level. The percentage of Ukrainians using the Internet regularly more than doubled to 18% within a year. Owing to access at work and through Internet cafes, there are more users than connections. According to measures of Internet traffic, Kyiv accounts for 51% of Ukraine's total traffic and other big cities for another 34%.[38] Facilitating more widespread Internet usage should be a key element in the government's sector strategy. This objective will require higher fixed-wire penetration rates, investment in broadband infrastructure and possibly local loop unbundling.

---

[37] In September 2005, Ukrainian Radio Systems was bought by Russia's Vimpelcom, which is co-owned by Telenor and Alfa Group. This deal, initiated by Alfa Group, was fought massively by Telenor, which fears a dilution of its majority stake in Kyivstar in case Kyivstar is merged with UKS. Telenor and Alfa Group have clashed repeatedly and the deep-rooted conflict between the two strategic investors remains unresolved.

[38] The survey of Ukrainians aged 41-59 was conducted by a market research company and the measure of Internet traffic was conducted by an electronic media company (*Kyiv Post*, 13 October 2005).

A rapidly growing market with significant trade potential between Ukraine and the EU is that of IT-enabled services. This market includes a wide range of services that can be transacted over the telephone or the Internet (i.e. trade in services through mode 1, cross-border supply). Examples are call centres, computer programming, database management, accounting, billing and various other back-office functions that more and more companies in developed economies are outsourcing to low-cost countries. Even though India has thus far been the primary beneficiary of the rapid growth in this multi-billion dollar industry, CEEC countries are increasingly benefiting from this trend.[39] With its well-educated workforce, low wage rates and geographical proximity to the EU, Ukraine would be well placed to compete in this market. An important precondition, however, would be comprehensive reforms in the telecom sector.

4.   Energy

Besides the specific integration measures in the energy sector outlined in this section, a more comprehensive approach to energy sector integration between Ukraine and the EU would be Ukraine's accession to the Energy Treaty between the EU and the non-EU countries of south-eastern Europe (SEE). The Treaty establishing the Energy Community was signed in March 2005.[40] It provides a roadmap for the gradual integration of the entire region into the EU energy market over the coming decade. Non-EU signatories are committing themselves to full adoption of the entire *acquis* for electricity and gas as well as compliance with competition and environmental rules. An estimated €15-20 billion of investments will be required to bring the energy infrastructure of the region up to EU standards.[41] One component of the regional strategy is a set of new pipelines from the Black Sea across the Balkans, which would diversify European oil and gas supplies from Iran and the Caspian region. A secretariat, mainly funded by the European Commission, will oversee the implementation of the Treaty. Both Ukraine and Moldova are observers to

---

[39] For a more detailed analysis of trade in IT-enabled services, see D. Müller-Jentsch (2004).

[40] The signatories are the EU and the countries of former Yugoslavia (Serbia, Croatia, Bosnia, Montenegro, Macedonia and Kosovo) as well as Bulgaria, Romania, Albania and Turkey.

[41] See *Financial Times Deutschland* of 2 November 2005.

this process, but have expressed their intention to become full members. A binding agreement in this regard would establish a clear framework for deeper EU–Ukraine integration in the energy sector.

Ukraine's energy sector is not only of great economic importance, but is also one of the most complex in terms of its reform needs. Since many of the policy issues at stake are intertwined, the government should develop a comprehensive energy-sector strategy that covers all forms of energy (oil, gas, electricity and coal) and all key issues such as national resource development, import security/diversification, energy transit, energy efficiency, investment plans, tariff rebalancing, competition, nuclear safety and environmental issues. There is significant potential for deeper EU–Ukrainian integration in this sector, but various cross-border barriers and distortions will have to be removed if the full potential is to be unlocked.

Few sectors are as prone to the abuse of market power and other forms of anti-competitive behaviour as the energy sector. Even in the EU, a decade of liberalisation has not yet managed to break up oligopolistic market structures. To achieve this, a pro-competitive regulatory regime and an effective regulatory authority are essential. If Ukraine wants to reform its energy sector in line with EU principles, a strengthening of the National Energy Regulatory Committee (NERC) will thus be needed. Steps to ensure its full independence from both the government and sector interests are needed (in terms of mandate, funding and staffing) along with a strengthening of its institutional capacity. For that purpose, the government should seek the technical assistance of a donor with the necessary expertise (e.g. the World Bank) and complement this by an EU-funded twinning arrangement with a successful energy regulator from a recent accession country in Central and Eastern Europe.

An important pre-condition for deeper EU–Ukrainian integration will be tariff-rebalancing throughout the energy sector. Currently, most energy tariffs remain below world market prices. This situation distorts cross-border competition and violates key principles of the European Single Market, as the following examples show:

1)   The export-oriented and FIG-dominated metallurgical sector relies on coke that is implicitly subsidised, as state-owned coal mines sell their produce below actual costs.

2) Ukraine's steel and chemical industries also gain an unfair competitive advantage through oil and gas prices below world market levels (including special VAT treatment for gas imports).[42]

3) If Ukraine were to export electricity to the EU, the fuel costs of the power plants would also have to be in line with international prices. As a precondition for fair trade, such explicit and implicit energy subsidies would have to be phased out.[43]

Cost-related energy prices would also provide an important incentive for greater energy efficiency and new investments.[44] With Gazprom pushing for higher gas prices, the gradual convergence of Ukraine on world market prices is inevitable.

Another set of issues that need to be addressed to create a level playing field for cross-border competition are environmental standards. In the EU, high environmental standards on emissions, fuel quality and nuclear safety are all factored into energy prices. As long as environmental standards in Ukraine's energy sector are far below their EU equivalents, cross-border competition will be distorted. Even though EU standards cannot be enforced in Ukraine overnight, those issues will have to be addressed in the medium term. One option would be an agreement

---

[42] The metallurgical sector accounts for 13% and the chemical sector for 11% of all gas consumed in Ukraine. Currently, gas prices for industrial consumers are $68/1000 m³, but industry observers expect that a gradual increase of gas prices by Gazprom will bring prices up to $180/1000 m³ by 2008. (See Concorde Capital, *Ukraine's Gas Issue: The Way Out*, Kyiv, September 2005).

[43] One important measure in that regard will be whether Naftogaz passes on the natural gas that it receives from Gazprom as a transit fee on behalf of the government (i.e. 29 of the 87 bcm of Ukraine's domestic consumption in 2004) to consumers – at least to industrial clients – at world market prices. A technically complicated problem that would have to be resolved for electricity trade is the export of nuclear power, with its low marginal costs.

[44] Energy consumption in Ukraine has been reduced by almost half since independence, but the country still has a very energy-intensive industry and energy efficiency across the economy remains very low. The only area where some degree of subsidisation might be justified is the household sector (which is not trade-related). But even here, targeted subsidies to low-income households would be much more efficient than general price subsidies.

on some minimum standards or compensatory mechanisms (or both) to eliminate the most significant distortions (e.g. through pollution taxes or import duties).

4.1   Oil, gas and coal

About 80% of Russia's natural gas exports to the EU cross Ukraine via pipelines (see Figure A.3.1). The transit fee to Ukraine is paid in the form of gas and meets a considerable part of Ukraine's import requirements. This is recorded as a service export and accounts for the country's surplus in services trade. The gas transit is of great economic and geo-strategic importance for both Ukraine and the EU, as illustrated by the high-profile conflict about gas prices between Russia's Gazprom and Ukraine in late 2005. At the beginning of 2006, both sides settled their gas dispute by agreeing on a five-year delivery contract that doubles the average import price from $50 to $95 per 1000 m³ – considerably below the $230 originally demanded by Gazprom, but comparable to import prices for other countries in the region.

Figure A.3.1 Europe's gas pipeline network

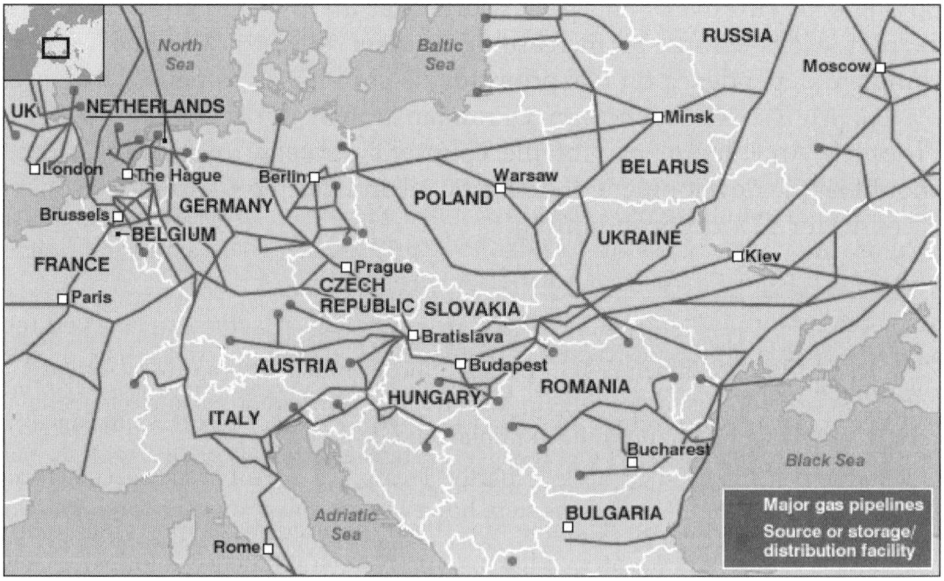

Source: Inogate (EU oil and gas transport cooperation programme).

There are indications that Russia's gas monopolist Gazprom tried to use the conflict order to gain control over the transit pipelines.[45] This tactic would be in line with its general strategy to control all transit routes to Europe: in mid-2005, Gazprom and its German partners EON and BASF agreed to build a controversial submarine pipeline through the Baltic Sea (in order to circumvent transit countries) and in December Gazprom managed to gain ownership over an existing pipeline through Belarus in a rather non-transparent fashion (no details of the deal were made public). The previous Ukrainian government and Gazprom had also concluded an agreement in 2002 to establish a joint gas consortium to operate the system of pipelines that cross Ukraine, but the new government stopped these plans to maintain control over these strategic assets. The EU has a natural interest in preventing Gazprom from controlling all transit routes to European markets and should engage in a strategic dialogue with the Ukrainian government on the future control and ownership structures of these pipelines.[46]

To reduce its dependency on Russian gas, Ukraine signed an agreement to expand gas imports from Turkmenistan in 2004. This deal, however, also involved Gazprom, which had already secured the right to buy most of Turkmenistan's gas exports over the 20-year period up to 2028 as part of its efforts to increase its market power.[47] Ukraine's almost complete dependence on Gazprom for its supplies is somewhat balanced by Gazprom's dependence on Ukrainian transit rights for its exports to Europe.[48] An integral part of the country's strategy to diversify supply should be the development of domestic oil and gas resources (domestic gas accounts for 22% of consumption).

---

[45] See *Financial Times Deutschland* of 2 January 2006 and *Frankfurter Allgemeine Zeitung* of 31 December 2005. During the conflict, Russia put forward a compromise proposal according to which price concessions could be made in return for a stake by Gazprom in Ukrainian energy assets.

[46] Ukraine has signed the Energy Charter Treaty – a cross-border agreement on transit and investment issues. This step, however, can only be seen as an initial one in the right direction.

[47] According to the agreement, Gazprom will increase the gas deliveries to Ukraine from 44 billion m³ in 2005 to 60 billion m³ in 2028.

[48] See Concorde Capital (2005, op. cit.). A more long-term option to diversify Ukraine's (and the EU's) gas supplies would be to build a pipeline to Iran.

Virtually all of Ukraine's gas market – from upstream exploration to downstream distribution – is being controlled by the state-owned company Naftogaz. The company is a sprawling conglomerate of more than 250 enterprises with low levels of transparency. The government should develop a comprehensive strategy for reform of the gas sector and for the restructuring of Naftogaz (e.g. for the streamlining of institutional structure, more transparent corporate governance and more effective commercial management). Compliance with the EU *acquis* in this sub-sector would require the vertical unbundling of Naftogaz (e.g. exploration, transmission and distribution) and the opening of certain activities to competition.

Ukraine also plays a major in the transit of oil between Russia and the EU and would like to position itself as a transit country for Caspian oil. The newly constructed Yuzhny oil terminal in the Black Sea port of Odessa and an oil pipeline between Odessa and the Polish border remained unused for some years before the Russian–British company TNK-BP reached a deal with Ukrtransnafta – the state-owned company operating Ukraine's oil pipelines – to reverse the pipeline. Since late 2004, the company has been pumping Russian oil to Odessa, where it is transferred to ships for export. A use of the pipeline in the originally foreseen south-north direction, however, would help both Ukraine and the EU to diversify their supplies away from Russia. Such use would require the construction of a connecting pipeline from the border to the Polish town of Plotzk, where it would link up to existing pipelines (with estimated costs at €500 million). Both the EC and Poland are advocating such a scenario and finding a common solution could be a priority cooperation project between Ukraine and the EU in the energy sector.[49]

Most of Ukraine's oil imports come from Russia, with Kazakhstan accounting for much of the balance. Four of the country's six refineries belong to Russian oil companies and one to a Kazakh oil company.[50] Even though this was originally meant to secure supplies, the Tymoshenko government accused the owners of price fixing in 2005. In response, the government introduced controversial price controls and abolished import

---

[49] See the Economist Intelligence Unit (2005), op. cit.

[50] These companies control 90% of the market for refined oil products and 75% of filling stations. The Russian oil companies that own Ukrainian refineries are TNK-BP, Lukoil and the Alliance Group.

duties for refined oil products.[51] In September 2004, a presidential decree provided for the establishment of a vertically integrated oil company through Naftogaz. A more promising strategy, however, would be to reduce market power through unbundling and pro-competitive regulation.[52] In addition, further privatisations and new concessions could help diversify the set of foreign investors, which would also stimulate competition. Austria's oil company OMV, for instance, is already active in several CEECs and has expressed an interest in entering the Ukrainian market. Growing car ownership is bound to increase future demand for refined oil products. The stock of passenger cars has risen by 75% since independence, but with 110 cars per 1,000 persons Ukraine still has less than half the level of neighbouring Poland (with 250).[53]

Coal accounts for almost a third of Ukraine's energy balance (twice as much as in the EU) and the country is one of the 10 largest coal producers in the world. Most of the loss-making mines remain state owned and the budget expenditures for the coal industry in 2004 alone amounted to UAH 3.6 billion. The metallurgical FIGs rely on coal for their coke supply and thus benefit from these subsidies. Other problems are the coal sector's damaging effects on the environment and the enormous amount of surplus staff. The challenges for the government will be to improve the profitability of state-owned mines, eliminate subsidies to privatised mines and industrial clients, close unviable mines and shed surplus labour in a socially acceptable manner, and reduce the environmental pollution caused by coal. The EU–Ukraine ENP Action Plan should incorporate some of

---

[51] The abolition of import duties is a market-based instrument to increase competition in the domestic market and it also promotes deeper integration between Ukraine and the EU in this specific market segment.

[52] This recommendation also holds for other segments of the energy sector. Horizontal unbundling can force dominant players who exceed a certain market share threshold to sell capacity (e.g. in power generation, oil refineries or gas stations). Vertical unbundling can prevent the extension of monopoly power from one market segment to another (e.g. between gas transmission and distribution or between power generation, transmission and distribution). Other forms of pro-competitive regulation include price regulation in monopolistic market segments or network access to gas pipelines or the electricity grid (i.e. natural monopoly functions).

[53] See the Economist Intelligence Unit (2005), op. cit.

these measures and the strategy implemented to downsize Poland's coal sector prior to EU accession could provide some guidance.

4.2 Electricity

Largely owing to the post-independence recession, Ukraine currently only utilises about half of its generation capacity of 56 GW to meet domestic demand. About 50% of the electricity generated comes from 4 nuclear power stations, 40% comes from 17 thermal power stations (gas, oil and coal) and 10% is hydropower. In 2004, Ukraine used about a third of its spare capacity for electricity exports to Russia and an agreement signed in October 2004 could soon double that figure.[54] In the longer term, however, there could also be significant potential for electricity trade between Ukraine and its EU neighbours (i.e. trade through mode 1, cross-border supply).

Most of the electricity sector remains government owned: the state still controls all of the country's 19 generation companies (energos) and 15 out of 27 regional distribution companies (oblenergos). The other 12 oblenergos were privatised in 1998 and 2001, but low tariffs and the poor payment discipline in the sector prevented further disposals.[55] In 2004, the government decided to transfer the remaining state-owned electricity assets to a vertically integrated company, the United Energy Company of Ukraine. This decision, however, runs counter to international best practice and to EU rules in the electricity sector, which require vertical unbundling between generation, transmission and distribution. The government should therefore reconsider its decision. Moreover, an expansion of trade in electricity through mode 3 (commercial presence) would require further privatisations of state-owned generation and distribution companies (transmission as the key natural monopoly should not be privatised).

---

[54] Ibid.

[55] The enactment of an energy debt-restructuring law, as committed to under the ongoing Programmatic Adjustment Loan (PAL) 2 from the World Bank should help to address this problem. Previous electricity-sector privatisations were apparently not transacted through concessions (which is the standard international practice), but through direct asset sales, with minority shares remaining with the government. Future privatisations in power generation are constrained by the fact that about half of the total generation capacity is accounted for by nuclear power.

Increased FDI from EU and other foreign companies (i.e. trade through mode 3) would help upgrade Ukraine's electricity infrastructure.

As far as sector regulation is concerned, Ukraine's electricity law is a framework law that still needs to be complemented through detailed regulations – and especially through effective enforcement by the sector regulator (as discussed above). Further privatisations should only be pursued after comprehensive regulatory reforms and they should be implemented in a pro-competitive manner – i.e. by packaging generation and distribution assets in a way that will create viable competitors that can compete on an equal footing.

Comprehensive electricity sector reforms along the lines of EU rules should be part of the deeper free trade strategy. Electricity is one of the backbone service sectors where the EU *acquis* seems well suited to Ukraine.[56] The EU's internal rules are largely in line with international best practice and were explicitly designed with the dual objective of achieving market liberalisation and cross-border integration. The main elements of the *acquis* relate to vertical unbundling (between generation, transmission and distribution), open network access, transparent regulation through independent regulators and the gradual introduction of competition across all market segments. As the EU's internal reform experience shows, however, the effective enforcement of these rules requires competent regulators with a strong mandate and full independence. Currently, Ukraine neither has a regulatory framework nor a regulatory authority that would comply with the EU *acquis*.

There are three basic models for cross-border power markets. Under the single-buyer model, currently used in Ukraine, a central entity purchases electricity from all producers and then resells it. This model, which does not necessarily require unbundling, limits competition. A second model offering open access (third-party) has more competitive trading mechanisms. Transmission systems are open to generators, who

---

[56] The main elements of the EU's economic *acquis* for the electricity sector are: i) the 1999 Electricity Directive (unbundling, non-discriminatory access to the transmission system, gradual market opening, etc.) and ii) the 2003 package that amended the Electricity Directive (completion of market opening, stricter rules on unbundling, the requirement for all member states to establish independent regulators, etc.), which complemented it through a separate regulation on cross-border trade.

can sell directly to distributors or large customers. Most trades, however, continue to take place through long-term contracts. A precondition for such an arrangement is the effective regulation of network access and preferably the unbundling of transmission. In other words, functioning cross-border power markets require complementary domestic reforms. The third and most sophisticated type of trans-national power markets are power pools or wholesale exchanges. Requirements for the operation of a pool are a well-developed regulatory framework and institutional structures (e.g. spot and future markets along with power brokers) as well as a sufficiently large number of generators of similar size to permit effective competition. EU countries have gradually moved along this continuum of deeper integration in electricity markets (the process is still underway). Eventually, the electricity relations between the EU and Ukraine should evolve along the same path.

Before deeper integration can become feasible, however, a number of preconditions must be met. Ukraine needs to progress with its domestic reform agenda. At the same time, technical and institutional barriers to network integration need to be removed. The key technical barrier to trade is the fact that Ukraine's electricity grid is not yet interconnected with that of the EU. The country's network remains linked to that of the CIS and only a small section near the Slovak border, referred to as 'Burshtyn island', is integrated into the continental European grid. Since this only includes two thermal power stations, there is little trade potential. If Ukraine wants to hook up to the continental European grid without disconnecting from the CIS grid with its different frequency, significant investment will be needed to finance new transmission lines with back-to-back stations that act as adapters between the two systems.[57] The costs for this would be substantial but not prohibitive. The physical integration of the Baltic States (who are also part of the CIS grid) into the European system could provide an interesting precedent in this regard.

Once electricity grids are physically interconnected, the joint system will also have to be managed. More than in most other sectors, the integration of national markets for electricity also requires some form of cross-border regulatory cooperation. This explains why the sector

---

[57] Ukraine will also need to stabilise the frequency of its domestic electricity grid. The link between the grids in Ukraine and Belarus was disconnected after the Chernobyl accident, but is supposed to be re-established.

framework for the Single Market in electricity not only consists of rules and regulations, but also has a strong institutional dimension. The main cross-border institutions are the Union for the Coordination of the Transmission of Electricity (for technical management of the interconnected grid), the European Association of Transmission System Operators (to ensure cross-border network access and trade) and the Council of European Energy Regulators (to coordinate economic regulation).[58] The gradual integration of Ukraine into these institutional structures (e.g. starting with an observer status) would be desirable.

5. Other services

5.1 Retailing and distribution

A service sector that remains poorly developed in Ukraine is retailing. Especially Western-style supermarkets and large-scale branded outlets such as IKEA are still very rare. This situation is in stark contrast to the that in the CEE accession countries, where large EU retailers have developed regional distribution networks and driven development. Leading European supermarket chains include Carrefour, Ahold, Metro and Safeway. Examples of specialised retailers are H&M, Zara, Marks and Spencer, and IKEA. These and other players could also potentially expand into the Ukrainian market. Even though there are no formal barriers to entry, the difficulty of not only acquiring land and building permits for suitable sites, but also Ukraine's low purchasing power and difficult business environment appear to have deterred market entry. Two EU supermarket chains that have launched operations in Ukraine are Metro of Germany and Billa of Austria.[59]

5.2 Tourism

Ukraine has significant unexploited tourism potential, especially along its attractive Black Sea coast, which includes such highlights as the Crimean peninsula and the seaside resort of Odessa. Other destinations with some

---

[58] For a detailed discussion of the EU's internal rules for the power sector, see D. Müller-Jentsch, *The Development of Electricity Market in the Euro-Mediterranean Area*, World Bank, Washington D.C. and the European Commission, Brussels, 2001.

[59] In 2004, IKEA announced $300 million worth of investments in Ukraine. But these seem to be geared towards production and not retailing (*Financial Times*, 15 June 2005).

appeal are the capital Kyiv, the historic city of Lviv and the skiing resorts in the Carpathian mountains. Most of the country's tourism infrastructure, however, dates back to Soviet times and is poorly maintained. There is significant potential for increased tourism trade Ukraine and the EU – through both mode 3 (commercial presence or FDI) and mode 2 (consumption abroad). On the one hand, European tourism companies could bring the investments and know-how needed to develop the sector plus the marketing skills needed to attract Western clients. On the other hand, Ukraine could serve EU tourists and thus export services through mode 2. To date, however, there have been no EU investment in this sector to speak of. The reasons appear to be similar to those that have thus far obstructed the entry of international hotel groups into the Kyiv market (as discussed in the case study in Box 6.2, chapter 6). In addition, an EU–Ukraine open skies agreement could help improve the transport access for European clients to Ukrainian tourist destinations.

ANNEX 4. ECONOMIC MODELLING

This annex discusses the application of economic models to assess the impact of Ukraine's integration into the main EU economy. In particular, a multi-country general equilibrium model is used to assess the potential economic effects of integration. This model is an adaptation of that used in a previous report for the Commission in 1999 by Paul Brenton and John Whalley.[1] Thus it can also be seen as an updated version of their work, taking account of changes in economic structure and trade patterns along with the actual or anticipated integration of Ukraine's neighbours to the west and south into the wider European economy (i.e. with the accession states of 2004, the anticipated accession states of the Balkans and the large neighbour across the Black Sea, Turkey). The model here is described in greater technical detail than in the Brenton & Whalley paper (see in appendix B, which also gives an equation listing for the current version).

The major difference compared with the Brenton & Whalley study, apart from the updated database and an increase in the number of sectors and regions studied, is the extension of the analysis from that of a simple free trade area to examination of deeper integration, under which Ukraine (in common with Norway, Switzerland, Turkey and many other neighbours of the EU) would adopt many of the regulatory and technical standards of the EU in return for winning virtual free movement for many products between Ukraine and the rest of Europe.

The modelling work carried out has been of necessity (given time and data constraints) relatively conservative in nature and this is reflected in the results. Although it indicates that trade reforms and deeper integration can potentially benefit Ukraine, the work we carry out here suggests that the effects of these reforms will have a major impact on the structure of

---

[1] The report by P. Brenton and J. Whalley is entitled *Evaluating a Ukraine–EU Free Trade Agreement using a Numerical General Equilibrium Trade Model*, which was prepared for the European Commission as part of the EES Project UK26, "Study on the Economic Feasibility, General Economic Impact and Implications of a Free Trade Agreement between the European Union and Ukraine", and submitted by CEPS in 1999.

Ukraine's trade, but will have only a limited impact upon welfare, perhaps raising it by up to 10% in the long run (while the impact upon the existing EU economies will be negligible – reflecting Ukraine's relatively small GDP). In other words, Ukraine's poor economic performance is driven by a long list of factors, ranging from institutions, competition levels and corruption through to acquisition of technology, education, infrastructure and investment, which orthodox models do not consider to be greatly affected by trade policy changes.

We consider this to be the 'conservative view' of Ukrainian integration – that it is beneficial, but still relatively marginal in its effect. We also discuss an alternative view of the integration process – that it can potentially reach much more deeply into the development of an economy, with effects upon institutions, competition levels, investment and so on that can extend far beyond the relatively superficial effects investigated in traditional general equilibrium approaches. We therefore follow on to discuss in more detail the kinds of effects integration might conceivably have, and the developments in economic modelling that are slowly beginning to take account of such effects. We might call this a more 'extensive view' of Ukrainian integration.

There is, however, considerable uncertainty about the effects listed in the more extensive view. First, the precise ways in which trade policy affects an economy such as Ukraine, which is still highly distorted by endemic corruption, are not easy to disentangle. Integration may well have beneficial effects in terms of opening up markets to foreign competition, introducing new technology, allowing people to bypass monopoly suppliers or corrupt local financial institutions. Yet, it would be naïve to assume that Ukraine can fully benefit unless the Ukrainians themselves undertake an ongoing internal programme of promoting competition, making institutions more efficient and transparent, investing in infrastructure and the like. Indeed, in the absence of such reforms, trade or financial liberalisation can often throw up unanticipated problems.[2]

---

[2] For example, subsidies and distorted pricing meant that, in many cases in the early post-Soviet days, many transition countries developed exports with negative value added at world prices, such as Poland's notorious export of hothouse flowers. Likewise, liberalisation of external capital flows, while local taxation and financial regulation systems were half-developed, led to large-scale capital flight, often of money from corrupt privatisations fleeing for tax-evasion purposes.

We cannot overemphasise that deeper integration should properly be seen as a package involving domestic policy and institutional reforms, as well as trade reforms. Indeed, it is hard to see how mutual recognition agreements, for instance, can productively be put in place unless and until Ukraine develops the institutions necessary to enforce the harmonised standard elements of the *acquis*. Nevertheless, there are strong reasons to believe that the potential long-term gains from an integration package, so long as it is understood to require such elements of domestic reform, are potentially very strong – probably much greater than the gains from piecemeal reform alone. If this is understood, it should provide Ukraine with the incentive to follow along a similar path to its more successful neighbours to the south and west.

1.   Types of integration

We investigate two main types of integration. The first, which was already discussed in the 1999 report, is a 'simple' free trade area (FTA) between the EU and Ukraine. An FTA is seen as more promising than a customs union because it does not involve harmonising Ukraine's external tariffs with those imposed by the EU. Unlike the EU accession states, Ukraine still trades very heavily with Russia and it would not make sense to impede this trade (for further discussion see the analysis and data in chapter 4 of the main report).

According to our (rather simplified) database, in 2004 Russia accounted for over 40% of Ukraine's imports and 18% of its exports, with imports from Russia being larger than from the then 15 members of the EU, while exports were of comparable size (but declining relatively). This degree of Russian dominance partly reflects proximity and size, but to an even greater extent the legacy of Soviet integration (reflected in technical specifications, existing trade contacts and even the pattern of transport infrastructure). We would expect the relative importance of Russia and the EU to be reversed if Ukraine engages in a long-term process of deeper integration with Europe, but Russian trade will continue to be very important for many years (and that with the rest of the Commonwealth of Independent States (CIS) will continue to be significant). For this reason it would not be sensible to bring Ukraine's external tariffs into line with those imposed by the EU. In practice, the sectors that will be most affected by removal of tariff barriers are meat and dairy products,[3] and food processing, along with light manufactures and metal manufactures (in the case of Ukrainian exports). Much of the projected increase in trade is two-way and trade between Ukraine and the neighbouring EU accession states is expected to gain in particular, with sizeable trade gains coming partly as a result of their accession to the EU, and hence preceding any specific trade deal with Ukraine.

Unlike the previous report, we also consider deeper integration between Ukraine and the EU.[4] In this context, 'deeper integration' is taken as meaning a combination of harmonisation and mutual recognition in the markets for goods and services, along the lines of the agreements with the accession states and with Norway, Switzerland and Turkey to reduce or eliminate those differences in regulations that are deemed to be barriers to trade. In particular, Ukrainian trade with Europe is strongly affected by sanitary and phytosanitary standards (SPS) (agricultural safety and disease-prevention regulations, which effectively block trade in meat and dairy products at present), technical specifications (most Ukrainian goods and services still conform to old Soviet standards), specifications over testing and labelling, etc. Border delays can be serious and subject to corruption. Tackling these barriers to trade requires a pragmatic approach, involving a mixture of harmonised standards and mutual recognition (as has been discussed in other chapters of the report).[5]

There is a considerable difference in economic terms between a tariff barrier and a regulatory barrier. Both may potentially reduce trade and protect local firms. But a tariff raises revenue for the country imposing it.[6]

---

[3] Unfortunately, we cannot specifically and separately model the effects on the meat/dairy sector of removing many of the SPS barriers, due to lack of data.

[4] In practice this means deeper integration with the whole of the European Economic Area (EEA).

[5] On the issue of trade barriers, readers are especially referred to articles by J.E. Anderson and E. van Wincoop, "Trade Costs", *Journal of Economic Literature*, Vol. 42, No. 3, September 2004, along with A.M. Le Jour, R. De Mooij and R. Nahuis, *EU Enlargement: Implications for Countries and Industries,* CPB Netherlands Bureau for Economic Analysis, The Hague, 2001 and K.E. Maskus and J.S. Wilson (eds), *Quantifying the Impact of Technical Barriers to Trade*, Chs. 1 and 2, Ann Arbor, MI: Michigan University Press, 2001.

[6] Voluntary export restraints generally raise 'quota rents' for exporting firms.

By contrast, resources spent on re-labelling, repackaging and retesting products, as well as the time spent waiting at border posts and so forth can be considered as a pure waste in economic terms. Consequently, a regulatory barrier that reduces trade by x% is generally much more expensive to the importing country than a tariff that has the same effect on trade volumes.

Removing regulatory barriers is not a costless process, however. In practice, particularly if adoption of the EU *acquis* were made mandatory, there would be considerable expenditure required by Ukrainian authorities and firms to redesign products, retrain staff, improve labelling procedures, reform laws, etc. Some of these costs would be passed on to Ukrainian consumers. Against this, EU product standards might be assumed to benefit Ukrainian consumers, and in the longer term, the reliability of business in Ukraine and the reputation of Ukrainian firms worldwide might benefit substantially. Unfortunately, assessing these effects requires industry-level casework rather than a more macroeconomic-level, general equilibrium study such as we are able to carry out here.

We hold that deeper integration between the EU and Ukraine can be viewed as a second phase of the integration process, so that it is likely to follow on from the formation of a free trade area. As a result, we only look at deeper integration in conjunction with the prior installation of an FTA (so we could call it 'FTA+').

2. An orthodox general equilibrium assessment of Ukrainian integration

We start by carrying out a general equilibrium model assessment of the two levels of Ukrainian integration with the EU. The model is laid out in detail in appendix B and is a development of that used in the Brenton & Whalley study in 1999. The model is a multi-country model, which attempts to simultaneously simulate the effects of trade policy reforms on trade patterns, production and consumption in a number of industries and a variety of regions. The word 'simultaneously' is what distinguishes a general equilibrium model, such as we are using, from simpler, partial equilibrium studies that look only at one industry and one country.

We look at a wider range of regions and sectors than the original Brenton & Whalley (1999) study. As shown in Table A4.1, six regions in total are considered:

Table A4.1 Regions

No.	New code	Region description
1	UKR	Ukraine
2	EU	European Union – 15 member states
3	CEECs	2004 Eastern European accession states
4	SEECs	South-eastern European countries + Turkey
5	RUS	Russia
6	ROW	Rest of the world

Source: Authors' compilation.

As shown in Table A4.2, we use an eight-sector breakdown of the economy, in order to separately examine a number of sectors seen as particularly sensitive:

Table A4.2 Sectors

No.	New code	Sector description
1	Food crops and animal prod.	Crops and animal prod.
2	Minerals	Minerals
3	Food prod.	Food prod.
4	Light manufacturing	Light manufacturing
5	Heavy manufacturing	Heavy manufacturing
6	Textiles	Textiles
7	Metals	Metals
8	Services	Services and activities NES

Source: Authors' compilation.

We had originally intended to split food crops and animal products, but these turned out to be hard to separate in the Ukrainian national data that was available.

Construction of the database

Detailed economic data on Ukraine has long been scarce, although the situation is slowly improving. Construction of a database has therefore been an important aspect of this study.[7]

---

[7] Thanks are due in particular to Ece Turgay-Brett at the University of Loughborough, who has carried out a great deal of data work for this project.

Since we are using a multi-country model, it was sensible to use as a starting point the GTAP (Global Trade Analysis Project) database, which integrates data on trade, protection, output and consumption by industry for a large number of countries/regions and industrial sectors across the world. Further, it comes with an easy aggregation package. The main drawback, however, is that there is, as yet, no specific 'Ukraine' region in the GTAP database, because much of the data is not available, so we needed to merge the GTAP dataset with information from a variety of other sources.

First, we obtained from our Ukrainian colleagues an input-output dataset (on a more detailed aggregation than GTAP, but one that suited our purposes except those regarding agriculture), for a corresponding year (2001). In addition, we found trade data from two main sources: the extremely disaggregated PC-TAS trade database (for a number of years), and also some more aggregate data on trade volumes and protection that were kindly supplied by Dean De Rosa of ADR Consultants.[8]

As the discussion in chapter 4 makes clear, Ukrainian trade has seen an extremely rapid expansion since 2001 (in both directions). For this reason, we have factored up Ukraine's imports and exports to bring them into line with 2003 levels. The rest of the model essentially still uses our 2001 database.

Data on protection

While tariff rates are published, these are generally at a more disaggregated level than those we are using for our model. Obtaining the average tariff for trade in a particular broad sector between a pair of regions in a multi-country model therefore involves a lot of weighting by sub-sector and by sub-regions. For this reason, we have used GTAP's 2001 tariff data (for goods from the CIS excluding Russia) for tariffs on Ukrainian exports, while Ukraine's import tariffs have been put together from a combination of GTAP and Dean De Rosa's more disaggregated database (Table A4.3(a)-(b)).

---

[8] Dean De Rosa has recently been compiling Ukrainian trade data as part of a general trade study on the Balkans region).

Table A4.3(a) Ukrainian tariffs (%)

	G1	G2	G3	G4	G5	G6	G7	G8
From	**Agric.**	**Minerals**	**Food prod.**	**Light manuf.**	**Heavy manuf.**	**Textiles**	**Metals**	**Services**
UKR	0.00	0.00	0.00	0.00	0.00	0.00	0.00	0.00
EU-15	10.65	1.33	19.56	15.02	5.69	6.43	6.70	0.00
CEECs	7.20	0.42	18.83	16.52	7.05	9.83	6.45	2.92
SEECs	11.48	1.72	17.70	12.06	7.39	12.95	5.34	0.00
RUS	1.88	0.01	6.09	1.71	1.45	1.26	1.29	0.03
ROW	8.12	0.66	12.86	12.37	3.99	13.66	5.21	0.00
OCIS	7.69	0.05	12.47	11.89	4.20	8.89	3.30	0.07

Note: OCIS refers to other CIS, excluding Russia.

Source: Revised from GTAP (2001).

Table A4.3(b) Tariffs on Ukraine compared with other CIS members (%)

		UKR	EU-15	CEECs	SEECs	RUS	ROW	OCIS
G1	Agriculture	–	0.54	2.06	9.48	0.06	13.56	9.02
G2	Minerals	–	0.00	0.54	0.87	0.00	7.60	0.10
G3	Food prod.	–	14.08	18.07	23.73	0.00	32.45	13.01
G4	Lt manuf.	–	0.54	6.46	2.07	0.00	7.49	8.66
G5	Hvy manuf.	–	0.51	7.88	4.47	0.06	5.90	4.25
G6	Textiles	–	7.47	13.19	7.27	0.21	11.22	10.83
G7	Metals	–	1.20	8.33	7.62	0.01	5.41	45.56
G8	Services	–	0.00	4.83	0.00	0.00	0.00	0.07

Note: OCIS excludes Russia.

Source: GTAP (2001).

Modelling the quota on iron and steel exports from Ukraine to the EU is also a tricky issue. Our understanding is that the way the quota is imposed will almost certainly generate quota rents for the major steel companies and their owners. Liberalisation will lead to a large expansion of Ukrainian exports, but this is likely to be at the expense of the steel companies' profits. The quota rents (which disappear after liberalisation) are assumed to be equivalent to the revenue of a 100% tariff on Ukrainian steel exports, but the tariff revenue is spent by the Ukrainian oligarchs in Europe (not Ukraine), although it is (perhaps questionably) counted towards Ukrainian welfare in our model.

The effects of the integration of product standards associated with the EU Single Market are central to understanding the likely effects of deeper integration. In common with other recent studies,[9] we infer the effects of the Single Market by analysing observed trading patterns using a gravity framework. This is a well-used method for examining the effects of national borders and regional groupings on trade patterns. Again, as a base, we use the 2001 GTAP database on trade flows for all of our sectors, based upon a 39-region breakdown of the world. The model assumes that trade between a pair of countries in a particular sector (say, food processing) is likely to be greater :

1)   the larger is the importing country's market for food products;

2)   the larger production is in the exporting country; and

3)   the closer together are the two countries.

In addition, trade will usually be greater if the two countries belong to the same trade bloc and this is the effect in which we are most interested. We measure this latter effect by a series of dummy variables,[10] for when both countries are members of the EU, when both countries are accession states (CEEC or SEEC) or when one country is in the EU and the other is an accession state, or when one country is an EU member or an accession state and the other is totally outside the bloc.

The tables in appendix A summarise our gravity regressions. In Tables A4.4(a)-(b) below we show the projected long-term effects on trade volumes among various groups of countries, first when the Central and Eastern European and the south-eastern European accession states join the EU and second when a non-EU country achieves deeper integration with Europe.

---

[9] See Le Jour, De Mooij & Nahuis (2001), op. cit. and T. Huw Edwards, *Implicit Trade Costs and European Single Market Enlargement*, Working Paper ERP 05-04, Department of Economics, Loughborough University, 2005(b).

[10] These are indicators included in a regression that take the value of 1 in some instances and 0 in the others. For example, the dummy variable 'EUEU' takes the value 1 when both importing and exporting countries are EU members, and 0 otherwise.

Table A4.4(a) Long-term effects when all accession states join the EU on their trade with key sectors (%)

	Food crops	Meat/ dairy	Minerals	Food processing	Light manuf.	Heavy manuf.	Textiles
EU	156.6	142.9	71.1	187.1	-4.3	28.7	25.7
Accession states	272.7	179.6	180.5	187.4	-11.4	35.9	121.9
Other	58.5	42.7	74.4	146.0	97.7	93.5	123.9

Source: Authors' calculations.

Table A4.4(b) Long-term effects when a non-EU country achieves Single Market entry on its trade with key sectors (%)

	Food crops	Meat/ dairy	Minerals	Food processing	Light manuf.	Heavy manuf.	Textiles
EU	217.7	276.8	113.4	122.8	22.8	6.1	158.6
Accession states	403.4	437.6	272.1	447.9	142.7	105.3	478.9

Source: Authors' calculations.

Interestingly, Table A4.4(a) shows that accession of the CEECs and SEECs to the EU would be expected to make them more, rather than less, open to trade with third countries such as Ukraine. As Ukraine already trades significantly with these regions (being a close neighbour) this prospect is likely to promote Ukraine's trade in both directions with these regions.

Stages of market integration

We start with simulations based upon our baseline (2001 but with Ukrainian trade volumes uplifted). Three rounds of simulations are carried out from this baseline:

Round 1. CEECs' accession to the EU; the SEECs and Turkey also are assumed to join both the EU customs union and the Single Market.

Round 2. Following the changes in round 1, the EU (and CEEC and SEEC/Turkey regions) forms a free trade area with Ukraine. Tariffs between these blocs are eliminated, as is the steel quota (which may in fact be removed earlier than this).

Round 3. Following the first two rounds, Ukraine also enters into deeper integration in the form of harmonisation/mutual recognition agreements with the EU. Owing to the absence of other data, the assumed amount by which deep integration reduces the costs of trading between the EU and CEEC/SEEC regions and Ukraine is derived from our estimated gravity model coefficients.[11]

We consider two model variants: short term and long term. The former is close to that used in the study by Brenton & Whalley (1999), while the latter assumes that there is much more flexibility for both production and consumer behaviour to change in response to price changes. Table A4.5 shows the numerical values assumed for the key elasticities.

Table A4.5. Numerical values for elasticities

Assumed elasticities	Short term	Long term
Transformation in production	2.0	4.0
Substitution between goods classes (top level)	1.25	1.25
Substitution between countries in trade (lower level)	2.0	4.0

Source: Authors' calculations.

Summary of results

Accession of the CEECs and SEECs to the EU (or at least in some SEEC cases to the customs union and Single Market) is expected to be beneficial to Ukraine. This result stems from our gravity model simulations, which indicate that once account is taken of differences in country size and distances, the CEECs and SEECs were less open to trade with third-party countries, such as Ukraine, than were the EU-15 countries. Provisionally, this enlargement could, in the long run, double trade between the accession countries and Ukraine, with Ukraine's textile and food processing industries benefiting directly and services also prospering as a result of rising Ukrainian incomes (see Tables A4.6(a)–(d)).

---

[11] Another assumption is that the gravity model estimated for 2001 reflects the 'long-term' adjustment of trade to existing (2001) trade blocs.

Table A4.6(a) Results of Single Market accession by CEECs/SEECs – Scenario 1, welfare effects (%)

Effects upon welfare	Short term	Long term
Ukraine	1.91	3.05
EU-15	0.11	0.17
CEECs (2004 accession)	2.09	2.60
SEECs (Balkans + Turkey)	2.08	2.43
Russia	0.94	1.12
Rest of the world	0.05	0.08

Table A4.6(b) Scenario 1, output effects (%)

Effects upon Ukrainian output	Short run	Long run
Agriculture	-0.77	-4.42
Minerals	-3.41	-8.56
Food processing	1.05	2.73
Light manuf.	-4.86	-11.15
Heavy manuf.	-1.33	3.56
Textiles	4.48	8.34
Metals	-4.46	-17.78
Services	5.52	8.38

Table A4.6(c) Scenario 1, changes in exports (%)

Change in Ukrainian exports by destination	Short term	Long term
EU-15	-0.02	-11.72
CEECs	2.39	101.64
SEECs	3.11	82.48
Russia	-4.41	-13.70
Rest of World	0.42	-12.50

Table A4.6(d) Scenario 1, changes in imports (%)

Change in Ukrainian imports by destination	Short term	Long term
EU-15	-4.77	-11.72
CEECs	26.13	101.64
SEECs	16.99	82.48
Russia	-5.15	-13.70
Rest of World	-4.65	-12.50

Source: Authors' calculations.

Although tariff and quota liberalisation between the EU and Ukraine would be expected to lead to significant further increases in trade (on top of those from the accession of the CEECs/SEECs), particularly in metals exports to the pre-2004 EU countries, overall welfare effects (once quota rents are removed) are small or even slightly negative. Food processing is a sector that gains significantly from the tariff liberalisation[12] (see Tables A4.7(a)–(d)).

Table A4.7(a) Results of a Ukraine/EU/CEECs/SEECs free trade area – Scenario 2, welfare effects (%)

Effects upon welfare	Compared with base		Compared with CEEC/SEEC accession	
	Short term	Long term	Short term	Long term
Ukraine	1.91	2.99	0.00	-0.06
EU-15	0.11	0.17	0.00	0.01
CEECs (2004 accession)	2.10	2.68	0.01	0.08
SEECs (Balkans +Turkey)	2.08	2.42	-0.01	-0.01
Russia	0.94	1.12	0.00	0.00
Rest of the world	0.05	0.08	0.00	0.00

Table A4.7(b) Scenario 2, effects on output by industry (%)

Effects upon Ukrainian output by industry	Compared with base		Compared with CEEC/SEEC accession	
	Short term	Long term	Short term	Long term
Agriculture	-2.34	-8.61	-1.58	-4.38
Minerals	-2.17	-7.31	1.29	1.37
Food processing	13.07	34.03	11.90	30.47
Light manuf.	6.23	14.63	11.65	29.01
Heavy manuf.	2.58	13.93	3.96	10.02
Textiles	9.92	22.39	5.21	12.97
Metals	6.38	54.12	11.34	87.45
Services	6.81	10.33	1.23	1.79

---

[12] The decline in food processing in this scenario may be a reflection of the limitation of our model, which does not have intermediate inputs. In practice, growing food-processing exports should lead to increasing demand for Ukrainian agricultural products.

Table A4.7(c) Scenario 2, changes in exports and imports (%)

Effects upon Ukrainian exports and imports by destination/source				
	Compared with base		Compared with CEEC/SEEC accession	
	Short term	Long term	Short term	Long term
EU-15	19.75	63.67	19.78	85.39
CEECs	26.79	147.07	23.83	22.53
SEECs	25.66	123.48	21.87	22.47
Russia	-4.24	-10.51	0.18	3.69
Rest of World	0.65	-0.21	0.22	14.04

Table A4.7(d) Scenario 2, changes in imports (%)

Change in Ukrainian imports by destination				
EU-15	0.86	-1.69	5.91	11.35
CEECs	36.96	133.78	8.59	15.94
SEECs	26.72	110.79	8.31	15.52
Russia	-9.65	-22.99	-4.75	-10.76
Rest of World	-7.50	-18.37	-2.99	-6.71

Source: Authors' calculations.

Provisionally, our modelling work suggests that deeper integration is likely to have similar-sized effects again upon trade volumes compared with tariff liberalisation, but this time bringing significant gains to Ukrainian welfare (see Tables A4.8(a)–(d)). Particular industries that would gain are food processing, metals and light manufacturing, but heavy manufacturing and textiles also gain, as do services (benefiting from rising incomes in Ukraine).

Overall, the Brenton–Whalley model structure provides a cautious assessment of the likely effects of reforms: it is clear that an FTA agreement is likely to be broadly neutral economically, while a deeper integration agreement produces significant potential benefits. On the assumptions of this model, it is very unlikely that a Ukrainian trade agreement would have any great impact upon any industry in the EU-15 member states, while there would be some small gains to Ukraine's near neighbours in Eastern Europe.

Table A4.8(a) Ukraine's deeper integration – Scenario 3, welfare effects (%)

Effects upon welfare	Compared with base		Compared with an FTA	
	Short term	Long term	Short term	Long term
Ukraine	6.50	9.86	4.50	6.67
EU-15	0.12	0.19	0.01	0.02
CEECs (2004 accession)	2.14	2.81	0.04	0.13
SEECs (Balkans +Turkey)	2.10	2.46	0.02	0.03
Russia	0.94	1.12	0.00	0.00
Rest of the world	0.05	0.08	0.00	0.00

Table A4.8(b) Scenario 3, effects on output by industry (%)

Effects upon Ukrainian output by industry				
	Compared with base		Compared with an FTA	
	Short term	Long run	Short term	Long term
Agriculture	-5.91	-22.58	-3.66	-15.29
Minerals	-29.90	-47.55	-28.35	-43.41
Food processing	22.18	55.23	8.06	15.81
Light manuf.	12.52	38.29	5.92	20.64
Heavy manuf.	10.27	28.95	7.50	13.18
Textiles	20.28	34.24	9.42	9.68
Metals	3.92	93.13	-2.31	25.31
Services	7.51	17.07	0.65	6.12

Table A4.8(c) Scenario 3, changes in exports and imports (%)

Effects upon Ukrainian exports and imports by destination/source				
	Compared with base		Compared with an FTA	
	Short term	Long term	Short term	Long term
EU-15	38.63	158.58	15.76	57.99
CEECs	41.78	239.03	11.82	37.22
SEECs	34.06	201.40	6.68	34.86
Russia	-14.46	-24.34	-10.67	-15.46
Rest of World	-7.37	-11.69	-7.97	-11.50

Table A4.8(d) Scenario 3, changes in imports (%)

Change in Ukrainian imports by destination				
EU-15	19.27	50.97	18.26	53.57
CEECs	55.44	204.67	13.49	30.32
SEECs	31.25	171.49	3.58	28.79
Russia	-9.46	-28.35	0.21	-6.97
Rest of World	-9.28	-29.45	-1.92	-13.57

Source: Authors' calculations.

Detailed effects on trade by industry

The detailed effects (along with the revised gravity model results for EU border dummies) are shown in the tables in appendix A. Key results to note are discussed below.

i) Trade between Ukraine and the EU-15

The CEEC/SEEC accessions marginally reduce trade between Ukraine and the EU-15 in both directions in most sectors.

The effects of scrapping tariffs (and the steel quota) are dominated by a huge percentage increase in Ukrainian metals. Ukraine's exports of light manufactures also benefit significantly.

Deeper integration has a very big impact on services trade in both directions, while agricultural and mineral exports from Ukraine to the EU-15 also gain significantly.

ii) Trade between Ukraine and the CEEC accession states

Trade in both directions rises sharply when the accession of the CEECs to the EU is incorporated. Particularly significant are the rises in metals and agricultural products, in both of which the CEECs have a significant initial trade surplus with Ukraine.

Steel liberalisation leads to a huge proportional increase in Ukraine's exports from a low base. Other tariff liberalisation with Ukraine boosts Ukrainian exports of agriculture, although the smaller percentage rise of trade in the other direction may well be larger in monetary terms, since it is from a larger base. The rise in Ukraine's food product exports is significant.

The deeper integration of Ukraine leads to sizeable increases in trade in both directions in agriculture, food processing, minerals and metals trade.

iii) Trade between Ukraine and the SEECs

The SEECs are a fairly minor market for Ukraine's exports, but themselves export around $1.5 billion a year to Ukraine, notably in heavy manufacturing, metals and minerals.

SEEC accession leads to sizeable increases in trade in both directions in most industries, except services, which declines. Services trade only rises sharply in the final scenario, where Ukraine has deeper integration.

With tariff reform, again the most notable effect is the large increase in Ukrainian metals exports.

3.   Scope for analysis of more 'extensive' economic impacts

As was indicated earlier, there are considerable reasons to believe that an integration programme, if seriously carried out and tied in with concomitant domestic institutional reforms (and perhaps with appropriate infrastructure and technical support from EU member states), could have a far greater impact upon the Ukrainian economy than indicated in the previous section. This conclusion is essentially the line taken by several recent trade integration studies of the 2004 EU accession (notably the work by Baldwin, Francois & Portes on European enlargement in 1997 and a more recent study by Edwards in 2005).[13]

In making this kind of assessment, it is worth starting by listing potential reasons why Ukraine's economy in the 1990s was almost the poorest in Europe, with GDP per head perhaps 10% of the EU average. A relatively autarkic and distorted trade structure (heavily weighted towards trade with Russia, Belarus and Kazakhstan at the time of independence) is only one of a whole list of factors. The list further includes:

- poor financial controls, subsidies and soft budgets (being reformed, but more slowly than in the EU accession states or even Russia);

- highly concentrated industrial production, with little competition either at home or from abroad;

- rampant corruption, aided by weak institutions and a lack of transparency, as well as privatisations and capital outflows for the sake of tax evasion;

- a dearth of new investment;

- poor technical standards and specifications along with a lack of quality control;

- widespread adoption of old-fashioned technology (e.g. wasteful open-hearth steel mills);

- poor transport and communications infrastructure; and

- a poor image for Ukrainian firms trading abroad.

---

[13] See R.E. Baldwin, J.F. Francois and R. Portes, "EU enlargement: Small costs for the West, big gains for the East", *Economic Policy*, April 1997, pp. 127-76 (along with the subsequent comments by D. Rodrik) and Edwards (2005(b)), op. cit.

Against this should be listed a reasonably skilled population, ample coal resources and a large endowment of fertile agricultural land.

Many of these negative factors interact with one another in a way that might be deemed 'cumulative causation'. For example, corruption may deter investment in new firms. Yet investment in new firms may bring in newer technology (particularly where they are Western joint ventures or subsidiaries). It also increases competition, which, ironically, would help reduce corruption. And by yielding tax revenues to the state, it could help fund infrastructure improvements, which might again draw in more investment.

If one views Ukraine's problems as essentially those of cumulative causation in this sense, then the potential of the linkages of trade and other integration policies with these other factors begin to grow much more significant. One could perhaps draw on the more encouraging experiences of the recent EU accession states (or indeed of Spain and Portugal beforehand) in emphasising this.

The possible linkages being discussed here and their effects increasingly being taken into account in newer generations of general and partial equilibrium models. They are also, however, more speculative, which needs to be borne in mind.

Perhaps a good way of considering these effects is that traditional general equilibrium models were initially designed to explain the impact of marginal trade policies in economies that are large, dynamic, relatively uncorrupted and open, and which possess efficient technology, management techniques and government ethos. There is thus little reason in such circumstances to expect that exposure to increased foreign competition would profoundly affect the economy, other than leading to some improvement in resource allocation at the margin. This is not the case with developing or transition economies, which is why we need to take particular account of the factors below.

Linkages between trade and competition

Trade is often seen as having a 'pro-competitive' effect upon an economy, especially where it is small and relatively closed to start with. This effect is particularly examined by 'new trade theorists' (such as Paul Krugman,

Anthony Venables or Richard Baldwin),[14] who have developed imperfectly competitive models of trade based upon a 'love of variety' model of consumer choice.[15] Liberalising access to trade improves consumer welfare through a number of avenues, most notably:

a)   an increased variety of e available consumer goods. When trade barriers are high, people in many smaller and poorer countries will only have access to very few varieties of cheese, shoes, types of fruit, etc. (This of course does not apply to the rich). Lowering trade barriers increases the variety available to consumers;

b)   reduced monopoly profits. Where a country is relatively small and dominated by a handful of local firms, these would be expected to charge high prices and provide poor service. Standard models of imperfect competition suggest that, as importing firms move into sheltered industries and take market share from the local firms, the latter will be driven to reduce prices and improve quality and service; and

c)   a clearout of surplus capacity. In many industries, firms need to operate on a fairly large scale in order to achieve low costs. When the economy is small and sheltered, although there are few local firms, these are still too small to gain economies of scale. Trade competition may lead to a reduction in the number of these firms, but those that remain are likely to be larger.

Links between trade and input costs

For similar reasons to those explained above, trade liberalisation can lead firms to gain better access to a better choice of input suppliers. This should in turn enable them to find better spare parts and support services at a lower cost than previously. Special emphasis needs to be put on liberalisation of the financial services and telecoms sectors, which should greatly facilitate the development of new businesses and improve the

---

[14] Baldwin & Venables' 1995 article on regional economic integration is probably the best summary of this type of analysis – see R.E. Baldwin and A.J. Venables, "Regional Economic Integration" in G.M. Grossman and K. Rogoff (eds), *Handbook of International Economics*, Vol. 3, Amsterdam: Elsevier, pp. 1597-644, 1995.

[15] General equilibrium applications of this type of approach to issues of European integration include Baldwin, Francois & Portes (1997), op. cit. and Edwards (2005b), op. cit.

efficiency of existing ones. All of these changes should feed through to greater efficiency and competitiveness in a wide range of industries.

Capital market effects

At present, even though Ukraine is a relatively poor country and desperately in need of updating its capital stock in many areas (notably in its transport and communications infrastructures), it is suffering a huge outflow of capital.[16] Trade and financial services liberalisation could help reduce this by:

a)   making Ukraine more competitive as a producer, so encouraging inward investment;

b)   reducing the cost or improving the quality of capital goods – many of which have to be imported, at least if Ukrainian firms want to equip themselves with efficient technology;

c)   reducing profit margins and increasing efficiency in financial services;[17] and

d)   cutting the risk premium on investment in Ukraine.[18]

Some very rough simulations indicate that these capital market effects might be expected to benefit Ukrainian GDP in the long run by around 10%. The welfare gain would be smaller, but still around 5% of GDP. (See Box A4.1.)

---

[16] Ukraine is currently running a trade surplus of around 10% of GDP. While newsreaders often see a surplus as a good thing, in Ukraine's case it actually corresponds to a large ongoing outflow of financial capital, at a time when local industry might well benefit from investment.

[17] Some very provisional results from data envelopment analysis (DEA) studies of bank efficiency across a range of post-Soviet economies shows that Ukrainian banks have improved their ranking considerably since about 2000, although from a very poor initial base. This trend may partly reflect the effects of the general economic pick-up following the initial Yushenko reforms. Nevertheless, we caution that the crude figures may still be putting considerable gloss on a sector where corruption and oligarch domination are still central features.

[18] This was an important feature of the study by Baldwin, Francois and Portes (1997, op. cit.) of EU enlargement, where their more optimistic scenario assumed removal of a 10% risk premium on capital.

Box A4.1 Some simulations with variable capital stock

In order to appraise the effects of varying the capital stock, it is necessary to make some assumptions about the substitutability between capital and labour making up value added in the Ukrainian economy. It is usually assumed that technological elasticities of substitution between capital and labour within an industry are well below unity; however, the ability to switch between capital and labour-intensive industries may raise the overall elasticity of substitution in GDP. Against this, our simulations suggest that changes in the composition of industrial output in Ukraine are likely to be small. We therefore assume value added is a constant elasticity of substitution (CES) aggregate of capital and labour, with a substitution elasticity in our low elasticity case of 0.5 and in our high elasticity case of 0.9. As regards the composition of GDP, the initial breakdown available is:

Table 1. GDP breakdown

	UAH billions
GDP	204,190
O/W taxes	30,720
(Less) Subsidies	-3,456
Employees compensation	86,440
Capital cost	44,616
Supranormal profit	45,869

Supranormal profit has been derived by assuming a 35% monopolistic mark-up on costs.

It is estimated that real marginal production costs consist of employees' compensation plus capital cost, and are split as 66% labour cost and 34% capital cost. This is the data used to calibrate an initial CES production function. It is assumed that deeper integration of Ukraine into the wider European economy will reduce capital costs in three ways:

- First, the cost of capital goods will be reduced by cheaper imports. As a rough guide to this, the price of utility (in our general equilibrium (GE) model runs) is divided by the average production price of goods and services. This suggests the capital goods price (compared with average output prices for Ukrainian industry) could fall by 2.6% in our low elasticity case or 3% in our high elasticity case.

- Second, re-branding Ukraine as a more reliable place in which to do business will reduce risk premia for investors. We assume, rather conservatively, that this reduces the cost of capital (measured as the annual rental cost) by 10%.

- Finally, we also assume that increased competition in the banking sector reduces the cost of capital by 5%.

Taking these three changes together, capital is assumed to fall in price by 16.7% in the low elasticity case or 17.1% in the high elasticity case.

Cheaper capital affects welfare via a complex route. First, the stock of capital employed will rise by 14.4% in our low elasticity case or 28.8% in our high elasticity case. GDP will rise, by between 4.5% (low elasticity case) and 8.8% (high elasticity case), compared with the estimates produced by our basic GE model with fixed capital. This will raise wages in Ukraine by between 8.9 and 9.7%.

As shown above, however, assuming the extra capital is in the form of foreign direct investment, there will be an offsetting outflow of interest, profits and dividends. Still, a cheaper cost of capital goods means lower costs for existing Ukrainian firms, while a lowered risk premium also makes life less risky for them (reducing the welfare cost of uncertainty). Yet lower profit margins in finance, however, are assumed to mean lower profits for Ukrainian banks.

The net effects of all these factors are that welfare rises by between 4.5% (low elasticity case) and 4.8% (high elasticity case), in addition to the trade gains identified in our GE model.

Effects upon corruption and waste

A growing body of economic literature[19] explains corruption, at least partly, not just in terms of local institutions and traditions, but in terms of 'rent-seeking'. In other words, particularly in a society with relatively undeveloped policing and legal institutions, bribery, intimidation, theft and the squandering of resources in criminal enterprises will be greater the larger are the potential gains from such activities. These gains are closely linked to either the rental income from property, such as oilfields or gold mines where property rights are insecure or subject to official allocation, or to the profits of local or national monopolies.

- In the case of Ukraine, a culture has developed where oligarchs, with close links to politicians (at least pre-2004) have inherited most of the large companies dominating both export and home markets. Entry of new competitors is difficult owing to corruption and intimidation and the oligarchs' domination of the financial services sector.

---

[19] See for example, C. Perroni and J. Whalley, "Rents and the Cost and Optimal Design of Commodity Taxes", *Review of Economics and Statistics*, Vol. 1, No. 3, pp. 357-64, 1998.

- The steel quota rent is a classic case of a monopolistic income that benefits oligarchs.

- Increased competition in many goods industries should lower profit margins, meaning that the potential gains from deterring or obstructing competitors by illegal or semi-legal means are reduced.

- Reform of the financial services sector and the entry of foreign banks should greatly help the start-up of new businesses, which could transform the climate of many industries.

- Some theoretical work[20] indicates economies subject to corruption can experience multiple equilibria (so that small changes in economic parameters can, under some circumstances, lead to a sea change from being poor and corrupt to being prosperous and less corrupt).

- The weakening of oligopolistic powers over resources will relieve the constraints on entrepreneurial investment by credit-constrained individuals; and the shifting of political power towards the entrepreneurial elite will result in economic policy and institutions which are more conducive to entrepreneurship and productivity progress.[21]

Firm selection effects

Most standard economic models assume all firms are equally efficient. This is clearly unrealistic. In practice, there are good and bad firms, and within a firm there may be good or bad divisions or plants.

- Increased competition from imports is likely to lead to a clear-out of the least efficient plants and firms in many industries, raising average productivity.[22]

- In general, only the larger and more efficient firms can profitably enter export markets.[23] Under many circumstances, trade

---

[20] See M. Kelly, *Developing Rotten Institutions*, Discussion Paper No. 5281, CEPR, London, 2005.

[21] See J. Falkinger and V. Grossman, *Distribution of Natural Resources, Entrepreneurship and Economic Development: Growth Dynamics with Two Elites*, Working Paper No. 1562, CESifo, Munich, October, 2005.

[22] See the forthcoming paper by T. Huw Edwards, "Who Gains from Restructuring the Post-Soviet Transition Economies, and Why?", *International Review of Applied Economics*, 2006.

liberalisation, which leads to the faster growth of export industries, will particularly benefit these firms, raising average productivity across the economy. This effect is sometimes seen as having helped lead to the very impressive post-war growth in the productivity of Japanese and Korean exporting firms.

- The more easily new firms can enter the market, particularly in export industries, the bigger these gains will be. The reason is that if plenty of new firms are entering the market, the most efficient ones will be the likeliest to survive, while the least successful will close. Again, financial services liberalisation and institutional reforms could have big effects upon this.

Outsourcing and the inflow of technology

Much trade these days, especially the rapidly growing trade in East and South East Asia, is driven by outsourcing by Western firms. Effectively this involves establishing an ongoing business relationship (often involving a takeover or a joint venture) that enables the Western multinational to invest in bringing in its more advanced technology, product brands and business techniques to the local firm. Although outsourcing is often stimulated by cheaper local labour costs, low wages alone do not drive this sort of investment. The major reason is that outsourcing relationships can be very risky, since the Western company is investing in a new country with a new legal and administrative environment, a different business culture and an often unreliable infrastructure and local suppliers.

- Greater trade openness (which allows the Western firm to use its customary foreign suppliers), along with finance, utilities and infrastructure reforms (which enable its local partner to carry out business more efficiently), are essential in driving outsourcing.

- Bringing Ukraine's business regulations and quality standards into line with the rest of Europe should greatly enhance its attractiveness.

- Investments in transport infrastructure are also likely to prove essential.

---

[23] See A.B. Bernard, S. Redding and P.K. Schott, *Comparative Advantage and Heterogeneous Firms*, Paper presented at the Conference on Globalisation and Firm Level Adjustment, held at the GEP Centre, Nottingham, June 2005.

Networking effects

Because overseas firms face a risk when they enter a new market, they will tend to place a great premium upon markets that are, to some degree, familiar. Their decisions may reflect historical patterns of trade or local ethnic ties (for example, China's economic boom is largely being driven by businesses developed by the Chinese diaspora across South East Asia, who in turn developed links with the West far ahead of firms in the People's Republic). But once pioneering firms have entered a market and shown themselves to be successful, others will more easily follow. The key thing, therefore, is to establish and nurture the initial, pioneering ties.[24] Whether Ukraine can attract new investors across a range of industries (other than, perhaps, in agriculture or metals manufacture) is a difficult issue – probably the best initial prospects would be in food processing, provided Ukraine could overcome the formidable problems of removing the SPS barriers on trade with Western Europe.

When firm-to-firm economic relationships and trust are important – as in many aspects of industry – the formation of reliable ties can be seen as a form of capital formation, requiring the 'investment' of experimentation with new partners. In a well-functioning economy, firms are able to develop wider networks of ties, whereas in poorly functioning economies, where institutions and trust are weak, close insider relationships among small groups of people or firms may dominate. This latter case is relevant to Ukraine, because the Soviet break-up meant the destruction of many previous economic ties. Under some circumstances (which seem to have dominated in Poland, Hungary and the other EU accession states), after an initial disruption the process of re-establishing wide-ranging economic relationships, both at home and with the West, seems to have gone on apace, as some theorists have indicated that it should.[25] In the CIS states, however, something quite different has happened – the post-Soviet chaos seems to have led to the domination of some of the former Soviet economies (those further from the EU, notably Russia, Ukraine and Central Asia) by small, corrupt networks of insiders – the oligarchs – who can

---

[24] See for example, T. Huw Edwards, "Import Search and the Path-Dependency of Trade", Mimeo, Loughborough University, 2005(a).

[25] See for example, P. Frijters, D.J. Bezemer and U. Dulleck, *Contacts, Social Capital and Market Institutions – A Theory of Development*, Working Paper, University of Vienna, 2003.

obstruct reform and block the entry of new players. The theory for understanding and modelling this process, or of how and under what circumstances institutional and trade reforms can help switch an economy from a corrupt one with poorly-developed networks dominated by insiders to a thriving one with widespread economic ties is still in its infancy.

'Re-branding' Ukraine

At present, 'made in Ukraine' is probably a sign of substantial negative value, for both potential customers and potential business partners abroad. By contrast, 'made in the EU' is usually a strong positive sign. It may well be that the best hope Ukrainian producers have of initially breaking into many Western markets is under the brands of existing Western firms, who outsource their production to Ukraine. Yet even attracting the outsourcers may not be easy, since they too will be deterred by Ukraine's reputation.

- The ultimate prize for Ukraine would be for local Ukrainian firms to be treated with a high degree of trust by foreign consumers and business partners. This potential benefit is probably the biggest, yet the most intangible one of deeper integration of Ukraine. The intermediate prize would be for in-the-know Western outsourcing firms to be prepared to lend their brand names to goods produced in Ukraine. Even getting to this stage would require considerable improvements to Ukraine's business image. This goal requires reform across a whole range of institutional areas, as well as in trade and competition policy, regulation and the product rules associated with deeper integration.

- For Ukraine to reach the stage of achieving mutual recognition with the EU across a wide range of goods and services would probably be the most significant step in re-branding Ukraine as part of 'virtual Europe'.

- From the EU's perspective, the benefits from re-branding Ukraine are mainly political. There has to be some caution, in the sense that the EU cannot be seen to bestow the brand of 'virtual Europe' upon countries that fall far short of EU legal and business standards – for fear of tarnishing the image of European businesses in general.

4. Deeper integration of Ukraine and institutional reforms

As summarised earlier in chapter 4, 'top-down' empirical estimates of the role of improvements in institutional quality (as discussed in the 1999 work by Daniel Piazolo)[26] indicate that an improvement of one-third in institutional quality would have a static effect of perhaps 10% on Ukrainian GDP, with ongoing effects linked to capital formation (including network and social capital formation) leading to eventual gains of 20 to 30%. It may even (looking now at studies based upon an 'endogenous growth' formulation) have an ongoing increase in the growth rate, that would cumulate over the years beyond this.

These estimates are clearly much larger than the orthodox general estimates of the effects of trade policy reforms (even when the reforms involve deeper integration), as was summarised above. There is a strong overlap, however, between the wider-ranging economic effects of integration, as outlined in the subsequent bullish assessment (and which are only now being incorporated into general equilibrium-type models) and those picked up empirically by studies such as Piazolo's. For example, capital accumulation effects could add 5 to 10 percentage points to Ukraine's national income (as indicated above), while if increased competition reduced the scope and incentives for corruption, the gains could be similar in magnitude.

Yet there are further effects that are perhaps not being captured. Some are related to institutional reforms in areas that do not relate so directly to trade.[27] Some may be more closely driven by capital infrastructure investment,[28] while some may reflect political openness. Again, some of the key aspects of economic development – we have already mentioned networks and social capital in the context of trade – are still very difficult to model.

---

[26] See D. Piazolo, *The integration process between Eastern and Western Europe*, Kieler Studien No. 310, Berlin: Springer-Verlag, 1999.

[27] Although, as deeper integration is increasingly seen as incorporating reform in services sectors, its effects upon regulation will be wide-ranging, particularly if integration is interpreted as requiring not merely the institution of regulations, but the creation and maintenance of the institutions required to police them.

[28] Such investment should, nevertheless, be seen as an essential element of deeper integration since a sound capital infrastructure – roads, railways, airports, hotels, etc. – is essential to maximise the benefits of economic openness, even if such infrastructure requires financial assistance.

The survey in chapter 4 shows that international agreements can 'anchor' institutional reforms, such that by linking reforms closely to trade or political agreements their credibility can be enhanced. Perhaps above all, businesses can operate in a climate where the economic and institutional direction in which policy is headed is clear. This aspect may play an important part in the development of wider economic networks, as previously noted.

Nowhere has the impact of this kind of institutional-trade-political linkage been more evident than in the cases of successive waves of EU accession states, from Ireland through to Spain and Portugal to Poland and Hungary. A deeper integration package with Ukraine cannot go quite as far. This conclusion may make it somewhat harder to instil the credibility element in Ukrainian reforms, although, as our modelling indicates, the potential gains from deeper integration are not negligible and our discussion of the more extensive effects indicates that they could be large for Ukraine.

ANNEX 4. BIBLIOGRAPHY

Anderson, J.E. and E. van Wincoop (2004), "Trade Costs", *Journal of Economic Literature*, Vol. 42, No. 3, September.

Baldwin, R.E. and A.J. Venables (1995), "Regional Economic Integration" in G.M. Grossman and K. Rogoff (eds), *Handbook of International Economics*, Vol. 3, Amsterdam: Elsevier, pp. 1597-644.

Baldwin, R.E., J.F. Francois and R. Portes (1997), "EU enlargement: Small costs for the West, big gains for the East", *Economic Policy*, April, pp. 127-76 (along with the subsequent comments by D. Rodrik).

Bernard, A.B., S. Redding and P.K. Schott (2005), *Comparative Advantage and Heterogeneous Firms*, Paper presented at the Conference on Globalisation and Firm Level Adjustment, held at the GEP Centre, Nottingham, June 2005.

Brenton, P. and J. Whalley (1999), *Evaluating a Ukraine–EU Free Trade Agreement using a Numerical General Equilibrium Trade Model*, Report prepared for the European Commission as part of the EES Project UK26, "Study on the Economic Feasibility, General Economic Impact and Implications of a Free Trade Agreement between the European Union and Ukraine", submitted by CEPS, Brussels.

Edwards, T. Huw (2005a), "Import Search and the Path-Dependency of Trade", Mimeo, Loughborough University.

———— (2005b), *Implicit Trade Costs and European Single Market Enlargement*, Working Paper ERP 05-04, Department of Economics, Loughborough University.

———— (2006), "Who Gains from Restructuring the Post-Soviet Transition Economies, and Why?", *International Review of Applied Economics*, forthcoming.

Falkinger, J. and V. Grossman (2005), *Distribution of Natural Resources, Entrepreneurship and Economic Development: Growth Dynamics with Two Elites*, Working Paper No. 1562, CESifo, Munich, October.

Frijters, P., D.J. Bezemer and U. Dulleck (2003), *Contacts, Social Capital and Market Institutions – A Theory of Development*, Working Paper, University of Vienna (retrieved from http://homepage.univie.ac.at/uwe.dulleck/).

Kelly, M. (2005), *Developing Rotten Institutions*, Discussion Paper No. 5281, CEPR, London.

Le Jour, A.M., R. De Mooij and R. Nahuis (2001), *EU Enlargement: Implications for Countries and Industries,* CPB Netherlands Bureau for Economic Analysis, The Hague.

Maskus, K.E. and J.S. Wilson (eds) (2001), *Quantifying the Impact of Technical Barriers to Trade,* Chs. 1 and 2, Ann Arbor, MI: Michigan University Press.

Piazolo, D. (2001), *The integration process between Eastern and Western Europe,* Kieler Studien No. 310, Berlin: Springer-Verlag.

Perroni, C. and J. Whalley (1998), "Rents and the Cost and Optimal Design of Commodity Taxes", *Review of Economics and Statistics,* Vol. 1, No. 3, pp. 357-64.

Posner, R. (1975), "The Social Costs of Monopoly and Regulation", *Journal of Political Economy,* No. 83, pp. 807-27.

Rauch, J.E. and V. Trindade (2003), "Information, International Substitutability, and Globalization", *American Economic Review,* No. 93, June, pp. 775-991.

ANNEX 4. APPENDIX A

TABLES

Table A4(a). Effects of reforms on trade between the EU-15 and Ukraine

Effect on Ukrainian exports to EU-15		Effects of each stage in turn		
		CEEC/SEEC Single Market accession	Ukraine/EU/ CEECs/SEECs FTA	Ukraine Single Market enlargement
	Base value			
Agriculture	139	-1.44	49.64	103.37
Minerals	28	-3.57	7.41	142.73
Food processing	395	0.76	98.49	18.11
Light manuf.	540	-9.07	65.38	18.14
Heavy manuf.	1,894	-3.43	22.42	9.08
Textiles	431	0.00	25.06	2.97
Metals	98	-4.08	1714.89	76.09
Services	1,031	8.34	1.79	194.25
Overall	**4,556**	**-0.70**	**64.83**	**56.88**

Effect on EU-15 exports to Ukraine				
Agriculture	517	-9.67	36.62	48.66
Minerals	753	-13.94	2.93	-2.72
Food processing	107	-7.48	64.65	6.71
Light manuf.	101	-18.81	25.61	-5.41
Heavy manuf.	1,594	-18.57	7.40	-6.89
Textiles	323	-3.41	4.49	8.74
Metals	1,173	-17.90	20.77	18.45
Services	1,279	1.09	0.08	140.31
Overall	**5,847**	**-11.72**	**11.35**	**35.58**

Source: Authors' calculations.

Table A4(b). Effects of reforms on trade between the CEECs and Ukraine

Effect on Ukrainian Exports to CEECs		Effects of each stage in turn		
		CEEC/SEEC Single Market accession	Ukraine/EU/ CEECs/SEECs FTA	Ukraine Single Market enlargement
	Base value			
Agriculture	49	38.78	48.53	184.42
Minerals	30	40.00	7.14	242.22
Food processing	158	9.49	97.11	27.80
Light manuf.	220	-31.82	65.33	-11.75
Heavy manuf.	618	62.14	22.26	83.45
Textiles	134	40.30	25.00	45.07
Metals	35	111.43	1,460.81	238.29
Services	137	-55.47	1.64	21.37
Overall	1,381	27.30	94.08	74.68

Effect on CEECs' exports to Ukraine				
Agriculture	260	131.92	21.89	282.12
Minerals	235	85.96	-0.46	109.04
Food processing	78	83.33	68.53	112.24
Light manuf.	71	57.75	41.07	83.70
Heavy manuf.	775	62.84	13.79	87.33
Textiles	54	53.70	24.10	74.60
Metals	425	198.12	12.39	307.40
Services	50	-58.00	4.76	8.82
Overall	1,948	101.64	15.94	162.79

Source: Authors' calculations.

Table A4(c). Effects of reforms on trade between the SEECs and Ukraine

Effect on Ukrainian exports to SEECs		Effects of each stage in turn		
		CEEC/SEEC Single Market accession	Ukraine/EU/ CEECs/SEECs FTA	Ukraine Single Market enlargement
Base value				
Agriculture	24	66.67	50.00	233.33
Minerals	9	55.56	7.14	262.96
Food processing	22	59.09	97.14	86.76
Light manuf.	98	1.02	63.64	29.08
Heavy manuf.	352	40.06	21.91	57.77
Textiles	67	28.36	25.58	33.11
Metals	21	19.05	1,500.00	93.15
Services	50	-58.00	4.76	8.82
Overall	**643**	**26.44**	**76.75**	**70.52**

Effect on SEECs' exports to Ukraine				
Agriculture	114	103.51	40.95	232.34
Minerals	205	73.17	7.61	91.76
Food processing	45	108.89	61.70	141.87
Light manuf.	17	117.65	16.22	153.08
Heavy manuf.	602	55.81	13.43	78.95
Textiles	30	33.33	37.50	52.73
Metals	412	143.93	9.75	235.71
Services	76	-50.00	0.00	17.11
Overall	**1,501**	**82.48**	**15.52**	**135.02**

Source: Authors' calculations.

Table A4(d). Revised gravity model results for EU border dummies

	Food crops	Meat/ dairy	Minerals	Processing	Light manuf.	Heavy manuf.	Textiles	Metals	Services
Ln Importer Demand	0.616349	0.728503	0.821643	0.969623	0.987661	0.863769	0.837337	0.887152	0.80653
Ln Exporter Output	0.539988	0.609558	0.69277	0.603089	1.085446	1.08863	1.001178	0.875404	0.779284
Dummies: ACCACC	-1.40039	-0.22928	-1.64254	-0.4556	0.581296	0.339263	0.237486	-0.29987	0.22903
EUACC	-1.02726	-0.08863	-1.14785	-0.45472	0.504223	0.393738	0.805418	-0.23926	0.309239
EUEU	-0.0849	0.798732	-0.611	0.600022	0.460205	0.645917	1.034391	0.010159	0.598301
EUOTH	-1.24074	-0.5277	-1.36912	-0.20087	0.254973	0.586825	0.084205	-0.96722	0.393391
ACCOTH	-1.70107	-0.88329	-1.92505	-1.10089	-0.42647	-0.07326	-0.72162	-0.10795	0.20874
Ln Distance	-0.74427	-0.54377	-0.93815	-0.74615	-0.73098	-0.7764	-0.80084	-0.52587	-0.2336
Constant	-1.55601	-6.54877	-3.28787	-6.91939	-12.0975	-10.9053	-8.09363	-6.21969	-13.0317
R-squared	0.427408	0.377883	0.470544	0.518433	0.725546	0.794017	0.669382	0.656759	0.794545
Adj R-Squared	0.423959	0.37369	0.466822	0.515769	0.724045	0.792897	0.667561	0.654855	0.793429

Notes:

t-stats significant at 99% level

t-stats significant at 95% level

Source: Authors' calculations.

ANNEX 4. APPENDIX B

TECHNICAL MODEL DESCRIPTION

The model is a multi-country, general equilibrium model, adapted from that used earlier by Brenton & Whalley (1999). Their paper describes the model in less technical terms, while this note is more technical in nature.

The modelling procedure is effectively as follows:

As with any general equilibrium model, we start by assuming a model structure, which lays out the way in which we model production, consumption and trade.

- Based on that structure, we then need to assume a series of elasticities, relying upon the literature for guidance.

- We then assume that our base data represents an equilibrium state of the world economy, in accordance with the model structure that we have assumed. Working on this assumption, we are able to calibrate a series of share and other structural parameters that help determine the equilibrium of the model.

- We then lay out the equations of the model. These contain a number of variables – which alter simultaneously as we change our assumptions about tariffs and other policy instruments – in order to calculate the new equilibrium.

- Then we insert our altered policy assumptions and calculate the new equilibrium, deriving the effects on trade, production and consumer welfare.

All our data is calibrated upon an initial data set. This set is a series of input-output and trade tables, where the world is broken down into six regions, and production and consumption are split up among eight broad classes of commodities.

In the equation listing as follows, our regions are indexed as either 'r' or 'rr', while commodities are indexed as either 'g' or 'gg', so that, for example, $CNS_{r,g,rr}$ denotes consumption in country r of commodity g produced in country rr. $CNS_{r,g,tot}$ denotes consumption in country r of an aggregate basket of commodity g from all countries.

1.   Variables used in the model

The following is a listing of the variables in the model. These variables are the economic series that we assume will alter in order to satisfy the equilibrium conditions laid down by the model, once certain assumptions on tariffs and so forth are changed.

$PRN_{r,g}$ production

$CNS_{r,g}$ consumption

UTP_r price of utility

INC_r income

$PRP_{r,g}$ producer price

$PRC_{r,g,r}$ consumer price

$CP1_{r,g,r}$ CES price aggregate

REV_r tariff and tax revenue

2.   Model equations

2.1   Production functions with derived supply functions

We start by modelling the production side of the economy. We are still using the production structure of the Brenton–Whalley model, which was developed in order to simulate a Ukrainian economy on which very little information was available. Consequently, production is not modelled in detail. Rather, the economy is assumed to operate on a 'production possibility frontier', so that it can only produce more of one good by producing less of another. The rate at which one good is substituted for another is determined by the elasticity of transformation, σt. For simplicity, however, the equations below are actually written in terms of a 'transformation parameter', ρt, which is directly related to the elasticity of transformation by the formula ρt=(σt-1)/ σt. Note that this formulation has no intermediate inputs and does not distinguish between factors of production (such as labour or capital).

2.2   Production possibility frontier (PPF)

This equation determines the trade-off between production of each good g in country r. $PP1_{r,g}$ is a share parameter, based on the base year structure of production in each country:

$$PPF_R = (\sum_g PP1_{r,g} \, PRN_{r,g}{}^{\rho tr})^{1/\rho tr} . \tag{1}$$

2.3   Supply function (all goods except good 8)

We now want to know how the production of each good varies as producer prices are altered. This has been calculated by determining the ratio of production of good g to that of good 8 (services) in each country. This ratio will vary with prices according to the elasticity of transformation:

$$PRN_{r,g} = PRN_{r,g8}((PP1_{r,g} \, PRP_{r,g8})/(PP1_{r,g8} \, PRP_{r,g}))^{1/(1-\rho tr)}. \qquad (2)$$

2.4   Modelling the consumer side

Income function with derived demand functions

Country r's total income is revenue from selling goods, plus tax and tariff revenue and aid received from abroad:

$$INC_r = \sum_g PRN_{r,g} \, PRP_{r,g} + REV_r + AID_r \,. \qquad (3)$$

Aggregate price for bundles of each type of consumer goods

Consumers are assumed to maximise utility subject to a budget constraint (given by INC$_r$, as derived in the equation above). Utility is modelled as a nested CES (constant elasticity of substitution) function, so that consumers choose on a top level among different classes of goods (such as between services and food products) and simultaneously on a lower level among different countries of origin for each type of good (for example between EU or Russian food products).

We start by calculating the 'average price' for the bundle of good g, chosen from across the range of different countries:

$$CP1_{r,g} = (\sum_{rr} CNS_{r,g,rr} \, PRC_{r,g,rr}) / CNS_{r,g,tot}. \qquad (4)$$

Consequently, we derive an 'average price' for services, food products, light manufactures, etc.

Top level demand for each consumer goods category

Having calculated the average price for each goods category, the consumer is then able to choose how to split expenditure among goods (e.g. between services and food products). This is calculated from how the consumer initially splits up expenditure (BENCNS$_{r,g,tot}$ is total consumption in country r in the base case of goods class g from any source), along with the changes in consumer prices, by way of the top-level elasticity of substitution in consumption, σs and related substitution parameter ρs=(σs-1)/ σs:

$$CNS_{r,g,tot} = CNS_{r,g8,tot} \times (BENCNS_{r,g,tot} / BENCNS_{r,g8,tot})$$
$$\times (CP1_{r,g} BENCP1_{r,g}) / (CP1_{r,g8} BENCP1_{r,g8})^{1/(1-\rho sr)} \quad . \tag{5}$$

Marginal cost of utility in each country

The model uses as its overall price index the marginal cost of consumer utility. This takes the form of a CES price function, where UP0 is a parameter calculated from the baseline data, in order to express overall prices as an index:

$$UTP_r = (1/UP0_r) \times (\sum_{gg} UP1_{r,gg}^{(1/(1-\rho sr))} CP1_{r,gg}^{(\rho sr /(1-\rho sr))})^{(\rho sr-1)/\rho sr} \quad . \tag{6}$$

Demand for goods from different national sources

We now move to the lower level of the consumer's utility function, which determines how the consumer allocates expenditure on good g (say, food products) among different regions of origin. Share2 is a share parameter, reflecting the way consumers chose in the base case to split up consumption among different countries of origin. These shares will change to reflect changes in relative prices (inclusive of taxes and tariffs), subject to the constant elasticity of substitution at the lower level, σs_2 and the related substitution parameter $\rho s_2 = (\sigma s_2 - 1) / \sigma s_2$:

$$CNS_{r,g,rr} = CNS_{r,g,tot} \times SHARE2_{r,g,rr}^{1/(1-\rho s2r,g)} \times (CP1_{r,g} / PRC_{r,g,rr})^{1/(1-\rho s2r,g)} \quad . \tag{7}$$

Balanced (household) budget

The consumer's budget constraint is that income equals expenditure. For simplicity, we do not allow for varying savings in this model:

$$INCr = \sum_{g} \sum_{rr} CNS_{r,g,rr} PRC_{r,g,rr} \quad . \tag{8}$$

Market clearing

For each goods class, g, total consumption across all countries equals total production across all countries:

$$\sum_{rr} CNS_{r,g,rr} = PRN_{r,g} \quad . \tag{9}$$

Zero profits

Again for simplicity, the model assumes all markets are perfectly competitive (although different countries produce differentiated products, and there are taxes, tariffs and other trade costs). The price to consumers equals the production price plus tariffs plus consumption taxes:

$$PRC_{r,g,rr} = PRP_{rr,g}(1 + TAR_{r,g,rr})(1 + TAX_{r,g}). \tag{10}$$

2.5 Government balanced budget

Each country's government gains revenue from consumption taxes and tariffs. These are redistributed in a lump-sum form to consumers, to spend upon goods according to their own choice (there is no direct government spending in the model).

$$REV_r = \sum\sum(PRP_{rr,g}TAR_{r,g,rr} + PRP_{rr,g}TAX_{rr,g} + TAX_{r,g}TAR_{r,g,rr}PRP_{rr,g})CNS_{r,g,rr}. \tag{11}$$

PRPr,g1 is fixed at 1 to act as the denominator for the model

$$PRP.FX("ROW","G1") = 1. \tag{12}$$

Modelling of changing border costs

As well as tariffs, we assume that traded goods face a border cost, ICB$_{r,g,rr}$, when they cross from region r to region rr. These costs are assumed to reflect the effects of regulatory barriers to trade, and are assumed to be in the form of a fixed proportional cost on the value of traded goods (an 'iceberg cost'). These costs reflect different technical specifications and product compatibility, labelling, testing and costs of border and customs checks. We estimate these costs by looking at how trade patterns among various regions differ from an idealised pattern, using a gravity model.

We assume that deeper integration lowers the cost of trading between Ukraine and the various EU regions, by reducing or removing regulatory barriers. The easiest way to model this within the Brenton–Whalley model structure is to adjust the lower-level share parameters. Effectively, if regulatory costs on Ukrainian exports to the EU of good g are reduced, then we assume that EU consumers are now able to obtain more utility from each unit of good g imported from Ukraine. This is reflected in a rise in the share parameter for Ukrainian exports to the UK:

$$SHARE2_{r,g,rr} = UP2_{r,g,rr} \times (1 - ICB_{r,g,rr})^{\rho s2r,g}, \tag{13}$$

where UP2 is the share parameter in the base case and ICB is the assumed border cost between the two countries.

ABOUT THE AUTHORS

Michael Emerson (Project Director), Senior Research Fellow at the Centre for European Policy Studies and former EU Ambassador to Russia.

T. Huw Edwards, Lecturer in economics, Loughborough University, and former Economic Adviser, UK Departments of Energy and Trade & Industry.

Ildar Gazizullin, Economist at the International Centre for Policy Studies.

Daniel Müller-Jentsch, Economist at the European Commission/World Bank Office for South-East Europe, specialising in service sector reforms in transition economies.

Matthias Lücke, Senior Research Economist at the Kiel Institute for the World Economy and former Senior Economist at the International Monetary Fund.

Vira Nanivska, Director of the International Centre for Policy Studies.

Valeriy Pyatnytskiy, First Deputy Minister of Economy and European Integration, Deputy Head of the Joint Parliament–Government Committee on Ukraine's integration with the WTO.

Andreas Schneider, Research Fellow at the Centre for European Policy Studies and expert on agricultural policies and trade.

Rainer Schweickert, Head of the project "Beyond Europe – External Dimensions of Integration" at the Kiel Institute for the World Economy.

Olexandr Shevtsov, Senior Programme Advisor at the United Nations Development Programme in Ukraine .

Olga Shumylo, Head of the European Integration and Foreign Affairs Programme, International Centre for Policy Studies.